SATISFACTIONS IN WORK DESIGN: ERGONOMICS AND OTHER APPROACHES

SATISFACTIONS IN WORK DESIGN: ERGONOMICS AND OTHER APPROACHES

Edited by
R.G. Sell
Work Research Unit
Department of Employment, UK.

and

Patricia Shipley
Department of Occupational Psychology
Birkbeck College
University of London

TAYLOR & FRANCIS LTD
10-14 Macklin Street, London, WC2B 5NF
1979

658.314
S 253

First published 1979 by Taylor & Francis Ltd,
10-14 Macklin Street, London WC2B 5NF

Typeset by Red Lion Setters, Holborn, London
Printed and bound in Great Britain by
Taylor & Francis (Printers) Ltd
Rankine Road, Basingstoke, Hampshire RG24 0PR

British Library Cataloguing in Publication Data

Satisfactions in work design.
    1. Job satisfaction—Congresses 2. Work design
Congresses 3. Human engineering—Congresses
658.31'42   HF5549.5.J63

ISBN 0 85066 180 3

Contents

Contents   vii

'Can exploration of the kind needed ... be tackled adequately by researchers whose devotion to "precise" measurement is such that they are inclined either to forget or to ignore deliberately the existence of possibly influential factors which lie beyond the reach of their cherished clocks and counters?'

A. Rodger (1959), Ten Years of Ergonomics, *Nature*, 184.

Overview

This book is for job designers, and it is also hoped it will be seen as relevant by their clients: workers, trade unions and management. In particular, it is concerned with whether ergonomists as job designers should be interested in the satisfaction and motivation of working people. The papers were given at a conference held in September 1977 at Fulmer Grange and organized jointly by the Ergonomics Society and the International Ergonomics Association.

Traditionally, ergonomics has been little concerned with meeting higher level human needs. In 'fitting the job' to the man it has concentrated more on the criteria of physical health at the individual level, and efficient production of the system at another level. If it is to have a larger role to play in this field, then ergonomists, we suggest, will need to acquire and apply a more comprehensive model and understanding of people as complete functioning beings with feelings as well as aptitudes. Having usefully applied in the past objective knowledge about man's physical and psychological capacities and limitations (his physical and mental skills) to the design of work, particularly the design of physical working conditions, the ergonomist's comprehension will need in future to encompass more of the emotional, attitudinal and motivational facets of working people. This, we suggest, can be done without sacrificing the strengths of ergonomics.

But this added direction will pose a new challenge to ergonomists and will lead to their greater involvement in problems and issues of mental health, psychological stress and human joy, happiness and pain, which previously fell outside their boundaries. Truly psychological features of work are growing in salience in advanced industrial societies.

The fundamental concept in the book is the complex and controversial one of job satisfaction, and the main theme is the interaction between job satisfaction and job design. Few attempts have been made in the literature to define job satisfaction before proceeding to measure it. It is assumed it is a valid concept with a meaning (the same perhaps) for all workers. It is also assumed that it is a need which has emerged only recently as a product of affluence and better levels of education. Such assumptions may be wrong.

Researchers tend to distinguish between overall or 'global' satisfaction and satisfaction with different 'facets' of the job. They also distinguish between 'intrinsic' satisfaction, supposedly emanating from the characteristics of tasks being done, and 'extrinsic' satisfaction bound up with the quality of working conditions, the context in which those tasks are done. And if job satisfaction is a valid and reliable concept, if we know what we mean by it, do we need to do something about it; should it be promoted for its inherent worth as an end in itself, or because it is a means to some other desirable goal like better productivity? In the language of science the concept may have predictive power (predicting output, strain, etc); its status may rest at the level of explanation or it may be no more than descriptive. Yet it may have no claim whatsoever to scientific status.

Many authors in this collection have used level of job satisfaction as a diagnostic tool to assess the quality of the job in 'humanistic' terms; the degree of freedom and personal control the job affords, the amount of challenge in it, and so on ... Over 30 years ago Nigel Balchin (1947) asserted that a job should have 'all the best ingredients of life itself'. Those familiar with British Government office typing pools may think that conditions have hardly changed since 1948, the date of the study reported in this book by Stansfield. The humanistic view is that work is important to people and a primary source of personal identity, and that humane as well as economic goals should be pursued at the workplace. Klein's view is that experiences at work should help people to grow and develop in a psychological sense, that job designers have choices available to them and the choices they make will depend on the values they hold. Those interested in promoting worker participation and democracy want to give workers themselves the opportunity to make informed choices at work, to restore to them a measure of control over what happens to them during a large part of their lives.

Singleton's paper projects an image of the ergonomist occupying a scientific position in defiance of what he thinks is a fashionable ideological movement or 'push'. His goal is system's efficiency, to which individual human needs and personal goals must be subordinated. Man is a biological and information-processing organism with feelings which are someone else's business. The energies of the scientist-ergonomist are precious and must be devoted to other ends. He should be striving after objective factual knowledge, concrete data, unbiased views and unambiguous statements and concepts. It is interesting that Ahrends reports in this collection specific and objective findings about workers with ability who do not perform well at their jobs because the jobs fail to motivate them: an example of what happens these days, even in less developed countries, if people's attitudes are discounted at the workplace.

But there are strengths in the scientific-ergonomics approach which deserve greater application in job design, and this point is expressed in Rohmert's paper. He proposes ergonomic solutions to the problems associated with the stress and strain by-products of modern complex technology. But his frame of reference does incorporate the individual's needs. Firm incontrovertible criteria and evidence enshrined in ergonomic guiding principles are required, he believes, for sound work design. This should be based on identified regularities or 'laws' of human behaviour and functioning. This is precisely the kind of material ergonomists seek to provide. Negotiated agreements and even legislation can be based more on misleading assumptions and ignorance, than on evidence, and used as pawns in the union-management power game, Rohmert states. Individuals are simply unaware often of the longer term risks to their health of certain practices at the workplace. But trade unions persist with their pay bargaining stance, to the neglect, one might argue, of other important considerations.

Rissler's paper is important because she draws attention to a particular psychological phenomenon for humanised work design: that of the adaptation over time by the individual worker to adverse working conditions which may ultimately lead to a breakdown in health. We should surely think harder about alternative means to meeting a system's goals which are less costly to individuals operating those systems? Cope recognizes this adaptation process in his theoretical contribution on worker motivation when he points to the adjustments people make to their expectations about their jobs in the light of experience. This process of expectation is implicit in some of Cox and MacKay's findings on women adjusted to repetitive work in British factories, and in Khaleque's study of women cigar workers in Belgium.

The link between job satisfaction and health is being explored independently in their research by Rissler, Cox and Shipley. Expressed job dissatisfaction may be a clearcut signal for changes to be made in the job which would result in a reduction in health risks. On the other hand, people are known by researchers to report job satisfaction in conditions which are unreasonably shortening their lives. Shipley found in her study that those expressing the greatest dissatisfaction also expressed highest levels of perceived stress with conditions of work, especially in so far as such conditions had an adverse effect on the quality of their personal (out-of-work) lives. Job satisfaction measures can be sensitive diagnostic tools in some circumstances.

Several papers reflect a concern with optimal workload as a priority goal in job design. This is easier said than done as an assignment given our present state of knowledge; but where standards have to be arrived at, sooner rather than later, there is good reason to prefer recommendations based on the human sciences approach to those which do not accommodate such human criteria. Moors recognizes in his paper that we need to try and get the workload right, and that a more sophisticated view needs to be taken than hitherto of such design parameters. In the relevant general literature findings are consistently reported of stress resulting from sub-optimal load; such as the excessive mental load of complex responsible jobs, work-rate stress and pacing outside the control of the individual worker, or serious underloading and underutilizing of an individual's skill or potential. We suggest that the quantification and more precise detailing of such humanized work principles for the benefit of the individual worker is a difficult but fitting task for the ergonomist. As Moors demonstrates, the 'blind' uncritical application of work-humanizing strategies like 'job enrichment' and 'autonomous work groups' can lead, in the absence of this more precise and objective knowledge, to undesirable consequences the designer did not intend, such as imbalances in workload. Quantification of such intrinsic 'work content' parameters could be added to the more obvious contributions expected of ergonomists in the extrinsic context of physical conditions of work; and this is clearly seen by Verhaegen in his article. Saari and Lahtela also alert us in their paper to the possible dangers for increased accident risk of unthinking and too rapid innovations in work re-structuring.

Corlett draws some interesting links between these humanistic job design goals and the early work, reported in the psychological literature, on the importance of the exercise of the primary drives of curiosity and exploration for learning and mastery of the environment. A substantial lack of opportunities for such exercise leading to acute sensory or social deprivation may be the precondition of disease. Such conditions and drives may hold the key to better understanding of the importance of intrinsic satisfaction for workers and their motivation, as in the case of Foeken's chemical process operators.

Several papers in this collection focus or touch upon the theme of individual differences and the variability in behaviour which must be a headache to the designer looking for fixed design solutions. The ideal is for individuals to be left alone, where possible, to find their own level and pace of work since they are in a position to judge their own personal needs best. Khaleque reminds us that boredom is not an attribute of jobs but of individual workers. Some women may enjoy repetitive work for instrumental and extrinsic reasons; as not particularly important to them in itself but a useful source of extra money and socialising. Many workers of either sex, it is sometimes said, do not want or are not ready for responsible and enriched jobs. White points out that, although it is difficult for designers to accommodate fully these differences between individuals, as a general rule the approach has been to expect a one-sided adjustment by workers to the fixed features of their working environment. Lindon proposes that inconsistencies in job satisfaction research could arise from the different frames of reference a worker has had to adopt by circumstance. He suggests that those in responsible jobs may take a 'self-referent' view when asked to evaluate their jobs because of the measure of control they enjoy over their work, and of their ability to judge from the standpoint of their own internal standards. Others may take a 'job-referent' view based on external standards and opinions.

Sweden has had a long history of social legislation and is committed to the extension of the egalitarian principle to the workplace. This is exemplified in Björk's description of the Volvo work restructuring project at the Kalmar plant. And it may be conjectured that effecting such change in that country is an easy task for the 'agent of change'. Sell devotes much discussion to a consideration of the intervention skills required of the job designer as potential change-agent. The Kalmar project owes its success primarily, he suggests, to the total commitment of the 'top man' in the organization. The paper by Damodaran addresses some useful suggestions to an important group of other potential change-agents; managers may feel their status threatened by increasing worker democracy or may simply lack the interpersonal skills required for bringing about their desire for more effective employee participation.

In her paper Shipley switches the frame of reference from the client to the academic researcher in the role of external consultant who is not formally trained for such a role and for whom the artificial laboratory in the ivory tower is a more comfortable milieu in which to do research than the complex and ambiguous reality of the outside world. The lack of skill and understanding in following the required 'participative' guidelines enlisting the help and commitment of the people who are actually doing the job, is why humanized work re-design so often fails, according to de Jong's analysis. Work design, he emphasizes, is a complex technology requiring specialized training. In agreement with Sell, he believes the designer should take a systems view of his assignment and recognize the conflicts and different viewpoints associated with the distinct frames of reference and value systems of all those involved, including the designer's own. No single person can ever have enough knowledge to deal with all the human and technical problems involved in design; there has to be more sharing of information, and a greater understanding of the approach of other disciplines and a willingness to cross boundaries. It is impossible to satisfy all the social, psychological, health, technical and economic criteria in the real situation, and some compromise is necessary. The client, alone, must make the necessary decision but he must be helped to know the benefits and costs of each option, which requires the various specialists to work together.

It is recognized above that the scientist-ergonomist has an increasing role to play in establishing on a firmer footing the content and subject matter for job design, such as identifying the boundary conditions of mental workload. So far, however, there have been significant gaps in his training with reference to the application of such knowledge: the process of intervention and effecting desirable change. It is as important, therefore, to get right how something is done, as to get right what is done. He needs the skills of communication to deal effectively with clients at all levels and with fellow team members both from within and outside his own discipline. Peacock's case study is of interest because the changes were attempted in a 'directive' manner with perhaps insufficient participation from those doing the actual jobs.

The satisfaction of the job designer is also of interest, therefore, not just the satisfaction of the individuals whose jobs he is seeking to alter. An understanding of the subtleties and intangibles of change phenomena should also form part of the skills of the effective designer. One category of change, the technological, continues its inexorable march. It is pleasing to the ergonomist to hear from Crawley and Spurgeon about their ergonomics investigation into the intrinsic work satisfaction of the Air Traffic Controller. So often automation and mechanization is introduced insensitively into the workplace, and takes away some of the worker's opportunity for the exercise of skill. We are put in mind here of the present threat from the widescale use of microprocessors which have the potential for displacing from jobs legions of people at all levels, particularly those doing routine and stereotyped work. Many unwilling and unready people could be projected into a frightening form of post-industrial society, with enforced prolonged idleness and without the education to make good use of their new leisure. Even if adequate financial compensation is made to the displaced, who may potentially share in the fruits of this new technology, can we ever really make up to someone for the loss of that special identity that goes with the job that one does and the role one has in society? Perhaps this is the rapidly-approaching new challenge to the human and social scientist concerned with promoting the quality of life.

Editors: R.G. Sell,
Work Research Unit,
Department of Employment,
United Kingdom

P. Shipley,
Department of Occupational Psychology,
Birkbeck College,
London University,
United Kingdom

Job design in action — the perspective of the practitioner

R. G. Sell
Work Research Unit, Department of Employment, United Kingdom

This paper looks at the problems which exist in both research and application in job design, many of which are covered by other papers in this book. When designing jobs in practice we have to be concerned with:
1. the job design adviser—the ergonomist and others,
2. production/systems/engineering designers,
3. workers as individuals,
4. managers and supervisors,
5. employing organizations, and
6. the trade unions involved.
We have also to be aware of the values, needs, satisfactions and motivations of each of these groups. It would be wrong to assume that they share many of them in common.

Unlike the laboratory, the real life world is complex with many different factors influencing any situation in ways which are difficult to predict in advance. Solutions are not obvious therefore to many of the practical problems and those concerned with job design do not always ask the most important questions. Ergonomists have usually had an education based on scientific methods with an emphasis on objective measurements, and thus they tend to ignore subjective factors and industrial relations aspects. In this introduction an attempt is made to bring out some of the questions which need to be asked in the practical situation. We do not have general answers to many of them; and answers from one situation are not easy to apply to the questions in another. When changes are being made there are costs and benefits (in the widest sense) to all the options available. All too often those responsible for making the changes fail to consider some of the possible human costs of their choice.

Factors to be considered

If the job designer is to achieve real success he must understand better the vested interests of the various groups of individuals, the power systems of his own and the client organizations and the reward system in operation. In particular, he must be able to differentiate between the behaviour people say is important and that which is actually rewarded. Organizations often say they believe in safety, individual responsibility, work structuring etc. The behaviour which is really rewarded, however, is that which leads to increased short-term output or reduced production costs.

In spite of increased democratization it is often the attitudes of the top man of the organization which determine the management style and whether there is a concern for the individuals who man the system. Volvo owes much of its approach to the beliefs of its Managing Director, Pehr Gyllenhammar. Glaser (1976), in his review of many reported cases, shows that those that moved from success to failure did so when the top man of the organization was changed. Personal experience confirms the need for very strong top management support to help the change process through the many difficulties with which it will be faced and to maintain momentum over the long periods of time which may be necessary.

It is important also to be aware of the effect of changing one person's job on that of others in the same organization. The usual examples quoted are the effect on supervisors' jobs when lower level workers are given more responsibility but there is also the effect on service jobs, such as maintenance or personnel, of giving more responsibility to the line function for these activities. It is necessary to involve all levels and functions in discussing proposed job changes.

There are a number of reasons for looking at the design of jobs for individuals or for an organization and it is often the value system of those initiating changes or carrying out the work which determines the approach. Is it to increase productivity, effectiveness, product quality etc as a traditional ergonomics or work study approach; or is it to improve quality of working lives, satisfaction, mental health as is now becoming more the stated reason? Values also determine which jobs are chosen for study in an organization. Whose needs are being most satisfied? Is it those of the individual worker, the organization or even the researcher? Is the main initial output the improvement of the quality of working life, of productivity or the publication of a paper in an academic journal?

Before work is begun there should be agreement on the aims of the study, the needs of the various parties, including those of the job design adviser, and how all are likely to be met. There are likely to be conflicts between these so there must be discussion on the necessary trade-offs. There is no agreement among the experts as to which approach is likely to produce the most benefits in both the quality of working life and productivity areas. The National Centre for Quality of Working Life in the USA believes that by endeavouring to increase satisfaction there is likely to be an accompanying increase in effectiveness. Other schools of thought claim that if a person is doing more effective work then there is bound to be an increase in their job satisfaction.

In the present climate of public expenditure constraints in the United Kingdom there are many people in public service who feel that, because of overtime restrictions, they are unable to devote the time necessary to carry out their tasks properly or, because they are not allowed the necessary facilities, that they are giving an inadequate service. They perceive therefore that their employers, and thus the general public, do not value their contribution and this produces a downward spiral of reduced satisfaction, reduced service, more dissatisfaction etc.

There are increased desires among all people for more say in the way their own jobs are carried out. These desires are felt by job designers as well as those they are studying. Also, those whose jobs are studied have valuable information on the tasks which should be taken into account in any re-design. Only they have had experience of all the operating difficulties which can arise, of the demands which customers make, of the effects of variations in raw materials etc. To ignore this information is to invite disaster.

There is a need to test out assumptions and to beware of applying one's own views to someone else's job. In a study (Raffle & Sell 1970) carried out on the then new Victoria underground line (this has an automatic system whereby the train operator has only to push two buttons to move the train from one station to the next) my initial view, based on a traditional view of skill, was that this was a de-skilled job. The train 'manager', as the operator saw his new role, had a different attitude. He felt released from the constraints of having to keep the 'dead man's' control depressed, and from the signals of the guard. He, alone, now decided when the train should move. Thus, in the job designers language, he had a new found autonomy, more discretion and increased responsibility, enhanced by the improved communication system of which the train operator now felt a part.

There are also assumptions about the boredom of assembly work, the acceptance of this kind of work, the attitudes of women etc. The attitudes of people are influenced very much by their expectations. People who are brought up to believe that they will be working on repetitive, boring jobs, or women who expect only to be employed in certain roles, are not disappointed when that is the situation. This is probably why those who express dissatisfaction at present, at least in the UK, tend to be those in higher level jobs who have been led to expect more autonomy etc than they actually have. Given the opportunity, training, managerial support and the time necessary to adjust to new ways of working it is likely that many people will prefer them. Once they have changed to working on these new 'enriched' jobs then they may be less willing to return to the more boring repetitive short cycle tasks.

Pay may also be a problem. In a rational pay system the main basis of payment is some form of job evaluation based on knowledge, skill, responsibility etc. There is often overlaid some compensation for bad conditions which are usually physical, such as heat or noise, but may arise from boring and monotonous tasks. There will be problems in seeking to reduce these bad conditions because usually it will not be possible to match the reduction in pay warranted by the improvements in conditions with a corresponding increase in pay due to increase in skill, knowledge etc. The people doing the job will be those who are prepared to tolerate the conditions for the extra pay and will be reluctant to accept less pay.

There are many individual differences in attitudes to work which must be taken into consideration. Where general recommendations can be made it must be remembered that they do not apply to everyone. Some people do not want responsibility. They prefer a fixed job they know they can do and have no need for social contact, especially if they are well paid in compensation. Most studies in the job design area have taken a total approach to the people concerned. We need to know more about what differences in attitude to work exist between the different categories such as men/women, fit/less fit, old/young, native born white/immigrant etc.

One aim of job design should be to offer choice in the way of working. Many people do not want to change because they cannot contemplate a different way of organizing their work. They have no experience of anything other than their previous methods.

There is an ethical problem in that some managements may, under the guise of participation, use subtle pressures to manipulate the situation to obtain implementation of their own ideas. Sometimes this will rebound on them when those being manipulated realize what is happening.

It is necessary also to understand the constraints in any particular situation and how these affect possible solutions. In particular, there are economic and social constraints which may mean that what is good and appropriate for one organization in one culture, such as Volvo in Sweden, may not be appropriate elsewhere.

Scientific approaches

Ergonomists, and other job designers, have usually been educated with a strong emphasis on measurement and the use of the scientific method. When changes are taking place, managers and administrators as well as researchers want to be able to measure, among other things, changes in performance. Unfortunately, the parameters which are commonly measured, especially as far as performance is concerned, are those which are easy to measure and not necessarily those which are the most important. This is especially so in respect of service industries. How is the performance of the police force, the work of park keepers or of a refuse collector measured? Usually, secondary measures are resorted to with the more important primary aspects ignored. Measures can thus be artificial and irrelevant; for example, the number of streets patrolled, the frequency of mowing the grass and the number of houses served. The more important measures, which relate to how well the jobs are done, such as public satisfaction and reduction in crime, the quality of the lawns produced and the amount of refuse uncollected or spilt on the road are rarely taken into account because of the difficulty in obtaining them.

There is also a tendency to concentrate on short-term measures of output increase, particularly by work study practitioners. Longer term measures such as absence, turnover, health and disputes may go in the opposite way to short-term ones. Where there is an increase in these aspects there is usually an increase in costs which may act to balance out some or all of the short-term benefits gained.

In many of the areas concerned the measures have a strong volunteer bias in that they rely on someone reporting an incident. The willingness to report depends on a number of factors such as the rewards for reporting and the reporter's own assessment of what action is likely to be taken. When safety is talked it is usually the reported injury frequency rate that is meant. If more attention is given to safety in a factory then interest will be heightened and people will be more likely to report minor injuries they might otherwise have ignored. The same is true of organizations like the police which rely on reporting of crimes and other incidents. If the public perceive the police are doing well they are more inclined to report these incidents. Thus by paying attention to these factors it is possible to change the measured value while the underlying situation remains the same. To a psychologist concerned with safety the measure which is of most interest is that of human error. This is the basic cause of most injuries, of poor quality of work and of plant damage. Unfortunately, it is a measure which it is almost impossible to obtain because the organizational climate is normally such that nobody will admit to making an error. Only if errors are obvious to others will they be reported.

There is no single measure of job satisfaction. Different measures may be more relevant at different times and in different situations. With measures such as absence and labour turnover, attention must be paid to the surrounding environment and for instance to the ease with which an employee can obtain another job. With attitudes, it is usually found that very few people express great dissatisfaction initially. Should the same questions be asked after a job redesign exercise, there may not be any apparent improvement because the respondent's frame of reference within which he makes his reply has now changed. He may, however, now see his previous job (from the vantage point of the re-designed job) in far worse terms than he did at the time of the first questioning.

The ergonomist is prone to retreat to his laboratory to carry out an experiment in an environment where he can control what he considers to be the most important variables and where the extraneous variables are excluded. It is often those aspects which can be measured easily which are considered rather than those which may be the most important. The subjects used in the experiments are those found easy to obtain; students, housewives, military personnel etc and they may not be the most relevant for the topic under study. People at work carry out their jobs for seven to eight hours a day; five days or more a week; whereas subjects in the laboratory rarely work for more than two hours a day over a short working week.

The design of power station control rooms can illustrate the problems that may be caused by a failure to consider all the relevant factors. The Central Electricity Generating Board spent a lot of time designing the control desk and panels for a boiler/turbine unit, so that one man from one position could monitor and control the system during normal operation. When the system was installed, however, the desks for six units were put in one large control room. The social factors that had been ignored in the design exercise now became important. In normal working, the unit operators tend to concentrate in a group away from the desks and rely on some form of alarm to tell them when they need to return to the operating position. Thus decisions taken about the size of dial needed for accurate monitoring from a distance of 6 ft. or so became irrelevant when the actual distances of the man from his control panel were so much greater.

Similarly the ergonomist who works on inspection problems tends to concentrate in laboratory experiments on the perceptual aspects. These, no doubt, are important, especially to the development of theory, but the problems as industry sees them are often more of the social-organizational type.

There is a desire to apply scientific method, including control groups etc, to practical situations. Where active participation of those involved is being practised, however, this becomes very difficult. If one group sees another getting improvements in the job then the first group will naturally feel unjustly treated unless special reassurances are given. This means that experiments in industry in which the real aims are hidden from the participants become difficult to carry out.

Government and legal initiatives

In a number of countries governmental action has been taken to improve the quality of working life by legislation or by sponsoring research and setting up advisory units. Legal limits are placed on the minimum length of the working cycle in Norway, Sweden and Germany. Many countries, including the UK, have established units which advise organizations on ways of improving jobs; a joint management-employee approach to the problems is usually required. As with all changes, there are costs and benefits. It is easy to introduce laws which are socially desirable but which have unintended costs; for example, Employment Protection Acts which are reputed to make employers reluctant to take on people, and the Housing Acts which make landlords reluctant to let accommodation. The police, for example, have not been exempt from the UK Sex Discrimination Act and women police are now, in theory, interchangeable on police duties with men. Unfortunately, violence is an increasing problem in British society and although some women can deal with this as effectively as men the majority can not. Policemen tend to protect policewomen in potentially violent situations and thus total effectiveness is thereby reduced. There is pressure to provide policemen with better protective headgear for dealing with public disorder, demonstrations etc, but women have virtually no protection. Are policewomen to continue to be unprotected or will they be seen on the street equipped with riot helmets along with the men?

Job design in action

It is essential, if he is to have any influence, for the job designer to start from the practical job and its problems and not from the standpoint of his own discipline. If any solution is to be implemented the problem under study must be 'owned' by the client; i.e. the operational client and not an offline representative deriving from personnel or work study. If this practice is not followed, then there is unlikely to be any change because people do not like to be told what to do.

There is a need for a multi-disciplinary approach to help the client analyse his problem, and to bring to bear the correct skills to enable him to solve it, instead of relying on the consultant applying a particular and ready made solution which is a part of his skill repertoire. The multi-disciplinary approach is necessary because, without it, there is a risk of implementing a proposal which while solving one set of problems may create others which could be worse. It is in this area that the integration of subjects represented by ergonomics becomes a necessity although all too often this integration is lacking.

There should be concern to ensure that the client is not left worse off through the raising of issues which cannot be dealt with and which would have been better left obscured. Care must be exercised that expectations which cannot be satisfied are not raised. It is necessary to explore in advance options which might be available and the cost-benefits of each, although it must be made clear that it is difficult to forecast all factors.

The client will not share important problems where trust is lacking and it is necessary to earn the right to be involved in serious issues. This means preliminary talking with those in the organization, without any commitment on either side, to allow an exchange of ideas and values. Alternatively, successful working on a low level problem can establish credibility and competence. Only when there is trust and a belief in competence will it be possible to explore deeply the serious issues. The work of Argyris (1970) is relevant in this respect. The Work Research Unit approach is to set up a management/union/worker steering committee to discuss the possible areas of work, the possible constraints, the monitoring of work in progress and to examine what effects there might be on other parts of the organization.

It is difficult to satisfy everybody. Principles which have been established in one set of studies cannot necessarily be applied to a new situation because each benefit has a cost and different people and different organizations see their balance in different ways. There is often a choice between enriching all the lower level jobs and thus perhaps removing a layer of supervision, or leaving the jobs at the lower levels as they are but with better opportunities for those who want to progress up the promotion ladder. Similarly, it is often stated that people should have complete tasks, including the associated paper work, but there are many who do not want to write up their work or prepare reports. Individuals or groups can have vested interests which they are reluctant to give up and there is no certain recipe for overcoming them. With strong top management support it becomes easier to solve problems of this type but even so there is no guarantee of success.

It is not an easy task to carry out the ideas discussed in this paper. In the present UK economic situation changes are unlikely to be implemented unless they increase output or reduce the numbers employed. It is difficult to increase output with low consumer demand and it is incongruent to introduce a change intended to benefit employees if it makes some redundant. There can be seen to be a choice between having more people employed though in boring and monotonous jobs, and having more people unemployed but able, in theory, to be creative in their own time. Unemployment is not, however, acceptable at present to the vast majority of the population.

It may be that in some situations, it is not possible to change the design of jobs and the best solution is to accept a higher rate of turnover as people get bored with the work and leave. This may have to be accepted as a form of job 'rotation' but it does raise the question of what is the value to an organization of a stable and committed labour force?

Ergonomists have more to offer in the field of motivation, job satisfaction, quality of working life but they also have much to learn. It is hoped that this chapter has shown some of the directions in which that learning should proceed.

Some conceptual and operational doubts about job satisfaction

W. T. Singleton
Applied Psychology Department, University of Aston in Birmingham,
United Kingdom

There is at the present time a particular ideological/political movement in the Western World pushing the proposition that workers should be caused to obtain personal satisfaction from what they do to earn a living. Such movements must necessarily be treated cautiously; they are sometimes no more than fleeting fashionable crusades and there is a perpetual danger that such crusades will result in overemphasis on a particular facet of the complex multi-dimensional problems of work design which is encompassed by ergonomics. On the other hand, politicians and ideologists do sometimes crystallize some fundamental trend in thinking within a society which cannot be ignored.

Ergonomics is concerned with issues which arise from human work; including the application of psychological knowledge to these matters. It would therefore seem reasonable that the ergonomist, as a scientist, should attempt some clarification of the concept of job satisfaction, including the development of techniques for the reliable and valid acquisition of relevant evidence; and the ergonomist, as a technologist, should consider whether there are measurable aspects of job satisfaction which might serve as relevant criteria for successful work design.

'Satisfaction' is an interesting word in that there seem to be two meanings connected respectively with gratification and atonement. In the work context it is presumably the former which is dominant, although there are undertones of the latter in that work is somehow regarded as undesirable and atonement is required for the sin of its imposition. In order to avoid the more obscure ideological issues, this aspect is best set aside so that we are left with the concept of something that 'satisfies desire or gratifies feeling' to quote the Oxford Dictionary. Thus job satisfaction must be primarily a conscious personal reaction and, superficially, it would seem that it ought to be possible for a person doing a particular job to state whether or not or how far he finds it satisfying. At least for the individual, increases or decreases in subjective job satisfaction ought to correlate with differences in specific objective aspects of jobs, such as autonomy, variety and so on. Hopefully there will also be consistencies between individuals, so that job characteristics can be identified which indicate job satisfaction. This is the direct approach.

Alternatively, we can treat job satisfaction as an intervening variable and look for relationships between changes in jobs and in performance. These can sometimes be traced to physiological origins (such as reduced energy expenditure) or informational origins (such as reduced processing load) but if these are not identifiable, and yet there are still consistent improvements in productivity or some other aspect of performance with particular job changes, then one can postulate an intervening variable which could be labelled job satisfaction. This is the indirect approach.

Thus job satisfaction can be treated either as a set of direct subjective feelings, or as a blanket term covering affective intervening variables. These are not mutually exclusive alternatives. Given the current uncertainty about objectives and methods in the job satisfaction field, there is no reason to discourage or to criticize particular groups of research workers following either of these approaches, providing that they are clear about what they are doing. Criticism is appropriate for those who do not trouble to sort out their own philosophy, but proceed arbitrarily to design studies and to acquire bits of evidence in the hope that meaning will emerge as the data are analyzed.

Research findings

Before looking at the studies which have been carried out, and the populations concerned, it is worth noting that the traditional image of the worker as the male on the shopfloor in mass-production manufacturing is long outdated. Ginzberg (1975) reminds us that in the USA there are now probably less than 5% of all employed persons working on assembly lines; that less than one in three of workers are actually producing goods; and that the proportion of female workers is still increasing. In the context of job satisfaction, women might be very different from men, as this is one aspect of the rather neglected individual difference parameter. (Lawler, 1976).

The evidence on job satisfaction and job performance has been collected by Brayfield *et al* (1955) and Vroom (1964) and is available in summary form in Blum *et al* (1968). Studies involving foreman's ratings and productivity measures, correlated with job satisfaction measures obtained by interviews and questionnaires, yield rather inconsequential results. The correlations are usually positive but low, less than 0.2 which indicates no relationship of practical importance.

Studies on absence from work and job satisfaction have been collected by Nicholson *et al* (1976). After reviewing 29 studies, mostly involving blue-collar males but some white-collar and two involving nurses, they show that the relationship is negative or zero in every case. Their own study, involving more than 1000 workers in 80 organizations, compares time lost or frequency of absence and an additional index with scores on a job satisfaction questionnaire modified from the Cornell Job Description Index. Only 29 out of 240 correlations were significant and, of these, 22 were negative. Again, this indicates no relationship of practical importance. Wild (1973) has generated another twist to this question by suggesting that manpower planning cannot be carried out successfully without reasonable prediction of labour turnover, and such predictions depend on assessment of job satisfaction. Although there is no general relationship between job satisfaction and labour turnover, this is because of the multi-dimensional pattern of job satisfaction attributes, and prediction only becomes possible at the individual rather than the aggregate level. Thus for each individual: age, marital status, personality, home and family background must be considered, as well as the job before assessment of satisfaction and prediction of likely length of service is possible. Such individual predictions could be reaggregated to obtain a human resource prediction for the company.

It can be argued that, although the benefits of job satisfaction are not revealed by orthodox measures of system performance (such as productivity and absenteeism) they may nevertheless exist—we may not be taking the right measurements. This is the view of Lawler (1976), who proposes that a necessary preliminary to research in this area is the development of more varied and longer term measures of organizational performance. Others (eg Elliott, 1976) go further and acknowledge that their purpose is to impose their own values on industry. From this point of view, the job satisfaction movement is a moral crusade; and presumably questions of theory or model building become irrelevant and data become a source of propaganda rather than evidence.

Discussion

There are at least three intractable problems pervading job satisfaction research:
1. the quality of evidence, based on introspection, when job satisfaction is treated as an affective parameter;
2. the quality of evidence from case studies, where attempts are made to relate variables from different domains of measurement, eg productivity and satisfaction; and
3. ambiguities in the modelling of the job satisfaction concept and its context within related disciplines and technologies.
Each of these aspects is worthy of separate consideration:

Introspection

The following are among the reasons why a worker may honestly consider and state that he is satisfied with his job. It will be noted that none of these reasons have any connection with the standard recipes for job satisfaction such as job enlargement, job enrichment, individual autonomy or group autonomy.

(a) Temperamentally he may, invariably, be satisfied. As a matter of common experience there are large individual differences along a dimension to do with being equable, phlegmatic or 'field-independent'. Some individuals will 'grouse' whatever the situation; others will tolerate any situation.

(b) Individuals react to changes rather than absolute levels. One important, but sometimes overlooked, aspect is that a stated reaction is not to the absolute situation but to the comparative situation; how it has changed, perhaps over a very long time scale, how it compares with the situation of others with whom the individual identifies himself.

(c) The job may be unpleasant but quite satisfactory because of extrinsic factors such as pay, ease of travel, companionship, or perhaps just familiarity.

(d) Achievement of the overall purpose may be so rewarding as to transcend the conditions of work: for example, the soldier in wartime, or the nurse in the geriatric ward, or, on a shorter time scale, the fireman coping with a disaster, or the long distance runner outpacing his competitors.

(e) There can be a paradoxical satisfaction in extreme unpleasantness. 'It's a man's job'. This presumably operates for sewer men, workers in tanneries, grinders of castings, drop forgers etc. Improving the conditions can reduce satisfaction, and thus there is no reason to do so where there are no health hazards.

Case Studies

The Department of Employment has summarized over 100 examples of work restructuring in the UK (Report No. 2), about 20 in Scotland (Report No. 5), over 500 in Sweden (Paper No. 3), about 100 in USA (Report No. 3), and has surveyed the situation more generally across EEC countries (Paper No. 5). Davis *et al* (1975) have recently provided a book of cases over a wider area covering industrial democracy and other organizational/structural changes, as well as design of jobs. There are many descriptions in the literature of projects which have succeeded or failed, with analyses of why, and consequent recommendations of how these things should be done in future, eg Willebois (1970) de Jong (1973) Ruehl (1974), Warr and Wall (1975) Wall and Lisheron (1977). These detailed and comprehensive accumulations of cases yield little respectable evidence about the relationship between job satisfaction and the traditional measures, such as productivity and absenteeism, because that was not why the projects were carried out. Manufacturers, and other systems managers, make whatever changes they consider most appropriate at any time to further their own concept of the system effectiveness. Inevitably, all data acquired in such circumstances are contaminated by inextricable complexes of parameters and changes, reactions, attitudes, leadership and so on. Purity of evidence is not their concern, and this is not something about which academics can legitimately complain. Managers are not in the business of making life easy for job satisfaction students. However, such case studies have their own importance. They may not contribute to scientific advance but they do allow a kind of folk wisdom, or set of recipies, to emerge about what to do and what not to do to get a 'successful' application of job satisfaction principles. These are summarized in the various Work Research Unit reports (op. cit). Job restructuring is introduced when there is a need to reduce production costs, increase productivity, improve quality, morale, labour turnover, recruitment, communication and all other attributes of efficiency. If the application is carefully done it will probably, but not necessarily, have some but not all of the desired effects, depending entirely on the individual case. There are always problems: adjustments of pay; unanticipated effects on others, not directly the topic of study but interfacing with it; short term gains may be counterbalanced by longer term problems; or revising recruitment and training policies and regression to the old norms. At this stage, that familiar uneasy '*deja vu*' feeling emerges. All we need to do is change the title and we have the same recipe which emerges from case studies of work study, operational research, ergonomics, cost-benefit analysis, 'management by objectives', in short for every management/productivity service which has developed since World War II.

Conceptual modelling

Management service disciplines are different, not so much because of what they try to achieve, but because each has a different model of what the issues are and how to resolve them. In the complex multidimensional situation of people at work, the ordinary investigator can only make progress if he is provided with a structured situation, usually in the form of a core topic or resource with other parameters described and understood in terms of their relationship to this core topic. Thus, for work study time is the core topic, and this must be used as effectively as possible, and other variables are considered in terms of what their effect is in time and in using time. For operational research there is no core topic; but in compensation there is unusual emphasis on describing as precisely as possible the relationship between various relevant parameters using mathematical models. For ergonomics the biological/informational organism is the core with everything else related to this human operator. Cost benefit analysis relies on the twin topics in the title itself and emphasises the problems of measuring them, not necessarily in the same terms, but at least in ways where their ratio and possible changes in ratio can be perceived. In 'management by objectives' the emphasis is obviously on classifying the purpose and relating everything else to this purpose. Looked at in this way, it is difficult to see how job satisfaction can rise to a corresponding level of conceptual clarity. There is no simple way of defining what we are talking about; its relationship with the key parameters of system efficiency is obscure; and there are all the complications of huge individual differences.

This fundamental vagueness perhaps explains why the literature is at present so conflicting. Broadly, the academics, eg Davis and Cherns (1975) Warr (1976), are generating books in support of the broad theme, while recognising the difficulties of obtaining evidence about either theoretical soundness or operational utility. Evidence continues to accumulate about the difficulties in basic theory, eg Wahba *et al* (1974); difficulties of relating job satisfaction to performance variables, eg Wanous (1974); and some of the parameters of individual differences are being explored, eg Fossum (1973/74). Some investigators, eg Parke *et al* (1975), are becoming increasingly critical. They point out that quality may improve with job enrichment, not only because of individual well-being, but because with fewer people involved in one product 'management gained the ability to pinpoint performances above and below standard ... the potential for buck-passing was severely restricted'. Frank *et al* (1975) describe a case study where goals of job satisfaction, higher motivation and operator productivity were not met because the jobs in practice changed very little, because the responsible vice-president was replaced by one more sceptical about job enrichment, and because the contract of the consultant involved expired during the project. These latter, of course, are typical of the practical variables which often confound research findings and which are not always reported in sufficient detail.

Research implications

The psychometric approach

An investigator's confidence in a particular technique rests on two foundations: his trust in the theory on which it is based and his experience of successful application as measured by some external criterion; in psychometric jargon this is content validity and criterion validity respectively. Each must be developed slowly and systematically with varieties of studies which hopefully coalesce into a gradually improving overall validity. In this context, job satisfaction studies have scarcely begun compared for example with studies of intelligence. The analogy seems to be quite close. In both cases we have a theoretical construct of dangerous apparent simplicity because it is widely used in ordinary life ('everybody knows that there is such a thing as intelligence/ satisfaction') but attempts to define such terms more precisely prove extraordinarily difficult, and measurement is correspondingly loose. There is the problem of whether we are talking about a general factor, with related subsidiary factors, or whether there are a set of overlapping basic factors, and if so how many and what are they. There are difficulties about separating maturational effects from learning effects. These are problems of how much the measurement is affected if the subject is more or less co-operative, or whether he makes more or less effort in completing his part of the proceedings. If the job satisfaction metric is to develop along the same lines and with the same time scale as the intelligence metric then clearly we have a long wait before anything emerges which is theoretically defensible and operationally useful.

The systems approach

The systems concept of attempting to separate an objective from a function, which is a component in the means of achieving that objective, provokes some interesting questions. Is job satisfaction an end or a means? The same question can usefully be asked of all the jargon in this field: job enlargement, job enrichment, individual autonomy, group autonomy. Do we try these things because they are worthwhile in themselves or because they further other objectives either of an individual kind, such as dignity or well-being, or of a system kind, such as productivity or quality?

Every system is a sub-system of a larger system, and a particular system can be over-optimized at the expense of the parent system or other sub-systems. How do we balance the needs of people who are components of a system with those of others who are customers of that system? This difficulty exists for all systems, but it is most obviously acute in direct people-service systems such as hospitals or educational institutions. What are the relative priorities in the needs and aspirations of nurses and patients, lecturers and students? How do these interact with the requirements of the people in the parent system who, in both the above cases, are the tax-payers?

Systems analysis could usefully be employed on a much larger scale in the clarification of job satisfaction issues. Since there appears to have been very little work of this kind, the first effect is likely to be obscuration rather than clarification. But, hopefully, the essential outcome would be a more soundly based conceptual map of what is happening and why, in a much wider context than the individual or the group working at an apparently isolated job. The assumption of isolation is a dangerous illusion.

The human resources approach

Job satisfaction can be perceived as just one facet of the enormously complex problem of the utilization of the human resource. The system under consideration might be of any size from the working group through the department, factory, region, country, continent to the working world. At the world level, we already have an impossible problem to allow each individual the satisfaction of using his available energy and meeting his particular aspirations—which may be little more than temporary survival. It might reasonably be argued that this is too big a problem, and has virtually nothing to do with the job satisfaction investigator working in a particular factory. However, this investigator must appreciate that, in world terms, he is indulging in an exercise for the privileged. Even just beyond the factory in the region and country there are now so many people for whom the problem is not one of making their jobs satisfying but of actually creating jobs for them to do. The purpose of this paragraph is not to deliver a moral lecture, but rather to make the point that job satisfaction is far from being all-important; and given a currently limited human resource of human resource specialists, not too many of them should expend their expertise on job satisfaction. There are other, more important, issues in the larger context.

Taking an intermediate view of, say, the level of a country or region over a few decades of time the problem is how to define and describe the available human resources so that these can be actively and purposefully employed without excessive expenditure of the limited physical resources of energy, material and space. If this kind of matching of community needs to resources can be done, even crudely, then job satisfaction can probably be left to take care of itself through the initiative of the individuals involved. An alternative argument would be that we need to clarify the concept of job satisfaction as one part of the business of making the crude match: but these alternatives themselves need further clarification. To repeat the question: is a knowledge of job satisfaction a necessary component of human resources studies or is it an intrinsic byproduct of effective human resource utilization?

Operational implications

Pursuing the theme that all management services have common application problems, but different models of the focus of investigators' attention, then the operational utility of job satisfaction studies must be assessed in terms of the power of the particular model as a problem solving aid.

The most highly developed technique for assessing existing jobs, in terms of potentiality for redesign, seems to be that due to Hackman and Oldham (Butteriss, 1975). Their job diagnosis survey (JDS) depends on five job dimensions (skill variety, task identity, task significance, autonomy and feedback), three critical psychological states (experienced meaningfulness, experienced responsibility and knowledge of results), and affective reactions (subdivided into general and specific satisfactions). These dimensions, states and outcomes are related to predicting the potentiality for individual growth and the implementing concepts which might encourage that growth.

A different approach has been developed by researchers at Texas Instruments. They suggest that there are four motivation strategies: communication, job design, management procedures and individual growth opportunities; and three maintenance strategies: pay and benefits, system opportunities and facilities. They incorporate individual differences by a seven level taxonomy of value systems; reactive, tribalistic, egocentric, conformist, manipulative, sociocentric and existential.

Returning to the total problem of providing a management service, or an individual worker service, this approach may be desirable and perhaps necessary, but it is certainly not sufficient. It does not encompass problems of physiological and information load. Verhaegen (1977) suggests that, in Herzberg terminology, these traditional problems of ergonomics are essentially extrinsic, or hygiene, factors so that their absence will lead to dissatisfaction but will not produce positive satisfaction. This is one way of looking at it. We are back to the problem of which is core and which is periphery. Leaving aside the larger problems of creating jobs and assessing community contributions of jobs, given a job to assess it would seem reasonable that we have three separable stages, the physiological problems, the informational problems and the affective problems. The current state of the art seems to be the struggle to develop this third category on a reasonable systematic basis.

The objectives of these studies remain what they always were: productivity and health with productivity incorporating efficiency and health incorporating well-being.

Some problems of theory and method

Lisl Klein
Tavistock Institute of Human Relations, London, United Kingdom

I am glad and interested to see ergonomists exploring outside their traditional boundaries but sorry that they have chosen to focus on 'job satisfaction'. It is a pity because it has led Professor Singleton to use his great skill for shooting down some not very relevant aunt sallies.

Job satisfaction is not a design goal. As far as I know, it has never been the goal of serious researchers and action researchers working empirically in the field of job design. It may be an indicator that one is reaching or failing to reach a goal, but even then it is not a very reliable one. National surveys consistently show something like 75% to 80% of people as being fairly well satisfied with their current work situation—but I do not know what that means. I can interpret comments indicating dissatisfaction because they are usually about specific issues. I can sometimes interpret comments about specific items on the positive side. But I do not know what to do with general aggregate measures of satisfaction except, very occasionally, as indicators of a trend, and I know of no-one who uses them as anything else.

The work of the Tavistock Institute of Human Relations has been one of the main influences in opening the door to the possibility of choosing from among alternative forms of work organization, or alternative job designs, according to criteria to do with people: and in that work you will not find job satisfaction mentioned. What you will find mentioned are roles (as distinct from tasks), role relationships, inter-dependence, and criteria for the design of jobs which are to do with learning, development and growth.

What this is about seems to me to be very simple and not to require all those tortured little models. Because a large part of man's waking life is spent at work, work should have some characteristics, and provide some experiences that are helpful to his development. This suggests that the design of jobs should incorporate design criteria such as the opportunity to continue learning, to relate to and communicate with others, to contribute to the setting of standards, to have feed-back on one's performance, to have some control over one's own work situation, at least over such things as pace and movement, to use and develop skills. Certainly criteria such as these are based on value judgement. I cannot ask clients to share this value judgement; but I can offer it to them to accept or reject, and I can offer them strategies for making their own values explicit. The problem is that you cannot ask someone whether he wants an apple if he has no previous experience of apples. You have to provide an opportunity to try apples before deciding whether to accept or reject them. Since any client population is in any case unlikely to be homogeneous, the challenge to the designer is to provide for opportunities which do not have to be taken up, or which can be taken up differentially. That is not beyond the bounds of ingenuity and that is what one's work is about.

I also cannot ask the ergonomist as a job designer to share my values, but I can ask as a scientist that he makes his own values explicit. Every job design has values implicit in it; and ergonomists, no less than people working in the 'softer' human sciences, have a responsibility to make their values manifest and to let their clients choose whether they share them, and not to pretend that they come from some realm where choices don't have to be made.

Let me change frames of reference for a moment from individual psychology to sociology and structure. If you separate the setting of standards from the meeting of standards and allocate these functions to different roles in the system, then I can predict that those who are being controlled will try to find ways to regain control. In any specific control system I can predict where the fiddles will be. If you set things up so that one set of people make decisions and a different set of people are required to carry them out, there will be structural division in industry. The people involved may or may not express satisfaction: I don't know. I do know that conflict will have been designed into the system and that the response will be either overt conflict or some form of withdrawal.

It may be that, in terms of psychological health, conflict is preferable to passivity. In any case, design choices are followed by adaptations and adjustments. There are in fact many people now who believe that structural division in industry is an entirely satisfactory state of affairs and should not be interfered with. Not very long ago, a young German trade unionist said to me that you must not do away with the machine-paced, mass-production assembly line, because the assembly line is the basis of 'die Kollektive', of collective organisation which of course it is. How you react to this realization is a political choice, just as much as his reaction is a political one. Design decisions have long-term behavioural consequences and professionals have a responsibility to take that seriously and not to play academic parlour games.

A non-political way of putting what I have just been saying is that people make adjustments and adaptations to the work situations in which they find themselves. When you re-design a job (and we are not often in a greenfield situation, working with new jobs), you are not only attacking the structure of that job, you are also attacking the adjustment and adaptation that people have already made to it. And that is the dilemma—we are working in a context.

It is not only an ethical and political dilemma, but a scientific one. Context is the problem surrounding the validity of findings in the social sciences. From the social science world come ideas with varying degrees of verification. Maslow's hierarchy of needs concept and Herzberg's two-factor theory of motivation, are examples of ideas which, in parts of the social science community, are regarded as inadequately verified; while in parts of the user community they are regarded as useful products of social science. There are probably no findings so respectable as to remain completely unchallenged. Absence of consensus about what are valid findings is partly due to the politics and career structure of academic life. To some extent the identity and worth of one's own work, or that of one's team or school, are established by challenging the work of others, and this may not necessarily be done by replicating the work but by using different methods which, in any case, are likely to lead to different findings. However, there is another consideration, which is more intrinsic to the subject-matter: the distinction between an idea and a valid finding is, in principle, less fundamental in the social sciences than in the natural sciences because of the greater influence of differences in context. Even in the same historical period, different ideas which are not apparently compatible are put forward simultaneously, but concerning which one can find evidence if one looks carefully enough. Even more, a different geographical or historical context will affect the evidence for the same idea. Differences in context mean that some investigations are not repeatable, or not repeatable in the same form. Differences in context and time probably constitute the greatest problem in establishing any fundamental parallels between the social and the natural sciences.

However, this does not imply chaos, and total relativism. There are underlying generalities over which different concrete manifestations cluster. In the field which is generally called behaviour in organizations—although this is a phrase I dislike—I can suggest three examples of such underlying generalities, which probably have a more than temporary validity.

Firstly, the structural characteristics implied by time, market, technology and control systems in an organization will have behavioural consequences. Secondly, within narrower systems boundaries, the structural characteristics of jobs and work roles have some psychological consequences for the people doing them; in turn, people can influence the structure of their environment to some extent. The technical and social systems are interdependent. Thirdly, process, as well as content, is relevant. This implies, first, that how things are done (for instance how changes are introduced) will be relevant to outcomes as well as the content of what is done. And it implies, secondly, that groups and organizations can learn to review themselves and treat the processes by which they work as subjects for explicit consideration.

When it comes to application, context again makes replication and comparison difficult; whether an organization is the first pioneer to try out a new concept, or the twentieth follower, or whether it is compelled into application by policy or by law, will make a substantial difference to the result, and this really complicates our work tremendously. The enthusiasm with which something is being introduced may be the most influential factor around. On the other hand, sophisticated subjects may become immune to the Hawthorne effect and some change strategies may not be effective when tried repeatedly.

Now, I have been in the habit of thinking that these are problems of social psychology and sociology, and that psychology is relatively free of them. But my attention was drawn to the 1977 Presidential address to the British Psychological Association, which I found quite surprising. This is Dr. May

Davidson speaking, having taken application in psychology as her theme: 'It is a common experience of applied psychologists that more is expected of them by some other human beings than they can in fact deliver. The psychologists, in turn, expect their discipline to provide better solutions to many problems than it can produce.' She ascribes the discomforts and conflicts currently experienced by many applied psychologists to the fact that they were forced to emerge from a 'safe and sterile' psychometric tradition by three things: (a) longitudinal studies which took into account the influence on behaviour of situational and environmental variables and emphasized the dynamism in human affairs; (b) the growing evidence of experimenter effects on behavioural research and the tendency to create situations leading to self-fulfilling prophesies; and (c) an explosive growth in behaviour therapy and behaviour modification, which turned the applied psychologist into an interventionist.

These dilemmas sound to me remarkably similar to the ones in my own field—it seems to me we are in not dissimilar positions.

Because of these dilemmas, and because the reality we are dealing with is so complicated, the concepts that have emerged to deal with it have been inadequate, in two distinct ways. They have either been concepts which only deal with a part of the reality, so that one will always find some part of the data that they have not accounted for. Or they have been formulated at such a high level of generality that they are not operationally very useful. Among the first I would include the Herzberg theory and the hierarchy-of-needs concept. They can be criticized, they do not account for everything. But they do make sense of some experience, of some of the data. There 'is something in' the idea of a hierarchy of needs—even the most objective design criteria will have different salience, different degrees of importance, in different economic circumstances. There is an area of usefulness between taking an idea literally and rejecting it altogether. Ambiguity is part of our situation and we have to learn to come to terms with it.

Systems concepts, including the concept of the socio-technical system, I take at the moment to be formulated at such a high level of generality as not to be, by themselves, operationally very useful. A great deal still has to be done to make them operational and, in the meantime, the attractiveness of systems concepts in theory should not delude us into thinking that we have the tools to deal comprehensively with the problems of job design in practice. Ambiguity remains part of our work situation whether we like it or not, so we might as well lie back and enjoy it.

Finally, I want to put forward two methodological problems, which I take to be key ones at the moment, and which present very exciting methodological challenges to us. The first is the problem of combining quality with quantity. At a conference last year a Swedish researcher gave a paper on the consequences of a job design project. The whole paper was concerned with the responses of two women in the project. One of them had flourished and developed in the course of it; the other had experienced difficulties, and the researcher discussed the work that had been done with her, the adjustments that had been made, and so on. That is, if you like, the ideal type of one tradition. In the British and Scandinavian context we are familiar with projects where great care is taken to work with a particular group, a department, etc.

How does one do that on a large scale? For example, I do some work with one of the clearing banks in England. I know how to work with a branch of the bank and I know how to work with a district in which there are a number of branches. But I have great difficulty in knowing how to work with something that has three and a half thousand branches and over 50,000 employees.

The German Government programme on 'humanising work', is very much in the other direction: it is about diffusion, it is about application on a large scale. Partly because public funds are being spent, and partly because of a particular scientific tradition, they are looking for knowledge which has general application and which can be incorporated into design strategies or administered via the law, via structure and via technology. And because of that—this is of course very much over-simplified—there is some tendency for individuals in the projects to be the rather passive recipients of design and research attention. I don't know how one handles both levels simultaneously, and I think it would be very exciting if we were to focus our attention onto this problem.

The second methodological problem is about relating different frames of reference to each other. I have mentioned the complexities of context. The only person who incorporates comprehensively all aspects of the context of a job is the person doing it. That is why design strategies involving the job-holders themselves are a greater safeguard than reliance on specialists and experts that important things will not be left out. It is not merely a matter of the ideology of participation. Insofar as professionals are involved, it is quite clear by now that there are a number of distinct frames of reference, all of which are relevant. Ease of operation, safety, personal development, interest groups; one could list quite a number. The challenge is how to relate them to each other. It is easy to say 'multi-disciplinary work', but I know of no really satisfactory way to do it. One must not create a mere mish-mash, one cannot simply 'unify'. There is much work still to be done, possibly painful, in learning how to relate frames of reference to each other. In the meantime, once ergonomists venture outside their traditional boundaries, it is not all unbridled intuition, philosophy and politics. There are empirical research findings, there are disciplined methods and there is experience, outside the boundaries of ergonomics as well as within them.

Ergonomic principles of work structuring

Walter Rohmert
University of Darmstadt, West Germany

Over a long period of development, man was so superior to the machine that he could always adapt himself to its demands as well as to his own needs. This has been changed by progress in technology and by the division of tasks. Now the content and environment of work are changed to such an extent that they can be inappropriate for the natural conditions of human life. Therefore every work design is obliged to consider all the needs of men at their work. There is an increasing need to consider the quality of working life.

Agreed criteria of quality of working life can be fixed and controlled by national or international laws, regulations and rules. If they go beyond guiding-principles they may guarantee work reaching the minimum laid-down conditions, but very often this produces negative or fatalistic attitudes among people. Workers, of course, are aware of a potential legal claim while management simply try to avoid violating the laws. Both groups develop non-creative reactions instead of looking for better solutions of work design. The German legislation on work places (Arbeitsstättenverordnung, 1975) for example, includes a special paragraph of 'exceptions', meaning that the employer is allowed to take other work design measures than those formulated in the regulations. But doing so he has to prove that his measure has the same effect. The burden of proof is on him; which means he will avoid taking risks and will not try to be innovative or experiment. It was accepted that there was a real necessity to develop a governmental action programme for research in humanization of working life (Bundesminister für Arbeit und Sozialordnung, 1974). Its purpose was to encourage industry to make more effort in improving human work content and working conditions by financing 50% of the necessary investment costs.

Tackling the problem in this manner is not only unattractive and ineffective; it is wrong. Work design is a cyclic process dependent on criteria which are fixed and accepted (see Figure 1). This paper goes into details as far as ergonomic criteria are included. The hierarchy of the aims of work design and the possibility of establishing guiding-principles for the ergonomic design procedure is shown.

Satisfactions in work design

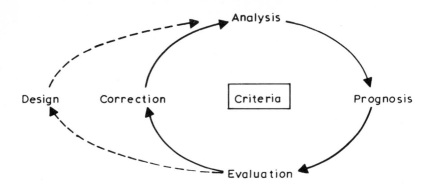

Figure 1.   Cyclic process of work design dependent on (fixed and accepted) criteria.

The ergonomic design process is a series of steps within a cycle. After analyzing the design problem the step of prognosis follows; the stress which will be imposed on the workers and their job satisfaction can be predicted. If the result of this evaluation procedure satisfies the fixed criteria which are accepted by all institutions and people concerned with work conditions, the design loop can be completed and the design can be realized. More often, however, the result of evaluation requires modifications which have to be re-analyzed. Then the design loop starts again.

Steps of work design and their limiting conditions

In general, the cyclic process of work design shown in Fig. 1 is negative. Corrections are necessary. The loop will be traversed several times. This means that the procedure shown in Fig. 2 will be carried out often. This procedure shows the state of each work design option (see circle at the bottom of the figure) which comes about as a result of the different steps of design and their limiting conditions. In general, each purpose and aim of a man-at-work system (see circle at the top of the figure) allows a choice among different kinds of technology. By selecting one, the first condition of work design is fixed. The next decision means the selection of the technology of production; at this stage of the design process the limiting conditions are determined by economic and technological factors as well as by regulations and laws of safety at work and in the community, and by the application of ergonomics. Then the degree of mechanization (Rohmert. 1969, 1971, 1972) has to be fixed. Among different alternatives a particular structure of work has to be chosen. This selection is influenced by a choice of the degree of functional division between man and man (job partition) or man and machine (allocation of functions), and by economic as well as by social or socio-political factors.

After fixing these general conditions the process of work design in the very detailed sense can start. At first we can design specific working tools, machines, places and environment in the course of which limiting conditions of ergonomics and industrial hygiene have to be taken into account, as well as legal postulates and the restrictions of labour law and negotiation agreements.

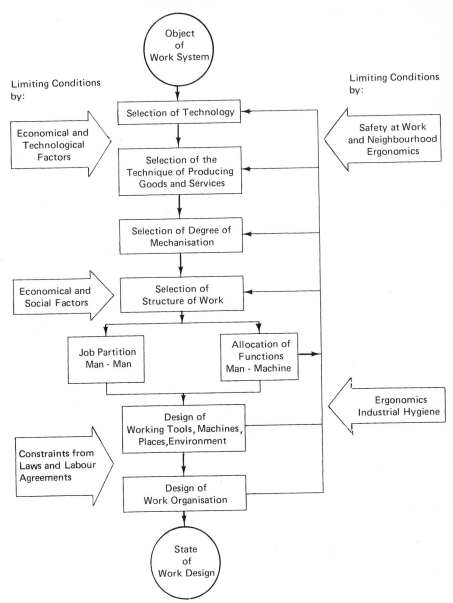

Figure 2.   State of work design resulting from different steps of design and their limiting conditions.

In the final step of the design, work has to be organized with respect to the working time (e.g. shift schedules, duration of shift, location and length of rest pauses). In this area, also, the same limiting conditions of design have to be respected. The result of the total design procedure emerges as a specific state of work design. Fig. 2 shows that there is a feedback from the final steps of the design process to the prior selections of design-options dependent on the criteria of evaluation of work and the limiting factors involved.

Humanitarian considerations and profitability as main design aims

When planning and designing work systems, the designer must have some knowledge of various alternative approaches to design, their effects on the goals and objectives of the work system and their effects on, or demands they make of, the work personnel. In planning and designing work systems the designer has to evaluate and select from various alternative designs. Therefore it is necessary to formulate design aims.

The interpretation of these aims is important as regards the proposed preparation and interpretation of design knowledge. The user of the knowledge must be aware of them in order that he can form his own opinion about the interpretation. The general aims of work design in the context of designing the man-at-work system will therefore be discussed briefly. The system design should, first and foremost, achieve the desired purpose of the work system (compare 'object of work system' in Fig. 2). However, other criteria must be used to decide the best way to realize the aims. These design aims may vary considerably from case to case, depending on the particular set of design problems. However, main aims can be defined, and the specific, detailed aims should contribute to these.

The efficiency of work systems under design or evaluation to fulfil a specific purpose, is always a main aim. There should be an optimum ratio of outlay to return, as this means that the most can be achieved with, or the greatest benefit derived from, the minimum of resources. However, as far as the benefit is concerned and how to achieve it, we find that it always comes back to people: as profit makers and profit losers. Consequently, work system design must always take into account the human contribution to doing the work and human needs with respect to what is produced by the work. Work systems designing must, therefore, include *human criteria* (that is to say, relate to human beings) and profitability as a work product must also serve humanity.

In our competitive economic and social system, profitability of individual economic units or organizations is a prime determinant. However, most research and experience has shown that man and his contribution to work can greatly affect the achievement of the economic purpose in a work system. Here we would simply remind you of the importance of motivation in output and production and in keeping down costs, and the long-term advantage to be gained from human capabilities given a suitable work-load as compared with the disadvantages of short-term exploitation of human working power. Therefore, while pursuing economic aims, we also have to consider humanitarian aims, lest we reduce the chances of achieving the economic aim in the long term.

Therefore, humanitarian considerations and profitability are always regarded as the joint leaders in the league of design aims. Of course, specific design measures will tend to promote one or the other more, but within the framework of a design project they must complement each other in a sensible way.

Construction of a hierarchical system of design aims

Primary design aims are too general, and cannot reasonably be used as a basis for stipulating the concrete factors and measures governing design. By looking for secondary aims which may contribute to the particular primary aims, we can construct a hierarchical system of aims. This will define specific aims, the relation of which to the primary aims can at any time be traced through the hierarchical system of aims. The secondary aims provide initially the direct starting point for the design process.

First of all, secondary aims have to be formulated. This leads to a list of aims which, understandably enough, does not include everything which can be pursued when designing work systems. Rather, this list is a selection of those aims which may play an important role in designing human work. It seems to be appropriate to use different lists. A basic list could be a classical ergonomic one with supplements related to specific aspects, e.g. safety aspects (Becker-Biskaborn 1975) and aspects of work structuring (Rohmert and Weg 1976).

These aims are formulated as desired changes in a situation, since the aim of designing is always to alter a given situation defined as unsatisfactory. This can apply to an existing work system which is to be improved, or to the original designing of a work system from scratch. Since the words here do not relate to a specific concrete design project, but are intended to be generalizations, they indicate the desirable way in which to change a given situation by active 'change' words, e.g. increase, reduce, ensure, facilitate, etc. The reference criterion to be changed is the noun at the beginning of the formulated aims, which also serves as a key word and ordinal word for the formulated aims. Fig. 3 gives some examples of the procedure described.

SERIAL NO.	CONTENT OF THE AIM	ORDINAL NO. (FOR AIMS SYSTEM)
AIMS AREA PROFITABILITY (P)		
2	TO INCREASE **PRECISION IN THE WORK**	P 62
11	TO REDUCE **FLUCTUATION**	P 34
24	TO IMPROVE **TIME UTILIZATION**	P 43
AIMS AREA HUMANITY (H)		
2	TO REDUCE **STRAIN**	H 43
20	TO FACILITATE **SELF-RECOGNITION THROUGH WORK**	H 45
24	TO AVOID **MAKING TOO FEW DEMANDS**	H 56

Figure 3.   List of aims for designing working systems (some examples)

The aims in the catalogue to Fig. 3 and in both the main areas of aims are equivalent. The evaluation of the aims is a subjective one and is related to decisions based not only on ergonomics but on other disciplines as well as on sociopolitical agreements. Often, achieving one aim contributes to achieving another. On the other hand, two aims can also conflict with each other. Therefore, the aims in the catalogue of aims should be arranged as an hierarchical aims system.

A detailed graphical description of the aims system under the aspects of work structuring is given by Rohmert and Weg (1976). All aims at a lower level in the hierarchy contribute towards the realization of higher hierarchical aims. When considering the relationships between aims in a means-end system, it is seen that a subsidiary aim can contribute to the accomplishment of a primary aim. Nevertheless, these relationships are not always causal but may be absolute and as such not to be accepted. It is also suggested that in such a system, covering the design for men as workers (ergonomic design), human motivation plays an important role in the accomplishment of the overall aims.

The position of an aim within the aims system does not indicate the value of the aim. It merely indicates that aims appearing further down are more concrete and specific than those nearer the top. In some cases, direct connections jump the intermediate stages. These are in addition to indirect connections (e.g. those assigned to a primary aim via several stages). This has been done if the intermediate aim does not completely exhaust the possibilities of the secondary aim contributing to the primary aim. For instance, increasing the precision of work helps 'to prevent mistakes', which helps to 'improve the quality of the product'; or 'increasing the precision of work' helps to 'improve the quality of the product', which applies if the quality is to be improved and not only maintained.

The various potential contributions of secondary aims to primary aims in the system cannot be quantified with weight, since this would depend too much on the particular man-at-work system under design. The weighting of specific measures has to be considered.

Some of the aims mutually contribute to achieving the aim (they are complementary aims), while others may be mutually obstructive, or even completely prevent the achieving of an aim (i.e. competing aims). For instance, 'increasing the work rate' and 'increasing the precision of work' are often in conflict. This is not specifically indicated within each aim area, since it must be assumed from the outset that the most important aim can only be achieved if all secondary aims have been achieved in the best possible way. Then, for each specific design, the importance of each secondary aim in achieving the particular aim is weighted accordingly.

The situation is rather different with respect to the connections between the two aim areas 'humanity' and 'profitability'. Here, there are characteristic conflicts between aims. For instance, intense concentration of the work may increase strain, which negates the aim of reducing stress. This in turn may have adverse effects on the efficiency of human work, perhaps because of increased fatigue, and this reduces output.

The aim system described is offered as a stimulus and an aid to the specific designing of ergonomic problems. Of course, we cannot claim that this system has absolute validity, since it must necessarily include judgements which can never have absolute validity but can only find general acceptance. Thus, the aims system proposed for the ergonomic designing of human work can be supplemented or modified.

A four-level hierarchy for assessment of work design

The aims system for designing human work shows the close links between the economic and human aspects of the design, and it is clearly quite illogical to pursue economic aims without considering human aims. Remember that, in a wider sociological context, economic aims must always be of service to humanity, otherwise, in the long term, they become self-destructive and pointless.

To assess the results of design of human work in the context of an overall man-at-work system design, apart from the primary aims of humanity and profitability, there are four cardinal criteria, the fulfilment of which contributes to the primary aims. Therefore, the evaluation of any concrete work design has to consider and to satisfy a four-level hierarchy: ability; tolerability; acceptability; and satisfaction.

The ability of man to do the job is a basic prerequisite for profitability. Human capabilities and characteristics must enable man to do the work before the work can be carried out at all. This limit of man's ability means a level of practicability of using human input. If the work design does not consider these maximal capacities, even if only required for a limited time by men at their work, then the designer is obliged to give up all claim to human power; the designer has to design a completely automatic work system. Therefore the level of practicability of human work sets imperative claims to cater for human functions (e.g. body dimensions, muscular strength, speed and accuracy of movements, sensory-organ functions, etc).

In most cases, we are not only interested in the 'one off' completion of a job (as in sports), but we require a daily repetition in the work during a normal shift's duration and over the total working life's period. Under these longer lasting conditions the demands placed on men have to be lower. The highest level of demand which can be endured to the end of the normal working life without any work-related damage to health or normal human functional abilities is called the level of tolerability. The qualitative and quantitative output of a man affects profitability. Then there is effectiveness in the sense of general efficiency. Not all working conditions are equally conducive to quality and quantity of output or to incurring minimum costs; this, in turn, affects profitability.

The cardinal criteria for assessing the humanity of work and working conditions are health, well-being and job satisfaction. However, it is important to see that well-being and satisfaction always include long-term tolerability of work in health terms. Therefore the second level of tolerability in assessing work systems also makes imperative claims on the designer as well as the worker and the trade unions, or the employers and the employers' federations.

The third criterion level means that working conditions should be accepted by those who are social partners on the shop floor or at the labour agreement level. Unfortunately conditions can be accepted by local agreement as well as imposed by labour laws which are not tolerable over the total life's period. Therefore the third level of acceptability of human work-design needs must respect the hierarchical level of tolerability first of all, but only after ensuring 'acceptability' working conditions. Understandably, social and perhaps individual values have a large part to play here. Also, there are likely to be changes in attitudes in the course of time. This is shown clearly when regarding the development of the modern slogan of 'improving quality of life'. There are, of course, human working conditions which were acceptable in the past or which will be accepted in times of high unemployment, which in normal conditions today are assessed to be inhumane. However, the more important postulate for humanity is to respect the conditions of long-term tolerability.

The hierarchy of assessment of human working conditions or design claims which starts with the individual level of man's ability ends at an individual level; the highest level of satisfaction. Both the levels in between are mainly oriented to more or less homogeneous groups and not necessarily to the individual. Striving for conditions of highest job satisfaction does not necessarily ensure tolerable conditions. For example, if someone is very content with his working conditions it might be, nevertheless, that his work load is intolerably high due to the fact that one stress factor, not necessarily its intensity but its duration, is too high. This can occur if a man works too much overtime or omits rest pauses, recovery periods and holidays under the illusion that he is doing a very satisfactory job. Also, the long distance jumper at the Olympic games will be highly content with his performance although he may never succeed in doing this maximal performance again. The two examples given show the importance of the basic levels in the hierarchy, as well as the necessity of setting and controlling design aims merely at these basic levels. Man does not know what is right and useful for him with regard to the defined tolerable conditions of health and well-being. This is shown by the examples of deciding for himself when to take meals or working time schedules and rest periods. There are very critical limits to the self-regulating of human working conditions. There is a real need in disciplines, methods, techniques and knowledge to adapt work to man and man to work to ensure 'tolerable' working conditions. Here is a real challenge for the human sciences, especially disciplines like ergonomics. Ergonomics may fix standards of work design primarily at the basic level of design assessment.

Fig. 4 summarizes the general principles of the four-level hierarchy of evaluating either the state of work design or the effects of work on man. For each of these four levels there are individual as well as collective standards which permit a rank order to occur in each case. Allied to each level we will find methods and techniques from different disciplines which are involved in the problems of designing and assessment. By this way one will find important subdisciplines of the human sciences. This is not intended as a claim for an hierarchy of scientific disciplines. Nevertheless, there is an important role for disciplines which use the methods and techniques of the natural sciences, the results of which have two important advantages in the context of man-at-work problems. Firstly, the results of applying methods of natural sciences to work design problems are reproducible; one can fix standards which can be measured. Secondly, these results (standards) have to stand the burden of being accepted and agreed, in accordance with human laws, as in mathematics. These two facts are, of course, extremely important in the application of knowledge to the field of work design where policies based on sociopolitical interests exist. In this context, ergonomics is classed with the natural sciences

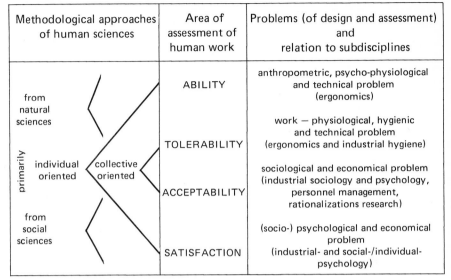

Methodological approaches of human sciences	Area of assessment of human work	Problems (of design and assessment) and relation to subdisciplines
	ABILITY	anthropometric, psycho-physiological and technical problem (ergonomics)
	TOLERABILITY	work — physiological, hygienic and technical problem (ergonomics and industrial hygiene)
	ACCEPTABILITY	sociological and economical problem (industrial sociology and psychology, personnel management, rationalizations research)
	SATISFACTION	(socio-) psychological and economical problem (industrial- and social-/individual-psychology)

Figure 4.   A four-level hierarchy for assessment of work design

and plays an important role in fixing standards of work design based on the evaluation levels one and two of the hierarchy; namely the level of ability and the level of tolerability.

Ergonomic guiding-principles of work structuring

Although there might still be a real lack of ergonomics knowledge, and of the results of experimental and empirical research of human sciences, ergonomics has tried often to summarize what is known and what can be applied. This way of presenting knowledge becomes important because design problems are complex, and knowledge is spread over many disciplines each with their own journals, documentation systems and different scientific languages.

Hitherto, the problem of processing and adapting ergonomic knowledge for practical application has been tackled by: research report and case studies; textbooks and manuals; data collections; check lists.

In these presentations two factors are usually missing: the aims of the design, that is to say, what is to be achieved by the design; and a procedure for redesigning as a synthetic process, a procedure which is both logically consistent and, at the same time, rational.

In particular, there is no suitable procedure which can be used to design an overall optimum plan for human work in its context, instead of the limited approach of optimizing some aspects of it. Therefore we used the approach of presenting 'guide lines for the design of human work'. Of course, with the means and time at our disposal it is impossible to process all the data in every sphere. On the one hand there is too much data to do this; on the other hand, much data are missing especially from research in the social sciences. However, examples from selected areas indicate the form further expansion of

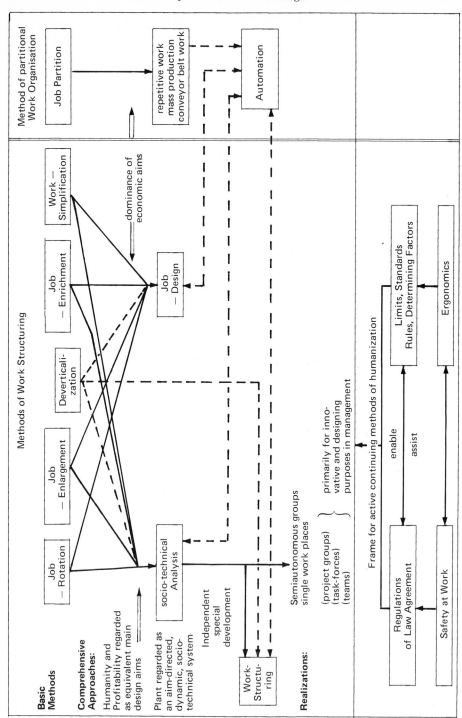

guide lines could take. We would therefore recommend publication of a further document to complete and extend the design suggestions in the various areas. This could form the basis of a new type of design manual.

Fig. 5 shows the relations between methods of organization of work classified into methods of work structuring and methods of job division. Finally some examples of guide lines will be illustrated for achieving those goals of work organization. At the end of each guide line the aims will be mentioned which should be achieved by this measure.

— As the *contribution of man*
(functions and parts of job to be done) consider man and his capabilities, which are superior to those of machines, mainly in:
  — predicting situations
  — interpreting situations
  — learning abilities and utilization of experience
  — flexibility in doing different jobs
  Aims: To improve the efficiency of human work
        To facilitate self-appraisal through work
— The *part of the work done by man*
should be performable with a free working rhythm and permit unimpeded growth of ability. Prolonged periods of time stress should be avoided, e.g. by
  — avoiding being bound to the rhythm of a machine (e.g. by an interposed buffer)
  — avoiding partial automation
  — avoiding being bound to the rate of other workers (production line)
  Aims: To reduce strain
        To enable ability to grow at work
— *Experience of older workers*
to be utilized, e.g. by
  — collaboration in designing projects
  — collaboration to improve known failings
  Aims: To facilitate self-appraisal through work
        To prevent mistakes
— For *structuring individual jobs* (job enlargement; job enrichment)
(scope of work for one worker) a rational work content should be provided, e.g. by
  — producing a complete intermediate product
  — carrying out all the processes of one type, including preparation and follow-up work
  — checking of own work including follow-up work
  Aims: To create interest in the work
        To enable ability to grow during work
        To avoid monotony
        To improve independent capacity
        To increase job satisfaction
— For *arranging several work places*
consider their interrelationship in terms of a larger task and facilitate co-operation, e.g. by
  — arranging for production flow

— setting up production groups
— team work (parallel jobs must be coordinated)
— seating workers facing one another
Aims: To improve cooperation
       To improve utilization
       To create interest in the work

More detailed examples, mainly guide lines in designing autonomous group work, will be found in the literature (Rohmert and Weg 1976).

The planning of new production systems

Lars E. Björk
The Swedish Council for Personnel Administration, Stockholm, Sweden

The changing background to work

This paper gives some reflections on the background and emerging new principles in the design of Swedish production systems.

During recent years there have been some new tendencies in Swedish industry. Many companies have decentralized their production. Many have started to get rid of routine tasks and some companies have tried a production design based on autonomous groups.

The development in Swedish factories and in Swedish society generally in the fifties and the sixties forms a background which can be valuable in the understanding of present trends. I will use three levels of description to picture the situation in Sweden 15 years ago. The levels are societal including both the community surrounding the factory and the whole nation; the second level is the company; the third is the individual.

Changes in society:

Many workers were made redundant during these years. The reason for this was the more and more systematized and high demands that were put upon the individual worker. The concept of a 'normal worker' underlying many of the most refined workstudy methods undermined the possibilities for older, or only slightly underperforming, workers of earning a living in many industries. One consequence for society was a rising number of people in need of help.

In order to handle the market forces in society the government had to take action against the stronger concentration of companies in the urban areas leaving a lot of workers behind in the less populated areas of Sweden. The answer to that was the so-called structural rationalization which sometimes had the effect of requiring workers to move to the location of the companies rather than the other way around.

Changes on the company-level

To combat high production costs more companies tried to rationalize their production. The models for these changes were based on Tayloristic ideas of specialization and mass-production. One tool in this specialization and division of work was the unnecessarily detailed use of time and method measurements in some factories. These systems were characterized by a very detailed measuring of the individual worker.

At the company level, rising absenteeism and labour turnover were symptoms that everything was not alright. The manufacturing companies, especially, had difficulties recruiting Swedish employees. The companies reacted in different ways. To fill the gaps in the shop-floor organization they started recruiting foreign labour. This immigration grew to proportions that far exceeded all previous waves of immigration to Sweden.

Many managers began to see that refining the methods of the individual worker was no longer a fruitful way to proceed. Some managers were inspired by the views of American and British behavioural scientists that the specific competence of man lay in mental work and not in repetitive, short-cycle, purely physical tasks. There were many human resources to be utilized if only you could organize the job to motivate your workers.

In Norway some companies had started experiments with autonomous groups that seemed promising. The group could be a more flexible unit in the production chain than an individual.

Changes in the individual

Many workers were involuntarily hit by the structural rationalization. The closing down of factories in the less populated areas created much distress.

The establishment of factories based on regarding men as interchangeable parts created both distress and stress. Many young workers felt that the gap between their own job and the society outside the factory was too wide. 'Why take on a 30-second repetitive job if I don't have to?' Many young people suffered a shock coming from school to industry. Figures seem to indicate that it was not primarily the physical environment but their lack of freedom and influence on the work-situation that repelled the youths. The results of these changes on all three levels were an increased demand for influence from the employees and their unions. The growing discontent among the workers caused over 100 motions to be delivered to the LO-congress (Trade union) 1971. No less than a quarter of all the motions from local unions all over Sweden dealt with the questions of increasing influence over the company and over the work environment.

One final result of this will be seen during 1978 when an agreement on co-determination between the parties on the labour market will follow the Act on co-determination which became effective on January 1, 1977. Besides this Act there are several others of similar purpose concerned with workers' safety and health, board representation of workers in companies bigger than 25 employees, etc.

In conclusion this means that the situation on the Swedish labour market is profoundly changed today. The set of new and more humane values, that can be seen in the new laws and demands from the unions, have created a drastically different situation for the company that is planning a new production system. Swedish companies are now trying to meet this new challenge together with the demands for productivity. One case that might be of interest is Volvo's three-year-old car factory in Kalmar.

A factory built in a changed environment

When Volvo built another factory in 1973 for the assembly of cars they based it upon the results of changes that had taken place during the last decade. They wanted to reduce personnel turnover and absenteeism, mainly because they thought that the quality of the assembly was negatively affected by continuous changes in the workforce. By reducing the adjustment and repair time the total number of man-hours per assembled car would drop.

The objectives of the new plant were spelled out by Volvo top management: 'This is a factory that, without any sacrifice of efficiency or financial results, will give employees the opportunity to work in groups, to communicate freely, to shift among work assignments, to vary their pace, to identify themselves with the product, to be conscious of responsibility for quality, and to influence their own work environment. When a product is manufactured by workers who find their work meaningful, it will inevitably be a product of high quality'. (Agurén, Hansson and Karlsson, 1976).

The new Kalmar factory was organized in 30 different 'work-shops', each with 15-20 workers and each with a certain function, e.g. putting in the electrical system. Of the total 640 employees 100 are white-collar and the rest blue-collar. The responsibility of the foremen usually covers two workshops. The car bodies are transported between and inside the workshops on battery-powered assembly carriers. They are steered by magnetic tracks embedded in the floor, but they can also be steered manually. This makes it technologically possible to have some choice in the way of organizing work.

The assembly carriers are interesting from an ergonomic point of view because the body of the car placed on them can easily and quickly be tilted 90° to facilitate work on the underside of the car.

Between the groups of workers there are buffers of cars making it possible to speed up the rate of production for a while and then take an eight-minute break in the staff-room directly adjacent to the work area.

How has this experiment worked out? One year ago the employers confederation (SAF) together with the workers' union (LO) submitted an evaluative report on the Kalmar plant made by their joint central SAF/LO Council on Rationalization. The study was requested by the works' council at the Kalmar plant. The report states that: 'The Volvo plant at Kalmar is better than a conventional car assembly plant. It is better to work in, and from the point of view of efficiency it is at least as good as Volvo's conventional car factories in Sweden' (Agurén *et al.*, 1976).

Nine out of ten workers work in groups and switch their tasks. 'And eight out of the nine think this is a good way of working'. Most of the workers have been interested in sharing the responsibility for the quality of assembly.

Up-to-date figures from the spring of 1977 show that the errors made on every car had gone down by 50% on the Kalmar plant that year. This puts the quality of the new factory well ahead of the conventional Volvo factories.

Today more quality and checking is carried out by the workers and foremen themselves, and less by the specialist function quality control.

In conclusion the Kalmar plant has proved realistic, and even superior to conventional car factories. This is, however, not a question of one single change but of changes in the underlying principles of organization and job design. And all these ideas reflect the rising demands of the employees for co-determination.

New ideas in design and organization of production systems

As shown above, the motives for changing the design and organization of production systems vary among different groups facing different problems. But despite conflicts in motives between individuals, companies and society at large, some new principles seem to emerge that are accepted by most parties.

The difficulty, though, is that these new principles almost always describe certain desirable ends or solutions, but seldom have recipes for reaching these end-states. We can thus divide the new experiences into two parts. First, normatively good end-states of factory-design and organization and, secondly, normatively good ways of dealing with the necessary change-processes leading to these favourable outcomes.

The employers' confederation (SAF) has compiled a number of new trends in design of production systems and condensed them into four criteria of 'good and effective production systems' (Lindholm, 1977).
1. Co-ordinated independence of small systems, meaning that the production could be divided into small units to raise individual job satisfaction and involvement and to cut administrative costs.,
2. A high degree of stability of the production system, which means both the systems patterns of material-flow, its reliability and its ability to handle variations and disturbances.
3. Attractive tasks, which means that, given certain levels of aspirations and demands from people in society at a certain time, the jobs offered by the industry shall be attractive to employees of different ages. This seems to mean group jobs of an autonomous character.
4. A good production environment in terms of minimized risks for health and safety and also a physically pleasant work environment.

As we can see there has been a strong shift in principles among Swedish employers. A shift from promoting the 'physical' productivity of every single worker over to the 'also mental' productivity and often in the form of a group, meaning fewer costs for detailed co-ordination and administration.

The change processes leading to rising employee participation have been described in detail by a research project in Sweden sponsored by state funds. Some of its findings can be summarized as follows (Björk 1976).
1. Changes in companies are often described in formal terms which obscure their dynamics. We must describe the changes in such a way that the opinions, intentions and interests of individuals, groups and local parties become visible. Then we can begin to learn from the change processes.
2. The employees should take part from the beginning in all change processes. This means that even problems formulated by the employees can be built into or generate changes.

3. Changes in the companies should be governed by the interests of both parties, groups and individuals.
4. An important part of the change process is the learning of all involved. This process cannot work overnight. The important thing is to try to facilitate the employees' influence over their own situation and to create a situation where influence and change can grow at the pace demanded by the employees.

These findings are representative of the last year's research on change processes in a Swedish industry and will probably be of use for effecting changes in other companies aiming at democratization.

Roles and instruments in work design and work re-design

John R. de Jong
Netherlands

Work re-design: some recommendations

In the last few years, it has been increasingly recognized that human tasks and work situations should be in accordance with the needs, capacities and abilities of the performers of the tasks. This recognition of the significance of taking into account 'human factors' has led—with varying success—to the re-design of a number of tasks and work situations which were felt to be unsatisfactory.

Comparatively-speaking, it may be concluded that in a material number of cases attempts to improve existing work systems have failed (i.e. they were not appreciated by the employees concerned and moreover often did not contribute to the effectivity of the relative sub-system). There are various reasons including: the employees in question were hardly (if at all) involved in the change process; they felt that the changes were insignificant; and changes of the equipment, processes etc. had not been considered (de Jong 1974).

We have come to the conclusion that it is essential to apply a 'systems approach' with these characteristics: simultaneously taking into account of functional demands (following from the purpose of the considered sub-system), and human factors demands; and taking notice of all system elements (the inputs, transformations and outputs; the equipment, individual and group tasks; the information and pay system, etc.).

Experience of our own work as well as that of others shows that the following conditions should be fulfilled.

Management must recognize its responsibility for the 'quality of working life' in its organization.

The representatives of the employees (the works council and the unions) should in principle concur with the redesign of unsatisfactory jobs and work situations.

The approach should be participative in nature.

The performers of the tasks should want the redesign of their jobs and of their work situations.

Data concerning present job contents, work situations, wishes and opinions of the persons concerned and probable future developments, should be collected and taken into account.

Not merely horizontal and vertical enlargement of tasks, but also the change of such factors like the work organization, the product design, the equipment and the pay system should be considered.

In general, job enrichment (vertical job loading) and increased autonomy of work groups should be given preference to horizontal job enlargement and job rotation.

The developed solution should be flexible in the sense that it permits alternatives in the individual tasks and performances (and sometimes also in respect of products and quantities to be produced).

These conditions may be expounded briefly.

Attitudes of management

If the management does not explicitly recognize its responsibility for the quality of working life in its organization—(and if the management has no perception of what this includes in respect of job contents, working conditions etc)—it must be expected that re-design projects may fall when organizational measures, investments, changes in the pay plan etc. appear to be necessary.

Endorsement of the unions and the works council

The endorsement of the representatives of the employees is a prerequisite of their cooperation in the development and implementation phases of the re-design process.

Participative approach

On the one hand the employees can usually contribute considerably to the development of a solution; on the other their resistance must be expected if they cannot take part in the various phases of the re-design of their jobs and their work conditions, in the widest sense of the term (de Jong 1974).

Required data

Although the re-design of a work system should primarily be based on functional requirements and human factors considerations, the indicated data regarding the present situation and probable future, and the wishes and objections of the persons concerned, are indispensable.

Which data are to be collected depends, of course, on the problem to be solved and the persons who are to play a part in the re-design process. We recommend generally a 'project approach', with the cooperation of key employees from the considered sub-system, one or more industrial engineers, personnel officers (with a social sciences background) and, if desirable, ergonomists, design engineers and others.

In the last few years, a large number of studies have revealed that the satisfaction and the behaviour of the worker are influenced by such factors as: work content; workplace, physical work environment, the work group, work organization, system inputs (e.g. raw materials, components, and information);

supervision (along with the leadership style adopted); participation; performance standards, objectives, budgets, etc; pay (along with the payment system
employed); promotion opportunities and job security; and objectives and
policies of the organization.

Researches conducted in industrial and other organizations have shown
what task attributes are generally experienced as important and are correlated
with job satisfaction.

Turner and Lawrence have on the basis of results of their studies, and those
of others, concluded that the following task attributes are the principal factors
which determine job satisfaction (Turner and Lawrence 1965): variety (variety
of parts, tools, controls, etc. and 'motor' variety, i.e. variety in prescribed
work pace, in location of work etc); autonomy; required interaction; optional
interaction (on-the-job and off-the-job); required knowledge and skill; and
responsibility.

They have developed scales for each of these task attributes. These make it
possible to 'measure' them and to compute the 'Requisite Task Attribute
Index' (RTA Index). This may be done with regard to (a) an existing situation,
(b) planned changes and (c) an altered situation, and so designed and implemented changes may be quantified and judged in this way. In what follows
about the recommended procedure for job redesign this method is one of the
'instruments' of which use is made.

Turner and Lawrence mention RTA Index scores between 13 and 63. It will
be clear that the object in view is not to attain in every situation the maximum
score, but to reduce the indicated discrepancies. That is to say: to achieve the
optimum index and 'profile' for the persons concerned.

The questionnaire and scales according to Turner and Lawrence can
provide more or less objective data. Indications about the opinions, wishes and
attitudes of the workers and their chiefs may be obtained among other
methods by means of the Job Diagnostic Survey (JDS) according to Hackman
et al. (1975).

With regard to satisfaction with work, separate scores are obtained
regarding general satisfaction, social satisfaction, supervisory satisfaction and
growth satisfaction.

Not merely average scores are of interest; at least as important is the spread
of the individual scores. This applies particularly to satisfaction with work,
work motivation and strength of the growth needs. A considerable spread of
the latter is indicative of the desirability of 'flexibility' in respect of the tasks: the
possibility of adapting individual tasks to personal abilities and wishes. This
may look difficult, but we know examples of departments where this is realized
(transport and equipment).

Scope of the re-design

Although job content is an important factor for job satisfaction and work
motivation, also the other factors that were mentioned (including the work
organization and the equipment) exercise their influence. Moreover their
re-design may be a condition of more satisfactory job content.

Forms of job re-design

Horizontal job enlargement and job rotation will mostly involve an extension of the task attributes: variety, knowledge and skill, and responsibility.

Vertical job enlargement (job enrichment) and increased group autonomy may influence all mentioned task attributes. Moreover the work situation is often changed in several respects. An analysis of 35 case histories concerning re-designed jobs gave the following picture (de Jong 1974):

In most cases the change was brought about by vertical job enlargement (job enrichment), while instances of job rotation were few. Frequently, job enlargement went hand in hand with organizational and technological improvements. In some cases, in view of assembly tasks, product design was altered. Repeatedly job enlargement was found to have improved quality and job satisfaction. In about half of the cases examined, labour productivity was mentioned; the general trend being upward. However, the effect on productivity tended to be less pronounced than the effect on quality. Recent years have shown a general decline in absenteeism and labour turnover after job redesign; previously, little or no attention had been paid to these two factors.

In general the use of job rotation would appear to merit recommendation only in cases where no other forms of job enlargement can be applied. In some instances the results of job redesign proved negative. The following causes, which were mentioned above, were largely responsible for the failure:

During the process of change no participation by the employees concerned had been allowed; re-design of the jobs had no significance for the employees involved (this may happen particularly in horizontal job enlargement); and job satisfaction and motivation were slight when work re-design was introduced.

Flexibility

The possible desirability of 'flexibility' in regard to job content (that is to say interindividual variety, in accordance with divergent abilities and wishes) has already been stated. Flexibility may also be essential in respect of present or future products and quantities to be produced. In work re-design the mode of working should satisfy the conditions that always apply, whenever a new (sub-)system be designed or an existing one improved. Among them are (besides a 'systems approach', already mentioned): after rational and analytical thinking, creative ('lateral') thinking should be furthered by the followed procedures; and alternatives should be developed and compared, because 'uncertainty' is usually a feature of the considered situations.

Interrelationships

In the foregoing the effect of job content on job satisfaction has been touched upon. Fig. 1 indicates this and other relationships: between the job and the work situation, job satisfaction, motivation to work, absenteeism, labour turnover, and a number of other factors. It can be assumed that motivation to work (5) depends on the employee's anticipated satisfaction with the consequences for him (8) of his effort (5) and performance (7) (his

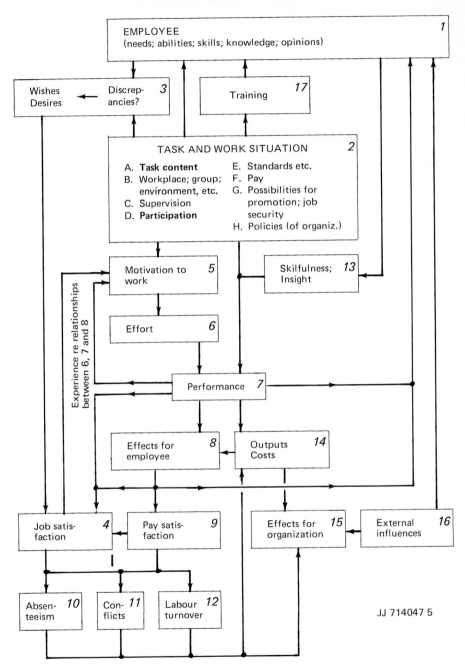

Figure 1.   Interrelationships between task content, work situation, the employee, his job satisfaction and motivation to work, and other factors.

'valence'), and on the degree to which he believes that these consequences are probable ('expectancy') (Vroom 1964). The employee can often choose between alternatives regarding his pace of work, work interruptions, assistance rendered to others, etc, each alternative having its own valence and expectancy. It is expected that he will aim at a behaviour with optimum consequences. If the re-design of a work system is considered, often a choice must be made between other alternatives (for instance in respect of tasks, tools, work organization and pay), once more with divergent valences and expectancies regarding the effects of the various alternatives. These may be different for the management and the employees concerned.

The figures 2 and 3 show relative models. In the middle of both figures 'variables' are stated between which a choice may have to be made. In fig. 2 the burdens and benefits from the point of view of the organization are indicated. To each alternative are attached certain performances, costs, benefits and operating results. The probable performances will be influenced by the expectations of the employees concerned, i.e. the burdens and benefits which they expect of a considered alternative (Fig. 3). The two models are in fact parts of one whole. Connecting elements are the performances and the incomes of the employees (costs of personnel). If the re-design of a work system is being considered, it is obviously important to know which relative reactions from the side of the employees concerned can be expected; this is one of the reasons why their participation in the design process is necessary.

Parts to be played

In the literature of work re-design quite divergent approaches in respect of those who played a part, have been described. In several cases, consultants have performed important tasks: sometimes with regard to the participation of the workers concerned, sometimes as problem solvers or designers of equipment.

In view of the many jobs and work situations that demand improvement and still more in consideration of the number of jobs and work situations that every day come into being or have been altered because of new products or new machines, processes, production systems and methods, it should be seriously considered how, in the majority of the cases, solutions are realized that are reasonably satisfactory from the point of view of human factors, inclusive of the job satisfaction and work motivation of the employees concerned.

We feel that each organization in industry and elsewhere therefore should be put into a position in which it is able to carry out system studies, fit for this purpose.

This implies: the availability of the knowledge and skill, necessary for the carrying out of studies as indicated in the foregoing and which are characterized by simultaneously taking into account the purpose of the (sub-)system and human factors; and adequate organization of the studies.

It was earlier pointed out that often project organization and the cooperation of representatives of the employees concerned, industrial engineers, personnel officers and possibly others, are recommended.

As the required specific knowledge and skill are often not available, it can

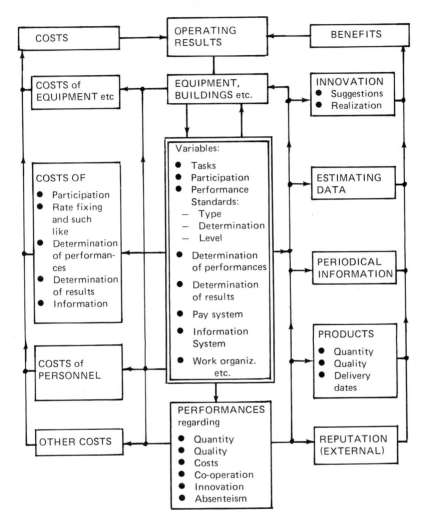

Figure 2   Costs and benefits for the organization, depending on job contents, work organization, information, the pay system, participation, etc.

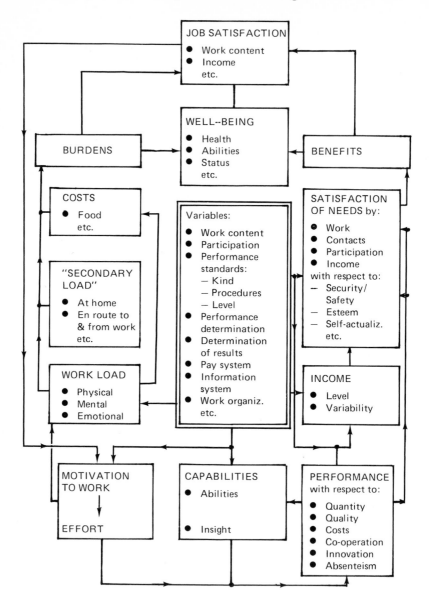

Figure 3.   Burdens and benefits for the employees as a result of job contents, work organization, information, the pay system, participation, etc.

be concluded that appropriate training courses are necessary. In the framework of the mentioned research project such courses are developed. The planned subject-matter is indicated in Fig. 4. The possibility of integration in more general courses is being investigated.

1. Theory
    * Aims
    * Relationships (job attributes, job satisfaction, motivation to work, etc.)
    * Forms of changing jobs and work organization
    * Possible effects
2. Various case histories
3. Recommended procedures
    * **Adaptation of the 10 steps in systems design**
    * **Project organization:**
        − project committee
        − participation
        − lower management
        − specialists
        − co-operation ind. eng.: personnel department
    * **Training in use of "instrumentarium"**
    * **Possible change in:**
        − layout/equipment
        − groups
        − information system
        − wage system
    * **Introduction of work re-design**
        − relative committee
        − information/discussion
            4 documents: · general information
                          · inf. top management
                          · procedures
                          · instrumentarium
    * **Feasibility**
    * **Orientation:** where start?

Figure 4.   Specific training in work re-design

Experience has shown that for various reasons production systems in particular and other sectors where change is inevitable (because of the replacement or change of products, the introduction of new processes, etc.) should be the object of the kind of systems re-design that was discussed in the foregoing. On the one hand, while other work systems are improved from the human factors point of view, this way new or altered work systems which do not meet ergonomics and motivational requirements are avoided. On the other hand, the return on the effort is often greater in the case of the design of new (sub-)systems, than if existing situations are improved.

Isolation and curiosity as sources of work attitudes

E. N. *Corlett*
Department of Engineering Production, University of Birmingham,
United Kingdom

In the consideration of work satisfaction there is emphasis on job organiza-tion, autonomy at the workplace and the important role of groups. In an earlier paper (Corlett 1974) a model of the work design process was presented, Fig. 1, which emphasized the inter-linking between extrinsic and intrinsic factors associated with work. Briefly, for any work to be performed efficiently it must be both possible and worthwhile to the doer. To omit the feasibility of the work is to suggest a lack of importance for the tasks themselves, not in line with the views of workers, as well as not recognizing that work is a process of getting things done which is part of a technical system. This system does not, by its nature, possess any optimizing processes which will ensure a good match between the work and the worker. Indeed, the situation is almost the opposite of this, in that those usually responsible for equipment or methods design have an absolute minimum of reliable information on human requirements and very little knowledge of how to apply it. Furthermore, at the machine design end there is virtually no link between designer and operator which permits the designer to learn the real human effects on the user of the product he has created. Machine situations thus tend to change very slowly, influenced by costs, fashions and traditions but rarely by reliable ergonomic studies.

In the last few years there has been rapidly growing interest in the design of jobs which people will find worthwhile, although the impact of this in practice is still quite small. Jobs usually arise as a result of technological needs and some widely held views on layout design and payment systems, giving rise to the typical shop floor organizations of today. Industrial workers have experience of the system and fit into it as best they can, although there is some evidence that new workers do not find it so acceptable.

The usual process at a workplace is adaptation and it is more of an adjust-ment process than an optimizing one. It is also an adjustment process which is one-sided, i.e. it occurs to the person but only, in a minor way to the equip-ment and organization. Why this should be so is worthy of some study. Even where opportunities exist for mutual modification they may not be used, as with the availability of adjustments to chairs. There appears to be no general

Satisfactions in work design

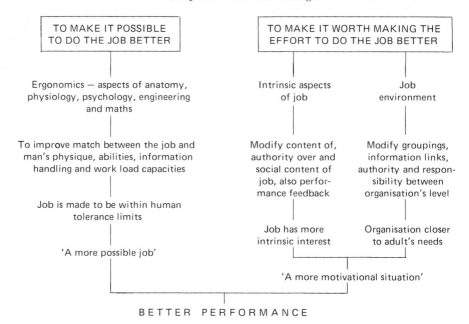

Figure 1.   An outline schema for work design.

predilection for the human mind to take a systems view of the work situation in which the person finds himself. Contemplation of the inter-play between means and ends is not one which is readily entered into, to permit a multi-disciplinary process to be explored, even randomly, for possible improvements. This may well be because equipment and organizations are perceived as immovable.

Changing this perception could lead to both a more holistic view by the people involved, and a change from an adaptive to an optimizing approach to the work situation. Some case studies, where work groups eventually control their own equipment design, layout etc. suggest that this does happen, but there appears to be no experimental evidence to this effect. So we do not have any real idea why people adapt themselves to their tasks—to their own physical and mental disadvantage—and why they will modify the available equipment only modestly, if at all.

The schema presented earlier makes an arbitrary division between problems of classical ergonomics, concerned with making a job more possible, and other areas of change concerned with changing the attitudes associated with work; 'attitudes' because we tend to think of work acceptability, of alienation, of satisfaction and motivation as the measures appropriate to this area of endeavour. These measures are often achieved through questionnaires and interviews, representing subjective assessments. By careful design and analysis, the investigator dissects the manifold influences which are integrated by the subject in his responses and relates these to measures of the job, environment or demographic factors.

With a major concentration on such measures, arising historically from the research having its roots in sociology and social psychology, possible contributions from the more experimental side of psychology may be neglected. Two areas are introduced below which may add some understanding to current discussions on job satisfaction and, also, to suggest that similar areas, when explored, may also contribute.

Sensory deprivation

There are two broad areas in which investigation has been pursued here; one concerned with the effects on adults who are variously deprived or isolated for long periods, and those studies dealing with deprivations in early life. There is no attempt to be comprehensive in the discussion which follows but the examples provide a reminder of the results of some recognized studies in each area so that we may consider if more such investigations should be pursued in order to improve our understanding of the effects of work situations.

We know that a constant and homogeneous sensory environment is equivalent to none at all and can be disorienting. Visually, we may quickly perceive no sensation under constant stimulation and the well-known study by Heron (1961) of subjects isolated and deprived as far as possible of all sensory variation for 2 to 3 days showed reduced intellectual and problem-solving abilities, hallucinations and increased susceptibility to propaganda. In less extreme situations, pilots have reported feelings of dissociation and hallucinations on long high-altitude flights. The tenor of such studies is that reduced variety and frequency of sensory stimulation lead to a degradation in performance on both mental and physical dimensions. These are described in the literature as resulting from relatively extreme situations and short exposures. There seems little to link these with less extreme conditions and longer exposures. Would the same mechanisms be called into play, resulting in the same effects (albeit at a different level) when people spend years working on monotonous tasks, or is the human system resistant to such influences up to a certain intensity and are the conclusions deduced from groups of subjects long exposed to particular work situations a result of a quite different set of psychological processes? Among these conclusions is the frequently noted relationship between socially isolating work and leisure activities of a non-involving kind, e.g. see Meissner (1971) or Torbert (1972). The direction of the influencing sequence 'work to leisure' is perhaps best supported in the words of Parker (1971): 'My view is that the causal influence is more likely to be from work experience ... to leisure experience ... than the other way around, mainly because the work sphere is both more structured and more basic to life ... ' The concept is that an enforced reduction in the range and variety of sensory change leads to adaptation towards a preference for reduced variation, since the individual's ability to cope with the uncertainties associated with variety is lowered. This reduction in the size of the individual's world leads to distorted perceptions of relationships, possibilities and expectations.

In the context of much industrial work, rapidly repeated and socially isolating work reduces the opportunity for a variety of physical stimulation and also a variety of social interactions. The social circle in many work situations is like that of the job itself, restricted to a small set of experiences constantly repeated and with little opportunity for comparison with a wider range of stimuli or points of view; there is a high degree of similarity between the stimuli from day to day.

But the sensory system is essentially comparative, recognizing changes in stimulation but not doing so well with absolute levels. Expectations are also derived from comparisons, either historically or by direct observation, of what a person has done and what others have achieved. If the experiences are not comprehensive, in the sense of being a true sample of the current range of feasible alternatives—then the expectations are likely to be less realistic. What is more, comparative isolation within a group which has only a small inter-change across its boundaries can lead to a reinforcement of the views held by those in the group and a drift from the current social norms.

Is it more appropriate, therefore, to consider the content of work and of its social needs in terms both of the availability of changes of movement and decision and of the opportunities to compare various points of view on the 'reality' of situations? Work can have meaning depending on its context as well as its content, some points concerning which are discussed in the following section. Hence work designs which lead to an increase in the variation of physical experience (a greater range of movements, forces etc called upon over time), which see complexity as a function of the numbers of alternatives with probabilistic outcomes (requiring knowledge and learning to deal with) and incorporate task uncertainties which require reference to others on occasion, so that the magnitude of problems is compared with the experiences of others, may be more realistically thought of as 'enriching' since they are aimed specifically at eliminating the consequences of 'deprivation'. The differentia-tion is not just a semantic one for it is based on observed effects on individuals of various intensities and dimensions of deprivation.

Job content and curiosity

Curiosity has been of interest to psychologists for at least half a century. Early published work demonstrated that the complexity of a problem in terms of, for example, the amount of material, its irregularity, incongruity or mixture of shapes, would attract attention and cause subjects to seek to complete their performance of tasks even after certain kinds of interruptions. Some psycholo-gists propose curiosity as a primary motive with hunger, sex drives, etc, but although the discussions of job content design are full of the implications of this research there seems to have been little attempt to explore, deliberately, the possible links between experimental studies of what has been called curiosity and the factors in jobs which lead to high or consistent performance.

It is true that a major trend in job design at the moment is to encourage people to specify their own jobs, indeed in practice this may currently be the most effective way of achieving productivity with satisfaction. It is not satis-factory, however, to have to assume that what is acceptable will be optimum, or even that this current social process will last. We obviously need more understanding of the underlying reasons and here is a possible experimental direction to further that understanding.

As an indication of what might be possible, a recent article by Kirkland (1976) presented a model of the growth of 'interest' as the fourth state in a chain which began with 'attention', followed by 'curiosity', the growth of 'skill' and finally interest itself. Attention he considered as a biological process arising from the incidence of unusual stimuli or changes in the environment. Curiosity was a stage of increasing the perception of the stimulus, during which satiation could arise, or of increasing knowledge of it. This increasing knowledge permitted better perception of the stimulus and its situation when, for human subjects, an increased understanding allows its potential to be explored: some skill with the model is being developed. Finally, under unforced conditions this skill could be utilized to 'play' with the new situation, meaningful thinking about it occurs, it is mastered and adapted to other purposes and playing with it is an expression of this.

Kirkland points out that animal studies demonstrate that the achievement of mastery via a play situation is more widespread than just with people. An implication from his paper, also, is that the arousal of interest arises from the exercise of skill under non-threatening conditions, i.e. conditions when the choice of behaviour can be made substantially by the subject alone.

What do such studies suggest for consideration in the work design context? Firstly, they suggest that we might start looking for job content variables which evoke curiosity and exploration but also provide opportunities for mental and manipulative exploitation. They suggest, too, that interest in a job arises from being able to deal with it with some considerable degree of independence from pressures to conform to laid down requirements, that the person should be able to 'play' with it in the sense that he can try out alternative routes revealed by his increasing understanding. If the work itself is to become important its performance must be free from factors emphasizing other priorities (hygiene factors?) and the purpose of organizational changes which give more personal control over quality, sequence, equipment maintenance etc is to permit this centralization of the work as a result of the 'free' environment.

What is suggested in this section is that we should pursue experimental studies to increase our understanding of the effects of job content on motivation and performance. If Kirkland is right, then we have a broad framework on which to build. Something is known about the capture of attention, of the maintenance of attention and of the learning of skill. In terms of a broad model of job interest the gaps are large and the focus of much of the work which has been done has not been appropriate for industrial activities. But the possibility exists that studies in this area, designed to look at the effects of individual differences, would give a clearer understanding of what is needed to make jobs interesting and would both support and illuminate other directions of investigation concerning factors relevant to job content, performance and satisfaction.

Discussion

There are three points in this paper which arise from a single assumption, that work is experienced by an individual and consequently the reasons for changes must be associated with the characteristics of individuals. Equally the behaviour and influences of groups should have explanations rooted in individual psychology and proposals for modifications should stem from these explanations.

The first point is that, where work is being designed, it is essential to see that it is possible to do it and the criteria for what is possible have now changed. Once, if it was not impossible it was considered to be possible, but today considerations of health and of productivity require more reasonable limits to be set. Here they are taken broadly to be current limitations as prescribed in the ergonomics literature.

The second and third points are also concerned with making work match the doer but in a wider sense than that expressed by the first point. The second point considers work-produced isolation and monotony as examples of deprivation, and work on social and sensory deprivation is quoted to suggest the similarities. Rather than consider 'working in groups' or 'enriched jobs' as desirable job change objectives, it is proposed that more precise criteria could be derived.

Although the quoted data have been negative, in that they have described the undesirable consequences of deprivation, the required job criteria would take a positive direction, perhaps proposing some mental health-related boundaries of the effects of jobs in relation to the personalities of the individuals concerned. It will be seen that this is a direct analogy with the physiological and psychological performance criteria used in ergonomics.

The final point concerns job interest, from which it is considered that motivation will arise and is, of course, also related to the enrichment of jobs. If interest in a task is correlated with the freedom with which it can be approached and also an ability to comprehend its overall intricacy and the operations involved in its performance, then some requirements for job structure can be deduced. Kirkland (op cit) suggested that 'when skills are applied freely, interest is the outcome' and the arrangement of the content and context of jobs to permit such interest requires a more detailed knowledge of the individual responses to various job characteristics than is currently available.

In short, this paper urges a closer look at job content factors in the study of job satisfaction. Important though job context is, and the attitudes and expectations arising therefrom, the purpose of most people at work is to do a job successfully and an ability to design acceptable jobs requires an understanding of the effects of all aspects of content if the work designer is to be successful.

Understanding the concept of job satisfaction

David Cope
Department of Applied Psychology,
University of Wales Institute of Science and Technology,
Cardiff, United Kingdom

An important reason for employing the concept of 'job satisfaction' must ultimately be to make assessments about people and jobs so that some action or improvement can be made in the jobs themselves, so that they are more satisfying for the people doing them, or that other appropriate remedies are taken to ensure in some way a better 'fit' between the individual and his job and organization. Yet the frustrating fact which seems to emerge from research is that improvements in jobs do not seem to be reflected in measures of job satisfaction. This is shown in a number of different ways. It appears that workers who have jobs that would be regarded by most people as unfulfilling, frustrating and dissatisfying nevertheless express satisfaction when asked. As Seashore (1975) has pointed out, 'individuals can, and do, report satisfaction with work situations that (from information not accessible to the respondents) are found to abbreviate their lives, threaten their family relationships, and unnecessarily narrow their future options.' Furthermore although large numbers of the workforce do mundane, repetitive jobs requiring little initiative, this is not reflected in their expression of job satisfaction. Taylor (1977) has shown that over a period of several years, 85% of approximately 20,000 people in a variety of occupations and organizations in the USA reported 'not being dissatisfied with their job'. Similar findings have been found in the UK in the General Household Survey (in 1975, the last year for which information is presently available, the equivalent figure was 90%). In our own research into the work attitudes of the nursing profession we again find that nurses express in questionnaires that they are 'satisfied' or 'very satisfied' with their jobs, yet we know from other evidence that they are very dissatisfied with many aspects of their jobs (Wallis and Cope, 1977).

Some of this difficulty resides in the concept of job satisfaction itself and its measurement. Despite all the work that has been done in this area—over 3,300 papers published up to 1976 (Locke, 1976), we are still unclear what we actually mean by job satisfaction and how we measure it. Indeed Bowles (1976) showed that there are very poor correlations between different measures of job satisfaction done on the same population!

Such difficulties have induced a number of advocates from the quality of working life (QWL) school (notably Davies, Cherns and Thorsrud) to concentrate upon the use of guiding principles concerning job design which, they would argue, experience has shown to be exemplary pointers to improved quality of working conditions (e.g. Emery, 1967; and Thorsrud 1972). These principles are now well known and include such factors as ensuring that there is: an optimum variety of tasks within the job; a meaningful pattern of tasks that gives to each job the semblance of a single overall task; an optimum length of work cycle; some scope for setting standards of quantity and quality of production or service and a suitable feedback of knowledge of results; the inclusion in the job of the auxiliary and preparatory tasks, and ensuring that the tasks included in the job should entail some degree of care, skill, knowledge or effort that is worthy of respect in the community and so on. Using the QWL approach means that changes are made in jobs without taking account of individual attitudes, wants or expressed desires.

Although such principles have some obvious advantages they have at least three important drawbacks.

First, there are an increasing number of jobs in skilled and professional groups where jobs already score very highly on the QWL factors mentioned above. Nevertheless, the occupants of these jobs can express great dissatisfaction, and it is clear that such jobs do still have room for improvement. Thus it may be that improvement of QWL may be contingent upon other types of factors in work organization and content than those which have emerged from previous research.

Secondly, a further weakness is that applying standard solutions, of the kind most commonly advocated, can mean ignoring individual differences. It may seem perverse of them, but nevertheless some people may not want their jobs improved in any of the ways so commonly advocated. (See, for example, Goldthorpe *et al* 1970).

Thirdly, as Seashore (1975) points out, these paradigms are essentially static with little allowance for changes in organization, jobs and individual needs.

Such difficulties mean, we believe, that it is still necessary to have some model of individual job satisfaction in addition to the usual job design criteria described above.

Job satisfaction theories

Perhaps the major difficulty in taking account of individual job satisfaction is having some theoretical model in which to measure, interpret and understand any findings and observations. At present there are many different theories which makes this task all the more difficult and confusing.

It is the intention of this contribution briefly to survey the field of job satisfaction and to try to synthesise the different approaches currently in use. A useful survey of the job satisfaction literature has been produced by S. Cameron (1973) who separated the theories into the three broad categories of Discrepancy Theories, Equity Theories and Expectancy Theories.

Discrepancy Theories typically outline some pattern of individual needs or wants and examine the discrepancy between what is wanted and what is, in fact, obtained on each of the factors identified. A large discrepancy is associated with dissatisfaction, whilst a small or zero discrepancy is associated with satisfaction. This conception of job satisfaction is the oldest, and consequently the greatest number of theories fall into this category. In many of these theories the 'ideal' standards of what is wanted are only implicitly stated, though they are usually referred to at least indirectly in the types of action required to improve satisfaction.

An important advantage of such theories is that they have generated a large amount of research and so have gradually evolved a comprehensive list and description of variables likely to influence satisfaction (eg variety, autonomy, etc) and questionnaires to measure them. On the other hand they generally make no attempt to describe or predict behaviour resulting from, or leading towards, satisfaction or dissatisfaction; nor do they provide for an adequate connection with motivation. Also there is no allowance for the 'distortion' of needs or wants in terms of social comparison or equity.

Equity Theories (eg Adams, 1963) suggest that the main way in which a person evaluates his job is by comparison with another person. This comparison is supposed to be made in the form of a ratio of the inputs in the job situation to the outcomes obtained from it. If this ratio compares unfavourably with that of the 'comparison other', then feelings of inequity and dissatisfaction result. One of the difficulties with this approach is to discover just which 'others' are chosen for comparison. Another difficulty is that such an approach ignores individual differences in evaluating the worth or value of any given factor.

Expectancy Theory provides possibly the most psychologically sophisticated explanation. It concentrates on performance, and attempts to explain just what performance should occur by reference to individual perceptions of the attractiveness (A) of any outcome, and the expectancies or beliefs they have about the probability that a particular level of action (or 'effort') on their part will actually lead to the behaviour or performance that they intend it to (P_1); and also, and equally critical, expectancies about the likelihood or probability that a given 'outcome' will follow their behaviour (P_2).

In any given situation an individual can conceive of a number of possible outcomes. The theory proposes that people will evaluate the product $A \times P_1 \times P_2$ (where by convention, A has a numerical value between $+1$ and -1) for each outcome and adopt the behaviour which leads to the outcome with the maximum numerical value for this product. Within certain limitations the theory provides a good explanation of observed behaviour. However, the theory affords an inadequate basis for explaining why certain behaviours should occur. It only tells us what behaviours are most probable.

One further factor must be borne in mind when looking at measures of expressed job satisfaction; as Thorsrud (1972) has pointed out—if workers' expectations are of low levels of QWL factors in their jobs, and these expectancies are borne out over the years, they are likely to adjust sufficiently to the circumstances to report 'feeling satisfied'. So it is possible that the basis of 'satisfaction' may be nothing more than a broad comparison with subjective expectations of various kinds; and thus 'job satisfaction' represents merely the individual's present state of adaptation to his work or job environment.

A possible synthesis

In the past, these different conceptions of the nature of job satisfaction have been regarded as alternative explanations, or even as rivals. But this need not be so. Perhaps the most interesting general feature of the theories is that they deal not with different conceptions of job satisfaction but rather with different aspects; and thus, rather than being rivals, they are indeed complements to any comprehensive understanding. Discrepancy theories describe the amount wanted of a particular factor and the gap between what is wanted and what is achieved, and give a list of the relevant and appropriate factors. Equity theories describe comparison processes and especially social comparison processes in the evaluation and assessment of rewards and wants. Expectancy theories focus on motivation, motivated behaviour and some types of job and organizational reward. Hence because these different types of theory focus on different aspects and parts of organizational behaviour it should be possible, at least in principle, to synthesize these approaches into a more general explanation.

The present paper seeks to outline the beginnings of such an explanation. We must start with an individual who has a set of wants or needs, which are fulfilled and unfulfilled to various degrees within the job. If any of these wants or needs are unfulfilled, that is unrewarded by the job or the job environment, then this leads to a discrepancy or tension (this idea of tension was first used by Morse, 1953). Tension, if unresolved can lead to a state of dissatisfaction. However the tension or discrepancy gives rise to motivation to reduce that tension. The behaviour which follows is governed or determined by the likelihood or probability of that effort resulting in the required performance and the probability, in turn, of that performance being followed by the appropriate reward. In other words the type of behaviour we might expect is that which is likely to result in a valued outcome, the precise description of the behaviour being given by Expectancy Theory. This performance and its subsequent outcomes react upon the tension level, hopefully reducing it; though it is possible that certain outcomes can increase it. Job satisfaction is related to the tension level; when tension is high, job satisfaction is low; and vice versa.

In addition to this there is a 'Balance Function' acting not only as a social comparison process but also, and more importantly, as a way of ensuring that the set of needs and wants represent realistic expectations from the job. It operates to balance wants with the perception of outcomes or rewards actually achieved. It is as though the individual says to himself, 'I will set my expectations as to what I want out of this job to the realistic level of what I believe I can achieve'. There are a number of elements in this Balance Function which include social equity, personal adaptation (cf the earlier reference to Thorsrud) and a belief as to what is possible or available in the situation (technological constraints come in this category). The result will be that tension levels will tend to be reduced and kept at low levels and, correspondingly, reported job satisfaction will tend to be more commonly expressed than would otherwise be expected.

In many ways it is easier to understand the model through the diagram shown in Fig. 1.

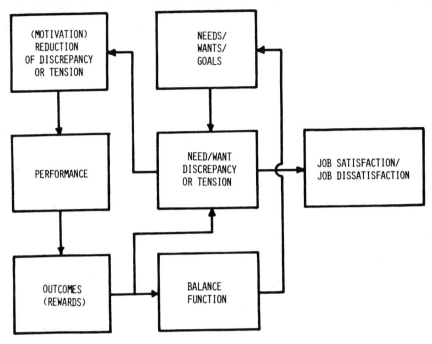

Figure 1.   Proposed model of the production of job satisfaction.

Conclusions

Such a model has a number of implications, not least in the ways in which studies of job satisfaction are attempted, and in the ways in which the concept of job satisfaction is employed.

More generally, it allows for a more comprehensive understanding of the factors underlying organizational behaviour by allowing us to place together in the one model variables which were previously theoretically unrelated.

The intention of this paper is simply to point out that such a synthesis can be made, and to sketch the form which we believe it should take. Because of this it is relevant only to give some examples which are in agreement with the model, rather than to present some definitive test. We are undertaking such tests, but they require far more space than is available here to describe accurately. Besides some of the parts which constitute the model have already been described and tested by other workers.

Previously it has been difficult to understand such relationships, but the introduction of a Balance Function allows us to explain these phenomena. The Balance Function adjusts expectations through the kinds of job-related wants which are introduced by the individual into his work situation. Each time the system works to maintain balance and equilibrium by adjusting wants to be in line with the rewards that can be achieved in the job. Thus we can explain the results of Taylor *et al*, reported earlier, where most people report feeling 'satisfied' with their job regardless of any objective assessment of that job. We would furthermore expect that such a balancing operation would take some time to function. We would also predict that most dissatisfaction would occur when the person was appointed to the job (thus labour turnover should be highest during the initial period of tenure—a fact commonly reported eg Rice *et al*, 1950) and that older workers should be more satisfied with their jobs than younger workers (again found by Walker, 1961).

In our work with nursing and other hospital staff, we have encountered a number of examples where individuals state that they are 'satisfied' or 'very satisfied' with their jobs, which from an outsiders' or QWL approach could be markedly improved. Nevertheless, if such improvements are made, then these staff are likely to respond in just the same fashion as before; that is by saying they are 'satisfied' or 'very satisfied'. Statements of job satisfaction per se, can therefore at times be an unreliable indicator of the underlying attitude we are attempting to measure. Although, of course, there are also other occasions when statements of satisfaction and QWL assessments of the job do coincide.

The Balance Function also implies that there should be an assymetric interpretation of job satisfaction statements. We should perhaps believe statements of job dissatisfaction and take them at face value, in that they point to areas of organizational life which could be improved. Statements of job satisfaction cannot be so interpreted. They may quite possibly indicate a situation which is indeed rich in opportunities for individuals to obtain fulfilment; on the other hand they may indicate a situation which is less than fulfilling and to which the worker has (reluctantly) adjusted.

The model also predicts that motivation to act can only be produced where tension arises from a set of job-related needs or wants being unfulfilled. Similarly (satisfactory) performance will only result when the outcomes or rewards fulfil individual wants. Furthermore, expressed job satisfaction would be independent of both motivation or performance. We have come across many examples where the system of organizational rewards does not coincide with individual wants, and where this has produced apathy and less effective job performance. Nevertheless job satisfaction, measured by traditional job satisfaction measures, has remained high.

Other workers have also found similar findings (eg Brayfield and Crockett, 1955). Such results are very difficult to explain by traditional models.

One consequence of thinking within the terms outlined in the proposed model is that such problems are much reduced. Instead of concentrating simply on measures of job satisfaction, it is also possible to incorporate other measures of individual wants and perceived rewards and to examine how people view the probability that effort will lead to the appropriate performance and hence to a suitable reward. Measures of the perceived availability of various alternative work methods and options and organizational policies can also be incorporated within the same conceptual framework. It may also be possible to assess change by asking whether or not the new working arrangements are preferred to the old.

However, there are a number of ways in which the model needs to be expanded: in particular by widening ideas of what factors can produce discrepancies and felt tension; and by examining broader effects of different principles of organizational design and operation than previously considered by QWL theorists. It can only be through such an approach that we can hope to explain the observation, commented upon above, that people in jobs already scoring highly on presently understood QWL variables can still express dissatisfaction.

Nevertheless the model would appear to present a generally comprehensive and meaningful picture of job satisfaction and motivation. It also enables us potentially to bridge the gap between traditional job satisfaction theorists and those of the QWL school. Further, it points to the reason why the two schools have diverged. It has conclusions which affect the data collected and suggests a fundamental widening of the kind of information which needs to be collected in most studies. It also has implications as to what interventions should be attempted. It may have a number of faults, but whatever replaces it must also surely aim at comprehensiveness.

An experimental investigation of the effect of different reference points on expressed job satisfaction

L. D. Lindon
Department of Occupational Psychology, Birkbeck College,
University of London, United Kingdom

The concept and measurement of job satisfaction

The voluminous literature on job satisfaction has been characterized by research which assumes that the individual's experience of satisfaction or dissatisfaction defines the quality of his working life (Seashore, 1975). This contention can be further elaborated as follows:

(a) that the objective features of the working environment induce corresponding attitudes of satisfaction or dissatisfaction,

(b) that this relationship is moderated by social and personal attributes that affect the individual's values, abilities or expectations, and

(c) that this relationship may well be tied to basic human needs.

Through persistent testing of these contentions, job satisfaction research has demonstrated that the overwhelming majority of workers are satisfied (Herzberg, Mausner, Peterson and Capwell, 1957; Quinn, Staines and McCullough, 1973; 'Which?' September 1977): that social relationships at work are a great source of satisfaction to a majority of workers (Herzberg *et al*, 1957; Mustafa and Sylvia, 1977): that the older the worker, the higher the status, and the longer the tenure the more satisfied the individual appears to be (Porter, Steers, Mowday and Boulian, 1974; Nicholson, Brown and Chadwick-Jones, 1976). There appears to be a division between blue collar workers who tend to value 'extrinsic' rewards, such as pay and security, and higher level workers who tend to value 'intrinsic' rewards, such as self-actualization or autonomy, from working (Gurin, Veroff and Feld, 1960; Centers and Bugenthal, 1966; Locke and Whiting, 1974)—relationships which may well be moderated by Rotter's (1966) Internal-External Locus of Control as noted by Evans (1973). Central to all these findings is the notion of adaptation of the individual's desires to a more realistic expectation of what working provides in the way of job satisfaction.

'Those workers for whom low skill level allows for no job alternatives which include an appreciable degree of intrinsic reward may find little sense in viewing their work as important for any reason other than its economic utility—irrespective of what they might prefer their work to be. Likewise, those whose jobs provide ample opportunity for challenge, achievement and responsibility may find the intrinsic rewards of work to be a source of immense satisfaction.' Andrisani and Miljus (1977, p. 18)

Thus as there is little realistic chance of the low level manual worker self-actualizing through working, the worker focusses on work aspects which can be more readily achieved—such as pay or security. This greater realism is demonstrated by the increasing match between the self-concept and occupational persona with increasing tenure (Brophy, 1959; Steffler, 1966), the more realistic expectations become as to the rewards from working (Schneider, Hall and Nygren, 1971; Hill, 1975; Wanous, 1976), and the less likely satisfaction is to be expressed. Satisfaction can therefore be viewed as a process of compromise between what is wanted, and what can realistically be achieved—with the onus upon the 'wants' end of the equation. As J.K. Galbraith (1967, p. 151) comments, the average worker has ' ... no illusion that he can adapt the goals of the organization to his own.'

Job satisfaction questionnaires have often focussed upon the organizational realities over which the individual has little or no control. To take the Job Description Index (JDI) (Smith, Kendall and Hulin, 1969) as an example, the JDI measures five satisfaction 'facets': the work itself, pay, supervision, promotion and co-workers. The worker has no control over his co-workers, they are a 'given'. His choice is limited to those co-workers with whom he may choose to interact in a non-instrumental manner on or off the job. Pay levels and promotion are decided by superiors utilizing a variety of objective (but more often subjective) factors, and hence there are limited chances for the subordinate to be able to influence his own pay or promotion—at least on an individual basis. Unions may be able to negotiate salary rises, the individual may be able to benefit from piece-rate or other bonus schemes, but there are few opportunities for the lone worker to award himself a salary rise, and fewer opportunities still for workers to promote themselves. Supervision is usually imposed, and a lot of effort is needed to effect a supervisory change. This, like pay and promotion is especially true at lower levels in the organizational hierarchy. The work itself, while subject to similar considerations, does give the individual more opportunity for control. While the actual work is a 'given', the ways in which the work may be done allow reasonable freedom of choice: especially as only a low percentage of workers are now estimated to be engaged in repetitive machine paced work (for example Blauner, 1964, noted that only 5% of automotive workers in Detroit were engaged in such activity) and effectively have no choice of work method. It is therefore not surprising that the work itself is such a significant factor in working life and satisfaction (eg Wild, 1970). In addition as Payne (1973) pointed out, the work itself facet sub-scale of the JDI accounted for the majority of the measurement variance of the overall JDI. Thus measuring instruments such as the JDI—widely accepted to be the most carefully developed job satisfaction scale to date (eg Vroom, 1964)—focusses the individual respondent on work areas over which little control is possible. The onus is more upon individual adaptation than upon organizational adaptation. Hence as Smith, Kendall and Hulin (1969, p. 70) cogently point out: ' ... (the worker's) responses have a job-referent, rather than a self-referent.'

In other words the JDI is measuring the satisfaction of the respondent with the job as given (job-referent), rather than the satisfaction of the job to the worker (self-referent). Self-referent refers to the ability to adapt the job to individual requirements; job-referent as the capacity of the individual to adapt to his job.

Research instruments which increase the amount of personal involvement have typically reduced the levels of expressed satisfaction (eg Kornhauser 1965, p. 160) presumably because the individual is urged to take a more self-referent view. This increased personal involvement may also alter the shape of satisfaction. The critical incident technique by reference to individually salient events yielded the now famed 'satisfiers' and 'hygiene' factors (Herzberg, Mausner and Snyderman, 1959)—a finding that may owe more to the increased personal involvement required by the methodology than to defects in this technique in comparison to the job-referent questionnaires that have failed to yield similar results. This conclusion is in accord with the work of the attribution theorists (eg Kelley, 1971; Enzel, Hansen and Lowe, 1975).

Typically, it is the job as extrinsically or socially rewarding that is being measured by instruments such as the JDI, Worker Opinion Survey (Cross, 1973) or the satisfaction scale of the Job Diagnostic Survey (Hackman and Oldham, 1974), which devote the majority of their questions to facets such as supervision, co-workers, pay, security, the firm as a whole and promotion satisfactions. Thus, even though Wild (1970 p. 161) concludes that: 'aspects of the actual work done were undoubtedly the major source of overall satisfaction, the difference between overall satisfied and overall dissatisfied being particularly marked in this area.' little has been done to extermine whether these consistent findings result from workers being more able to use a self-referent view when responding to 'work itself' questions than for other job satisfaction facets. The 'work itself' is the job area in which there is the greatest probability of worker control, in which he or she is most likely to attribute personal causation for satisfying events (de Charms, 1968), and in which the chances of intrinsic motivation and of expressing a self-referent view are maximized.

The present research is an attempt to get to grips with the self-referent/job-referent dichotomy and represents the first empirical test of the theory. An experimental methodology was chosen to investigate the possibility of effecting systematic changes in the 'shape' of satisfaction expressed via the introduction of an experimental set. Clearly if no systematic changes were observed, it was thought unlikely that such a dichotomy in reference points existed in situ. Hence the approach taken had the objective of determining if the reference points hypothesized were meaningful to respondents, rather than approaching the issue more indirectly by attempting to analyze non-experimental data on a post-hoc basis, without recourse to the perceived meaningfulness of the theory to respondents. The research reported here is the first step of a programme designed to determine if job satisfaction is dependent upon the job or self-referent viewpoint of the respondent—and is essentially exploratory.

The experimental investigation

Sample

An homogenous group of sergeants (n = 48) from the armed services participated in the study. The armed services were selected as an occupation in which the division between work and non-work is very much less clear cut than in most other occupations. This was intended to minimize the self-referent view as reflecting little more than an indication of work as the central life interest. As the armed forces largely control residence, and hence to a large degree free time opportunities, it was felt that this group would be fairly homogenous in terms of work as central to life. A sergeant group was selected in order to reduce the salience of intrinsic rewards—as a 'blue collar' group rather than the 'white collar' officer group. Once again this was done to minimize any artificial exaggeration of the effect of the self-referent view-point, which would be expected to have a greater effect upon an intrinsic reward seeking group as officers were more likely to be. The sergeants were selected at random. At the time the research was carried out the subjects were all undergoing a variety of training courses at an establishment different from their usual work place. No two individuals came from the same location, so factors idiosyncratic to a particular base were unlikely to have any appreciable effect on the results. Subjects were assigned at random to the different treatment conditions.

Design characteristics:

As the objective of the study was to examine the effects of experimental manipulation of reference point upon responses to the JDI, an essential pre-requisite was to isolate the experimental stimuli which would adequately convey the self-referent and job-referent orientation. To this end, a pilot study was conducted with a group of army sergeants (n = 19) utilizing six statements (3 for job-referent and 3 for self-referent) in an individual interview situation. The results demonstrated unambiguously that the two reference points could be meaningfully discriminated.

The experimental design was an extension of the Solomon (1949) four-group design, with four experimental and two control conditions. This design can be represented as follows:

Groups	Pre-test	Experimental manipulation	Post-test
Control 1	01		02
Experimental job referent 1	03	A	04
Experimental self referent 1	05	B	06
Control 2			07
Experimental job referent 2		A	08
Experimental self referent 2		B	09

This design was selected as a powerful control upon factors extraneous to the experimental condition; and to assess the reliability of the JDI. The experimental stimuli were delivered as a verbal and written instruction to respond to the JDI only:

(a) 'In terms of your perceptions as to what your work can reasonably provide' (job-referent) or,

(b) 'In terms of your own individual wants, in the context of your life' (self-referent).

These phrases were printed in addition at the beginning of each JDI scale in the experimental conditions, but in all other respects the standard version of the JDI was administered to all subjects. The control group had no special instructions.

Measurement

The JDI was used for three reasons. Firstly Smith, Kendall and Hulin (1969), who developed the instrument, explicitly state that it has a job-referent effect. Secondly, the JDI has been used extensively for job satisfaction research; and finally, the JDI has been shown to relate well to other satisfaction measures (eg Smith *et al*, 1969; Schneider and Alderfer, 1973; Evans, 1972).

Before the research was carried out the JDI was piloted to remove items that appeared to be culture bound (ie 'Healthful' was replaced by 'Keeps you fit', 'Smart' by 'Quick') or that were inappropriate to the armed forces group. The armed forces do not have profit sharing, so the pay item 'Satisfactory profit sharing' was replaced by 'Provides satisfactory incentives'.

Data analysis—a prelude to results:

At this point it is appropriate to address the issue of ordinal versus interval measurement levels with regard to job attitudes, an issue which is often both important and difficult to resolve. It was decided that differences between subjects measured were reflected in roughly equal differences between scores. Hence even though the author is convinced that the actual level of measurement is open to debate, it was decided to treat the attitudinal data collected as interval. This is not only in accord with the bulk of literature in the area, but also recognizes that psychologists are more comfortable with interval level statistics than those deriving from ordinal level measurement. There is considerable support in the literature for the use of interval level statistics as appropriate unless the data were collected via a ranking procedure clearly resulting in ordinal scale measurement (Lemke and Wiersma, 1976; Nunally, 1970). Finally, even though the intervals obtained in this study may not be exactly equal, the assumption was made that these differences were small and unlikely to bias any conclusions arrived at through assuming interval level measurement (Harshbarger, 1977) especially as the analysis techniques selected (analysis of variance and factor analysis) are statistically robust, and the methodology designed to remove sampling error.

As recommended by Campbell and Stanley (1963) post test and unpretest scores only were used in a simple analysis of variance design. The asymmetries of the design ruled out gain score analysis of variance. A covariance analysis of pre-test versus non pre-test conditions (01-06) was attempted, but terminated when the differences among the group regression coefficients was found to be significant ($F = 5.49$ with 2 and 18 d.f.) $p < .05$. Regression slopes were as follows: Control (0.67), Job referent (0.86), Self referent (2.23). The control and job-referent treatments were in general additive; the self-referent treatments were not.

The hypotheses being investigated were as follows:

1. There would be no significant differences between pre-tested and non pre-tested control and job-referent groups.
2. There would be no significant differences between job-referent satisfaction and control group satisfaction (as according to the above argument, they are both measuring the same thing).
3. There would be a significant difference between total JDI satisfaction scores between the control groups and the self-referent groups.
4. There would be a tendency for any experimental manipulation to decrease the levels of expressed satisfaction for both individual facet and overall satisfaction scores owing to the likelihood that treatments would increase personal involvement. This is the major reason that the self-referent groups were not hypothesised to be significantly different from the job-referent groups.

Findings

The results of the analysis of variance for the groups 02, 04, 06-09 (k = 6) yielded insignificant F scores on any JDI facet or in total. Thus it was concluded that all the treatment means were estimates of the same population value. To aid in parsimony, the groups for each treatment were collapsed to yield three groups; control (n = 16), job-referent (n = 16), and self-referent (n = 16). The analysis of variance for these three groups is given below:

Table 1.   Analysis of variance for three treatment groups (n = 48).

JDI facet	Source of variation	Sum of squares	d.f.	Mean square	F
The work itself	Treatments	153.9	2	76.95	0.83
	Within treatments	4147.4	45	92.16	
	Total	4301.3	47		
Pay	Treatments	9.3	2	4.65	0.10
	Within treatments	2114.6	45	46.99	
	Total	2123.9	47		
Supervision	Treatments	714.6	2	357.30	2.73
	Within treatments	5889.9	45	130.89	
	Total	6604.5	47		
Promotion	Treatments	151.6	2	75.80	1.16
	Within treatments	2938.9	45	65.31	
	Total	3090.5	47		
Co-workers	Treatments	282.2	2	141.10	0.77
	Within treatments	8269.3	45	183.76	
	Total	8551.5	47		
JDI total	Treatments	6621.8	2	3310.90	3.58
	Within treatments	41649.7	45	925.55	
	Total	48271.5	47		

Once more all the F values were insignificant. Hence hypothesis (1) was confirmed. However, as Edwards (1972) points out, it is not necessary for the values of F to be significant in analysis of variance in order to make multiple comparisons among treatment means. The treatment means for the control, job-referent and self-referent groups are shown in Table 2.

Table 2.   Treatment means for control, job and self referent groups.

Facet	Control (n = 16)	Job referent (n = 16)	Self referent (n = 16)
Work itself	39.0	37.8	34.8
Pay	8.6	9.6	9.3
Supervision	47.6	41.4	34.7
Promotion	20.5	17.6	16.3
Co-workers	47.1	44.6	39.2
JDI total	162.8	151.0	134.3

Duncan's (1955) multiple range test was used to assess the significance of differences between treatment means. The following differences were found to be significant:
1.   the control group JDI total mean was significantly higher (p .05) than the self-referent group;
2.   the control group mean was significantly higher than the self-referent mean (p .005) on the supervision facet.
Hence hypotheses 2 and 3 were supported. Finally as a cursory view of Table 2 demonstrates, hypothesis 4 was supported by four out of the five JDI facets, and for the overall satisfaction scores. The only exception to this decrease in score for experimental groups is the pay facet, the only area with which all groups were dissatisfied.

In order to achieve a greater understanding of the underlying dynamics of the control, job-referent and self-referent groups, facet scores were factor analyzed using principal factoring with iteration (PA2), all factors with latent roots greater than unity being entered into a VARIMAX rotation. Each group was analyzed separately to highlight group differences in underlying factor structure. With so few scores being entered into the analysis, a conservative estimate of the number of factors is to be expected (Cattell, 1952). In addition, factoring facets is equivalent to a second order factoring, JDI facets themselves being the result of factor analysis (Smith *et al*, 1969). Stringent conditions for factor loadings were appropriate, and applied, using the Burt-Banks formula (1947). Only facets loading at the 1% significance level on a factor were selected as being highly contributory to that factor. The Varimax analyses are shown in Table 3 below.

For every group, Factor II is clearly a 'promotion' factor. Pay loads significantly on Factor II in the job-referent group, but the loading of this facet on any factor is precluded by the exceptionally low communalities for Pay in the control and self-referent conditions. Factor I represents a 'Social' factor in both the control and job-referent conditions, the highest loading in each case being seen for Co-workers, followed by Supervision. Factor I is

Table 3.   Varimax analyses of JDI facets by treatment groups.

JDI facets	Control			Job referent			Self referent		
	Rotated factor loadings		Commu-nality	Rotated factor loadings		Commu-nality	Rotated factor loadings		Commu-nality
	I	II		I	II		I	II	
Work itself	.50	.39	.41	.47	.43	.41	.71+	−.16	.53
Pay	.05	−.15	.13	.07	.78+	.61	−.03	.17	.03
Supervision	.72+	.36	.92	.71+	.36	.64	.78+	.21	.65
Promotion	.11	.96+	.94	.28	.66+	.51	.26	.82+	.73
Co-workers	.95+	.43	.70	.90+	.05	.81	.69+	.61	.86

+ Indicates loading significant at $p < .01$ applying the Burt-Banks formula.

somewhat different for the self-referent group, and perhaps could be labelled a 'stimulation' factor. Supervision loads most heavily on this factor, followed by the Work itself and Co-workers.

Implications

This preliminary study offers some support for the notion that the reference point taken by the individual can have effects not only upon the level of satisfaction expressed but also upon the shape of that satisfaction. The results for all three groups support the view that social factors are highly significant for job satisfaction as demonstrated by the factor analysis performed by Mustafa and Sylvia (1976). Compared to the other groups, the self-referent group showed an increase in factor loading for the Work itself, and a decrease for Co-workers. This may imply that self-referent satisfaction places more emphasis upon intrinsic satisfactions at work than those more purely social in nature.

In this study, satisfaction with pay was low (compared to a possible maximum score of 27, the actual means were around 9) in stark contrast to the other facet means which were much nearer to the maxima (promotion, 27; the work itself, supervision and co-workers all 54). This suggests either that the pay dimension is being separated from the other facets of satisfaction in response to Phase II of governmental pay policy (it being in some way inappropriate to allow dissatisfaction with pay to affect overall satisfaction), or that pay satisfaction is qualitatively different from other job satisfaction facets.

Postscript

As an experimental study using an homogenous and rather atypical work group, it would be premature to draw conclusions about the existence of a 'natural' self-referent point being held by some workers. The author's research (Linden, 1978) has shown that approximately a third of workers (both management and blue collar) are looking for psychological growth through work, the remainder for social or security satisfactions from their employment. Hence it is possible that a reasonable proportion of the workforce are adjudging their work from a self-referent point, a clear example of such a group being given by Lachter (1971). There are implications from several studies, including the research presented here, that this area warrants further study. The author is presently engaged in further research using a battery of job satisfaction, career orientation and need satisfaction measures set against organizational backgrounds. The objective of this work is to try to isolate those factors which may help to describe adequately the differences in reference point used to assess job satisfaction by the individual.

Acknowledgement

The research outlined in this paper was funded by the Social Science Research Council.

Job design and individual differences

G. C. White
Work Research Unit, Department of Employment,
United Kingdom

In the process of designing and improving existing jobs to take account of human as well as technical and commercial factors, we are faced with a number of problems posed by the range of individual differences. These differences are to be found in contributions that can be expected from people to the way the organization functions and to the tasks that it carries out. They arise also in what people themselves expect from their working lives and therefore in the ways they react to aspects of the content and context of their jobs. These human characteristics present problems for the design of work systems when attempts are made to prescribe specifications for work organization translating into practice the principles widely acknowledged to form the basis of good design.

Problems arise when a static model of job design is adopted, when it is found to be almost impossible, except within very wide limits of tolerance, to define many of the capacities needed. Moreover, some characteristics (eg skills and knowledge) can be modified by training to improve the fit between people and their work. Other characteristics, like 'job satisfaction' or 'motivation' are not so much attributes of individuals or of their jobs but of the relationship between them. This, too, can show considerable difference between individuals and can change for one individual over time. Attempts, therefore, to design into jobs a degree of 'motivating potential' or 'job satisfaction' have not been wholly successful.

Several strategies can be identified for coping with the somewhat uncomfortable fact that people differ and are not easily interchangeable. First, it is possible to ignore differences, expecting individuals to change and adapt or to conform to general assumptions. These may include assumptions about people's needs from work based on general theories of human behaviour. Social scientists as well as managers face this dilemma of reconciling the uniqueness of individuals with generalizations based on characteristics they may or may not share with others.

It is usually expected that people will have sufficient characteristics in common for job design to be based solely and satisfactorily on technical and

Satisfactions in work design

commercial criteria. When this expectation is not fulfilled, the pay system is relied on to improve motivation, or tasks may be simplified to reduce the level of skill needed to cope, or people are moved to other tasks or discharged.

Differences may be acknowledged but their impact reduced by giving training, increasing supervision and providing for inspection, work-checks and the rectification of errors. Induction training and other, less overt, methods are used to assist the socialization process so making it less necessary to accommodate a wide range of individual differences. Recruitment and selection procedures can also be seen in this context as a powerful strategy for reducing the variance for some characteristics.

All these strategies are to be found in traditionally designed work systems in which organizational effectiveness and the well-being of individual employees are objectives which tend to be pursued independently. Indeed, they are frequently seen as conflicting, each being pursued at the expense of the other. Improvements in organizational effectiveness are seen as being achieved mainly by technical innovation, by changes in the design of the product, by opening new markets to absorb increased production or reducing costs. Individual well-being at work is catered for by physical health and safety measures, reinforced by legislation, by welfare provision and 'progressive' employment conditions, negotiated and bargained for by individuals or organized groups of employees.

Attempts to add human to technical and commercial factors have not had signal success in acknowledging the needs of, and giving scope to, individuals. Although the application to the way organizations operate of socio-technical analysis has helped many of them to improve their functioning as well as the efficiency of their output, individual employees are not universally reported as regarding their needs as being better met. The reaction against the gospel of 'job enrichment' has been partly due to neglect in finding out whether employees are ready to respond as predicted, applying uncritically a recipe which appears to have been successful elsewhere. Of those who have criticized attempts at improving jobs in this way some, like Mitchell Fein (1974), argue that it does not work, and that what is reported as improvement is largely fictitious. Fein suggests, somewhat complacently, that 'we should learn to trust workers' expressions of their wants. Workers will readily signal when they are ready for changes'. He overlooks the possibility that these signals may be ignored, or be unclear, misinterpreted or given after considerable suffering has occurred. Some attempts have been made to gauge the needs and readiness of workers to respond to changes in their jobs (Oldham, Hackman and Pearce, 1976). It is not unusual to find an attitude survey being carried out to discover the difficulties and distastes of present employees. These efforts do not entirely overcome the problems of designing work systems to make allowances for, let alone make full use of, differences that exist between individuals including those not yet in the organization.

A strategy currently being applied in a number of organizations, including those with which the Work Research Unit of the Department of Employment UK has been associated (Jessup, 1977), provides an approach to the problem of individual differences at work. This strategy for job design has two objectives:

(a) improving individual well being, and

(b) increasing the effectiveness of the enterprise in meeting its objectives.

The strategy is to extend the 'democratization' of work to include the process of change. Individuals are not only given some areas of independence and control over their jobs, but are involved in the change process itself and indeed in the evaluation of its effects. As developed by the staff of the Work Research Unit in their consultancy work the strategy has three lines of attack.

1. The first course is the collecting of data from individual employees about work difficulties and distastes. This is collected by exploratory interviews, by questionnaire enquiries or structured interviews and by discussion with groups of people at the same level or in the same work group. These are not alternative courses; but all may be used.

2. The second line of attack lies in involving individuals in planning and organizing the work system, and implementing changes in those parts of the organization where they are themselves concerned. In practice, it may be necessary to set up a two or three stage process of consultation in companies where numbers are large and there are many links that prevent independent action. In one such organization, there is a steering committee on which all functional interests are represented and which can authorize agreed changes. On this body, trade unions are represented. Because this body tends to be large, with some dozen members under the chairmanship of a senior manager, a nucleus of four people, with the WRU consultant as adviser, has established itself as a project planning and management team. On this team are people from the department where changes are to be made, with skills and knowledge applicable to that department. Their job is to formulate proposals in consultation with people whose jobs are involved and to implement the changes authorized by the steering group. Each individual worker has, consequently, several channels for influencing the nature of the changes. He can give his views initially about problems, difficulties, distastes and ideas for improvement. He can be represented on, or participate in, the project planning team. He can participate or be represented through a nominee from his work group as well as by his trade union official on the steering group.

This is an iterative process rather than 'once for all time', allowing modification in the light of information about what other people say and as a result of further experience and information.

3. The third element is the application of a principle which can more readily be aimed at than applied. It is not easy for management to accept a degree of uncertainty, or positively to avoid planning and specifying the duties and responsibilities of jobs. Nevertheless, it seems to be important to allow for individual differences by giving some scope for individuals to decide independently how, what, when, where and with whom they work. Faunce and Dubin (in Davis and Cherns 1976) suggested that job specifications should include only what is minimally required for adequate performance and co-operation with others. Capacities required might, for example, be described in terms of thresholds below and above which individuals may find the job too difficult or not sufficiently demanding, and that this 'zone of indifference' should be large enough

to give adequate opportunity to people to do the job their way. Cherns (1976) and Davis (1977) have also included this in their list of principles for job design, distinguishing between objectives and means, suggesting that while objectives may need to be specified after discussion with the jobholder, it may rarely be necessary to be precise about how the work is done. In most organizations, there seems to be too much specificity in this respect, some of it redundant, some obstructive, leading people to make unofficial arrangements to get work done in spite of the rules and procedures laid down.

This same principle could be extended to include not only the way jobs are done but the way in which other systems in the organization operate, giving individual employees a wide range of alternatives from which to choose to meet their specific needs. Flexi-time is one example of this. It has also been advocated for salary, pension and retirement provision by organizations. The policy might, with advantages to the organization and individuals, be applied to movement between jobs within an organization. It would help the organization to be more flexible and resilient. It might help individuals to plan their future more effectively.

Another area where individual differences may need more positive attention is in work systems which use semi-autonomous or self-regulating work groups. It is not uncommon for work groups to exert pressures on, or to exclude altogether, individuals regarded as deviant in ways which are perceived as disadvantageous to the interests of the group. The power structure, and other features of the relationship between individuals in a working group and between one working group and others, can be expected to have an effect on performance and on individual satisfactions. They are therefore too important to be left to chance. This suggests that there should be alternative work systems in the same setting, which would cater for those who prefer to work in a particular way and whose loss to the organization is undesirable. It also suggests the importance of safeguards in the way groups are formed and in the pay system as well if this links individual pay with group output.

One example of the provision of alternatives is offered by an insurance office, in which claims are processed and cheques sent out or otherwise paid to clients. Since large numbers of claims are made, the need for equitable treatment is paramount, and speed in payment is crucial to recipients, the procedures are standardized and, for the most part, carried out with the help of computers. Although the procedures are standardized, there is considerable scope for alternative working arrangements even within a branch office employing between 30 and 90 people. Most branches have been forced to abandon a 'flow line' type of system in which each individual specializes in a single task such as linking correspondence with claim documents, rating complicated claims, checking, or answering queries. This system is too sensitive to staff absence. It is unable to cope easily with fluctuations in work load or with a large proportion of new and inexperienced staff.

Work teams of 8-10 clerks, including a supervisor, have been set up, each team being allocated a share of the work load. In some teams, individuals specialize to some extent as resources of knowledge on particular subjects for the team; although the most boring tasks are shared and, when there is a rush of work, it is a case of 'all hands to the pumps'. In other teams, the supervisor arranges the work and allocates tasks to individuals on the basis of their level of skill and knowledge, their training needs and the need to share out those tasks that people would avoid if they could. In other teams, impetus provided by the deadlines seems to be enough to ensure that the work gets done. The supervisors act as a resource for difficult problems, and as contact with other teams and senior management. Team members do what needs to be done and what they currently are able to do, changing tasks when they arrange with others to do so and when (as with the checking task) they find their error detection rate dropping. In interviews with staff, supporters for each of these variations can be found. From the management's view-point, there is not much difference in throughput or accuracy. Some specialist functions, like the financial and legal departments, are separate from the work of the teams. Team loyalty tends to be high and people are reluctant to transfer or to accept work from other teams. Nevertheless, the variation of working systems within each branch can accommodate a wider range of individual differences than any single system.

Other experiments, for example, those described in Philips (1977), have typically started with small, sometimes volunteer, groups with the objective of extending the 'new' system of working once it had been tested. To have different arrangements existing side by side, with perhaps different pay systems, may be regarded as untidy. Nevertheless, it is possible that a mixed system might, in the longer term, offer advantages in flexibility and in the way it meets the needs of a wider range of people.

In summary, the ways in which individual differences in capacities and inclinations are likely to be ignored or countered both in traditional work systems and in those designed with assumed needs of human beings in mind have been indicated. It has been suggested that one way of allowing for individual differences in the design of jobs and work systems is to provide for workers to be involved in the process of design and change. This has been tried in practice but there is still need to make positive provision for individual choice and to leave unprescribed some areas for individual discretion and control.

Work satisfaction in present-day working life: ergonomics and work satisfaction

Paul Verhaegen
Psychology Department, Catholic University of Leuven, Belgium

In this paper we try to answer the following questions 'What does ergonomics have to do with work satisfaction? Is there more satisfaction when ergonomics principles are applied in the design of work? Is ergonomics important for work satisfaction?'

We start by defining the concept of satisfaction. Then we discuss different theories of motivation and satisfaction and try to formulate the logical consequences of those theories for the relation between ergonomics and satisfaction. We shall incidentally make a few general comments on opportunities for satisfaction in modern industry and conclude with some ideas about the significance of ergonomics for satisfaction.

The definition of work satisfaction

'Job satisfaction may be defined as a pleasurable or positive emotional state resulting from the appraisal of one's job or job experiences' (Locke, 1976). Although such a definition is still vague and non-operational, it is probably the best we can do. It seems to be impossible to arrive at any better definition because of the very nature of the subject. Summarizing causal models of job satisfaction, Locke (1976) makes a distinction between models using the notion of expectancy and models having as their basis the notions of needs and/or values.

Expectancy theories

The general idea underlying expectancy theories is that people have more or less intense expectancies about the possibility of their achieving goals, that have more or less high values for them, by doing certain things. Their motivation, i.e. their willingness to expend the effort to do these things, will be high when they see these efforts as appropriate instruments to reach goals for which the expectancy-valence product is high. Insofar as people suceeed in reaching what they expect and value, they will be satisfied.

Vroom (1964) has formulated a quite elaborate valence-instrumentality-expectancy theory. His so-called theory, in common with most theories of motivation, lacks the general applicability that one expects of a theory, and so should rather be called a model. In any case, Vroom's model is difficult to test in real situations, although the general idea seems applicable to a large set of situations, as is indeed the case with all motivation 'theories'.

Locke (1976) has several criticisms of this model. For example, it is not true that people generally act to maximize their 'valences'; satisfaction should not be equated with pleasure; the theory seems to accept hedonism and determinism as valid.

Coming to the question on the meaning of ergonomics for satisfaction within the framework of this theory, we would like to suggest that ergonomics will perhaps contribute to motivation and satisfaction to the extent that it is valued by the people concerned and implemented in their work situation. For people, who know about ergonomics, the application of it to their own jobs may logically become a factor in their work satisfaction.

Needs and values

Locke (1976) rightly points out that a distinction should be made between needs and values. 'Needs are the objective requirements of an organism's survival and well-being'. To know these objective requirements, scientific research is indispensable. It may be safely stated that all physiological and psychological needs of the human organism are not yet completely known. Values are what people wish to acquire or to realize. People will be satisfied when they reach their values. However, if values do not correspond to real needs, they will not be able to guarantee satisfaction in the long run; e.g. smoking or drinking may be values for some persons, but too much of either will not guarantee their satisfaction in the long run.

So Locke (1976) states that job satisfaction results from the perception that one's job fulfils or allows the fulfilment of one's important job values, providing, and to the degree, that those values are congruent with one's needs. We should perhaps add as a supplementary note that satisfaction with one's job can also result from the fulfilment through one's work of some values outside work; eg, work that in itself is neither interesting nor satisfying may be assessed subjectively as fairly satisfying in the context of a total life style if, for example, the work provides a high salary and so allows better education of one's children.

Authors of 'need'-theories, mostly mean 'value' when they speak of 'need'. In summarizing these theories, we shall frequently use the word need, as most authors regrettably do, knowing that it means value. Motivation theories are always satisfaction theories. Motivation means a willingness to expend effort to pursue a particular value. People are motivated to realize or reach their values. If they succeed, they are satisfied. If they do not succeed, they may be dissatisfied. We should observe, however, that the effort of trying, even without success, may represent an important value for some people.

The problem of work satisfaction reduces itself to the problem of values connected with work or of values that are only instrumentally reached through work. Since different people have different values, they will be motivated in different ways and become satisfied by different objects. If we speak of values instead of needs, we can easily see that motivation and satisfaction are brought about by different objects and in various ways in different cultures and sub-cultures and at different times in their history. Theorists on motivation have tried to describe different categories of needs, to develop fairly universally acceptable taxonomies of needs (values).

Maslow's theory

One important theory is Maslow's (1970). This author describes a hierarchy of needs: first the physiological needs, then, successively, the need for safety in the sense of social security, the need for social contacts, the need for self-esteem and for esteem from others, and finally the need for self-actualization. Only when a need lower in the hierarchy is fulfilled does the next higher one become psychologically real and move the person to seek gratification. For example, as long as physiological needs are barely satisfied by work, the needs for social security or social contacts in the work situation are not strongly felt. But once the former are reasonably satisfied, the latter increase in intensity.

Concerning Maslow's theory, it must be pointed out that, at least in advanced countries, most lower needs can be fulfilled by work quite easily. These lower needs are real needs. Research is indispensable to know them in detail; e.g. there is a need for food, but it is not so clear what qualities and quantities of different foodstuffs are really needed in order to increase health and longevity. Lower needs can, in principle, be easily satisfied by work, but they are frequently not too well satisfied in the work situation itself. (Consider all the toxic chemicals in workshops.) Ergonomics evidently is concerned with the satisfaction of these lower needs. However, since they are still largely unknown, and hence not valued by workers, failure to satisfy them does not lead to dissatisfaction in the short term. Because they generally have a fairly high educational level, many people in advanced countries are also developing strong needs for 'self-actualization' (an ill-defined notion as Locke (1976) points out), which they want to see fulfilled in their work.

This is not always easy to realize. Consider process industries, or more particularly, a glass factory. It consists of an enormous fully automated machine system. Its development and construction admittedly created an opportunity for self-actualization for a small group of high level technical people. But once it is in operation, it has to be serviced routinely by large groups of workers who cannot satisfy any need for self-actualization in doing so. This fact perhaps creates problems in Western culture.

Incidentally, it must be pointed out that in our crowded world providing for one person's self-actualization in work may frequently only be done by denying it too, or severely limiting it for, someone else (Weijel, 1975). On the other hand, there is no reason to think that this need for self-actualization has the same urgency in different people and in different cultures; or, more correctly, that it is an important value in every culture. It has been remarked that, in the Western world, this 'need' has its origin in the Renaissance period and that it does not have the same general importance in other cultures, even today. For instance, in Japan people are not much concerned about self-actualization, but are quite concerned about the maintenance of harmonious relations within the groups of which they are members. So they look for and try to achieve such relations in their work setting (Van De Meerssche, 1977). Because it is strongly related to Maslow's self-actualization, McClelland's (1961) theory on achievement motivation should be mentioned. This theory claims that some people are motivated by a need to create things, to achieve something. In the framework of Maslow's theory, ergonomics is mainly associated with the lower needs. Ergonomics, eg good seating arrangements, clean air, work not causing physical or mental overload, etc. will be more valued and give satisfaction, once it is better known.

Herzberg's theory

If we think of needs to be fulfilled or values to be reached in connection with work, a distinction can be made between those needs whose objects are outside work and those needs that concern work itself. In the case of the former, work activity is merely instrumental to the needs or, conversely, the needs concern secondary aspects of work (eg agreeable material surroundings). Such needs, actually most of the lower ones in Maslow's hierarchy, can be called extrinsic needs. Other needs from Maslow's taxonomy are work intrinsic i.e. the need to have creative work, the need for self-actualization. This very important distinction between work intrinsic and work extrinsic factors has been made by Herzberg (1966). He argues that only intrinsic factors are really motivating, i.e. that cause people to expend effort. Consequently they would be the only ones that lead to real work satisfaction. Extrinsic factors, on the other hand, could never be motivators. The non-gratification of extrinsic needs leads to dissatisfaction. Their fulfilment produces some neutral state, but never real satisfaction. For Herzberg, satisfaction and dissatisfaction are not opposite poles of one continuum but two unipolar variables depending on qualitatively different stimuli.

According to this theory, human factors, or ergonomics, are exclusively concerned with extrinsic factors in Herzberg's sense. Of course there is a semantic problem here. Ergonomists try to design work, machines, environments and systems so that they can be operated easily and will not constitute a threat to health and safety. They do so, of course, by designing the work itself. But in Herzberg's terminology intrinsic factors mean something else: opportunities to use one's skills, capacity to take decisions and initiative, etc.; extrinsic factors are material work conditions, supervision, etc.

It is not always clear whether a given aspect of work is intrinsic or extrinsic; in fact, it may be different for different subjects. The pleasure that some drivers find in smoothly changing gears, or that some computer operators find in retrieving information from their system, seems to be intrinsically motivating. Do systems, successfully designed with the human operator in mind, contribute perhaps to intrinsic motivation?

Nevertheless, generally speaking, if we accept Herzberg's theory we can only conclude that ergonomics cannot lead to high work satisfaction (except, of course, for the designer himself) but that the absence of ergonomics can possibly lead to dissatisfaction.

Of course, not all students of work satisfaction agree with Herzberg. It has been pointed out that his results are confirmed only by researchers who use the same techniques he worked with (see Thierry (1968), aptly summarized by Biesheuvel (1975)). Even then his results are not always confirmed. Konings (1974), using Herzberg's technique of critical incidents in a study of motivation and satisfaction in 70 automobile factory workers, found that extrinsic factors were associated with 84% of the negative events elicited and with 75% of the positive events. Consequently in this study extrinsic factors were as much responsible for satisfaction as for dissatisfaction. Using a questionnaire on the same subjects, Konings got comparable results, again not confirming Herzberg's theory.

It may, however, be argued that intrinsic motivation cannot be produced in a conventional automobile factory with the result that subjects can only generate stories about extrinsic factors, when they are invited to tell about situations that were highly satisfying. Aertssen (1975) and Taels (1978) performed a similar study on nursing personnel in a psychiatric hospital. Using the critical incident technique they got results confirming Herzberg's theory, but this was not the case with questionnaires filled in by the same people. The questionnaire data showed that intrinsic and extrinsic factors were connected both with dissatisfaction and satisfaction.

It has been pointed out (Farr, 1977) that some results obtained by the critical incident technique may be attributional artifacts: people tend to attribute successes to their own activity (intrinsic factors) and negative experiences to the environment (extrinsic factors), although the real causality may be different. But even if this is true, or just because it is true, one may wonder whether we should not try to design intrinsic or motivational aspects into work tasks whenever there are opportunities to do so, in order to create the possibility of highly satisfying experiences.

Anyway, most researchers in this field admit that satisfaction and dissatisfaction are two poles of the same continuum and not unipolar states.

Intrinsic factors can perhaps be much more motivating and lead to much higher degrees of satisfaction than extrinsic ones, but the latter also can really motivate and bring satisfaction. Much depends on the type of work, on the existing needs, etc. Satisfaction depends on need fulfilment. Needs are very different as between individuals and they change over time. Satisfaction will be obtained in different ways by different persons. Some aspects of the work situation lead to satisfaction in some people, to dissatisfaction in others. That is the reason why, for practical purposes, each situation must be studied individually both from the point of view of the needs of the workers, and of the imperatives and characteristics of the system.

Further comments on Maslow's and Herzberg's theories

In commenting on Maslow's views, we stressed the difficulty of designing work in such a way that self-actualization in the work situation would come within reach of most people. This same idea can be expressed using Herzberg's terminology. Many production systems, designed in perhaps the only way possible to make them compatible with high productivity, do not allow the fulfilment of needs connected with intrinsic factors for most employers. Thus, an important avenue to higher work satisfaction is closed to people who, by virtue of their educational backgrounds, have developed these values and have such needs. The importance of intrinsic motivation, of autonomy in work settings, etc has been stressed again by a recent, very extensive, literature review (Srivastva *et al.* (1975).

There is some irony in the fact that highly efficient large scale production systems exclude intrinsic motivation for many workers. For example, producing eggs and chickens is done very efficiently in large scale chicken farms by employees who probably do not get very much intrinsic work satisfaction. On the other hand, many people get much satisfaction from keeping some poultry in their backyards and so producing eggs and chickens in a rather inefficient way ... In general such 'archaic activities' (Sivadon and Amiel, 1969) are by their very nature highly satisfying to their performers.

Designers of work should take into consideration all the needs and values of the people who will be employed in their systems and they should take great pains to design systems in such a way that these needs and values can be fulfilled. Nevertheless, trade-offs frequently will be inevitable and one may wonder whether, for many people, gratification of higher needs such as self-actualization and creativity actually will, in the future, be limited to their leisure time activities. For that reason the present trend towards a decrease in working time and an increase in leisure time should be considered a favourable one.

Concluding remarks on work satisfaction

To summarize: the level of satisfaction experienced with one's work is a complex function of (a) the degree to which different values connected with work and with its concomitant results are attained, (b) the opportunities perceived for the attainment of these values, (c) the relative advantages and disadvantages of the work situation compared with that of other people, and (d) personality and cultural determinants.

If this view is correct, it seems quite difficult to do scientific research on satisfaction and to reach conclusions that are sufficiently general and applicable in practice. Moreover, by the nature of the subject, research on satisfaction can only be carried out with questionnaires and interviews, i.e. techniques that are unfortunately susceptible to attributional artifacts.

Of course, absenteeism and turnover have something to do with satisfaction, but they are influenced by so many other factors, that only in some concrete situations can differences in absenteeism be related in an unequivocal way to differences in satisfaction. Progress in this field will depend on longitudinal studies, in which people are questioned over years on their concrete, changing, job-connected values, and the aspects of their work to which they attribute their satisfaction or dissatisfaction. Moreover, work tasks must be correlated with changes in satisfaction, not over six months, but over years, in order to exclude short-lived Hawthorne effects.

The importance of ergonomics for work satisfaction

As already suggested, ergonomically-designed work will not, in and of itself, produce high degrees of satisfaction, but absence of ergonomics in design will frequently be connected with some dissatisfaction.

Once people are knowledgeable about principles of ergonomics, they become motivated to get these principles implemented at their work place. That in turn will generate some satisfaction. If it is true that extrinsic factors are also motivating and create satisfaction, ergonomically designed work will become more satisfying, once workers have understood the importance of ergonomics for their long term health and happiness; in other words, once ergonomics is experienced as a value.

The significance of being informed about ergonomics is shown by the fact that, in interviews with air traffic controllers, we learned that they merely questioned the work load caused by high traffic density but that they downright refused to use the bad seats in their work room. They had been informed about the ergonomics of seating but not on possible solutions for high traffic density problems. Once a need for ergonomics has been recognized, a lack of it seems to lead to dissatisfaction.

Of course satisfaction and dissatisfaction can be obtained in different ways. For example if workers get higher wages because their work place is not ergonomically designed, its redesign will lead to dissatisfaction.

In many countries, experiments on work structuring are presently under way, based on the idea that more autonomy leads to more satisfaction. In many cases, semi-autonomous groups of workers are set up and at the same time changes are frequently made to create an ergonomically better design of the work and of the work place. But in some experiments there has been an exclusive interest in social psychological aspects; eg during a field experiment in an electronics plant an assembly belt was broken up and replaced by 10 semi-autonomous groups of 8 persons each, who were going to perform enlarged and rotating jobs. An increase of work satisfaction was expected, but the researchers did not get it until after they reduced the hidden excessive work load that was present in one of the tasks (Moors *et al.*, 1975(b) and 1976). These facts suggest that ergonomics has some significance for work satisfaction and that social psychological efforts to enhance work satisfaction cannot easily succeed without taking into account human-factors principles.

Typing pools: a study in satisfactions in work

R. G. Stansfield
London, United Kingdom

This early practical study of 'the quality of working life' was made in the context of operational research of the time, late 1947 and early 1948. It was in response to a challenge to apply to a large organization's immediate problem—shortage of typists—the general ideas in a lecture by Nigel Balchin (1947). It studied the life of typing pools in the then Ministry of Works, to establish the satisfactions and dissatisfactions, actual and potential, for their members. Written in March 1948 for those responsible within the organization, the report contained recommendations for action. To preserve its authenticity as a record and as an early operational research report, and to make clear what seemed important in 1948, it was not rewritten to take account of subsequent developments of theory (cf Farr 1977) and of research practice. The present paper is a short version: the context of the study is set out more fully in the published Abstracts of the 1977 Conference (Stansfield 1977b).

At the time of the study, 2½ years after the end of the 1939-45 War, attitudes to work, and especially to supervisor-authority, were changing rapidly. England was deeply involved in the problems of post-War reconstruction and readjustment. In line with 'progressive' thinking in the United Kingdom about possibilities of making work more satisfying (eg Mace 1948; Madge 1948), Balchin (1947) pointed out that a person works for three types of reason: because he must; because he should; because he wants to. In industry, work was traditionally accepted as an unpleasant necessity. For 50 years the aim had been to make it less unpleasant, with little conscious use of positive satisfactions arising from work itself. Balchin suggested that industry should try to give the average man what many people already enjoyed—a job which was not merely a means of 'earning a living', but which had in it all the best ingredients of life itself. He protested: 'and to do that we have to scrap all our lingering prejudices about work ... Why should the professional pleasure providers have a monopoly of the emotional satisfactions?'.

The study was carried out 11 years before the appearance of Herzberg's 'The motivation to work' (1959; cf Farr 1977). It was made in the same year as the invention of the transistor, the device essential to so much present-day office equipment. The observations below on the dictaphone remind us that material technology can change much faster than social technology. Regarding the art of carrying out social research in practical situations, the study gave early experience of the problems of reporting-back discussed by Dalziel and Klein 1960, Appendix II; Klein 1976(a). The satisfactions found in work may be compared with the satisfactions of London office secretaries studied by Mrs Silverstone (1974); in the author's opinion, the differences between pool typists and secretaries were due more to the great differences in their working relationships than to changes during the 25 years between the two studies.

For the study, the author spent a number of days in each of seven typing pools in central London, partly in general observation of the life of the pool and partly in individual discussion with the people there. Each pool, except one, occupied a single room. After the author had been introduced as a scientific observer and had explained the purpose of the study, he spent some time there examining the attendance registers for several years past. These provided a good introduction to the character of the pool. The information obtained on staff turnover and sickness absence is summarized and analyzed in the full report. The task of abstracting data provided an occupation for the investigator during a period which enabled him to observe what went on, and also to come to recognize and be accepted by the members of the pool. Next, the subject of the study was discussed, first with the supervisor and then with a sample of other members, in confidential interviews. These were as informal as possible, usually at the person's normal workplace at a time chosen to minimize disturbance. The aim was to interview a typical cross-section of the pool members. The study was exploratory, not attempting to use a strict sampling technique: the interview procedure was not standardized, nor was any attempt made to cover a specific list of topics with each person. Rather, each person was left free to discuss whatever topics she selected as relevant, though effort was made from time to time to bring the conversation to particular topics likely to be valuable. Because of the unstandardized approach, no attempt was made to draw quantitative results from the interview data. Users of the typing services, hereafter referred to as 'clients', were outside the scope of the survey.

The typing pools studied were social communities of from six to 30 people, each under a Superintendent, organized for the purpose of carrying out the typing work for a specific part of the Ministry. Administratively they formed part of the typing service under the controller of typists and were not part of the division or section which they served. Although the Ministry staff was predominantly male, the typing pools were all-female communities, except that two each had one male member; a far cry from the nineteenth century 'commercial monasteries' criticized as early as 1801 by Dr Thomas Beddoes (1801), who also made ergonomics-style recommendations for improving the desks and working conditions; cf Silverstone (1976). Both the men appeared to fit quite normally into their jobs and said that they did not find any difficulty as men in a job customarily held by women; neither showed any sign of feeling self-conscious, nor did the other members of the pool appear to think their presence strange.

The individual members of the pools were diverse. They ranged from the middle-aged, unmarried woman for whom typing had been a career and who, left with a house and semi-independent means, continued as a typist partly for the extra money and partly for the occupation and companionship which she found in the pool, to the young girl who had recently left school and whose parents wished her to be a typist in the Ministry because her home was near and her mother also worked in the Ministry; from the married woman who needed to earn by holding a part-time job to the young wife who said frankly that she lived with her parents-in-law for lack of better accommodation and worked full-time, not for need of the money but to be out of the house while her husband was away at work. Nevertheless, each pool had an individual character of its own. This was manifestly much influenced by the character of the Superintendent; other factors were also important, such as the size of the pool, the nature of its work, its past history and the general composition of the personnel.

The pools appeared as clearly-defined social entities, each with a strong community life of its own which manifested itself not only in the conversations and activities during the morning and afternoon rest-breaks but also, for example, through the Christmas decorations in the pool rooms and in group support for a sanatorium. The isolation of each pool from the rest of the organization was very striking. Its members' contacts were among themselves. They had little personal contact with the members of the division for which they did their work and in whose building they were located, or with members of other typing pools, even pools in the same building. Such outside contacts as they had were chiefly with the messengers who came in and out of the pool room carrying 'copy', plus those made by the shorthand writers who went out to take dictation. Users of the typing services rarely visited the pool; when they did, they usually dropped work into the 'in' tray and exchanged a few words with the Superintendent, without making contact with the typists. Contact with the administration was normally by the Superintendent, using the telephone.

Within each pool the social structure was also evident. The existence and membership of informal sub-groups, apparently formed more by naturally-congenial people becoming seated near each other than by friendships developing from physical proximity, were especially clear during the morning and afternoon intervals when work stopped and the groups drew together to chat and drink tea. Sub-groups appeared to range in size from two to about six members. It was noted that the larger groups were more talkative than the smaller, which were based more on silent companionship. The pool Superintendent was in a special position. Her official position deprived her of the companionship of equals enjoyed by the other members of the pool. In most of the pools her social remoteness was emphasized and physically expressed by the distance separating her desk from the compact array of the desks of her subordinates, an array which she confronted in the pre-war style of a teacher facing a class. Across this gap she had mostly to watch the active social life going on in her pool. Spending almost all the working day in the pool room, isolated from people outside, she had little compensation from contact with congenial equals elsewhere. The loneliness of the Superintendent and its ill effects are discussed elsewhere (Stansfield 1977a, b).

One pool was engaged mainly on typing order forms. It was so much in arrears that many forms were being written out by hand elsewhere in the building, by clerical staff working overtime. The Superintendent was so worried by her belief that her staff were not doing what they could that the investigator got permission to put to the group, informally during a tea break, the situation as he saw it. There was a moment's silence; then a young typist, an informal social leader, said 'I *didn't know* that orders were being written by hand!' This initiated frank discussion between Superintendent and typists. The discussion made clear to the investigator, by then a bystander, how absent had been a sense of purpose (one remark was 'just the atmosphere that keeps us going') and how complete was the lack of contact between the pool and the division it served.

Physical conditions of the workplace indicated outsiders' lack of contact with the people in the pools. These conditions were important because they too were felt by the typists to express the regard in which their work was held by others. Rooms gave the negative impression of being kept clean but with little effort to make them attractive or pleasant. 'Why should the Director get his room done up, when we are the people who do the work? ... I'd come in on Sunday to scrub it, but I'd be told I'm a mug': the typist's comment on her own room indicated how the division of labour for cleaning had generated as a by-product the attitude that members of a pool should have no responsibility for the appearance of their own workplace: (cf Balchin's 'Perfect working conditions—but what appalling living conditions!'). In one room, a black-and-ochre original drawing of a building cared for by the Directorate revealed an attempt by higher authority which had missed its mark: 'It's supposed to brighten up the room ... but it's the same colour as the walls'. The typists seemed quite capable of choosing pictures—one named van Gogh for brightness—and the report made recommendations about what could be done.

The dictaphone was just appearing in the Ministry as an alternative to shorthand, an early sign of coming technological change. The author was asked to pay special attention to believed problems in the pool which had a couple of machines. Because of typist shortage, the new system implied no threat of redundancy. There seemed to be some resistance to it as a novelty, and the shorthand typists felt dislike for it as an eventual threat to their craft skill. The author thought that if the dictaphone replaced shorthand, it could easily weaken the already-poor links between a typing pool and the people for whom it worked. The personal contacts made by shorthand writers going outside the pool room to take dictation provided some opportunity for the typists to obtain greater insight and interest in the work which they did, to feel more closely associated with the persons responsible for their work; they helped a sense of society with the persons giving dictation.

The immediate problem was identified as stemming from the way the dictaphone had been introduced. Because of local past events, the pool where the machines were, and another pool in the same building, felt threatened in identity and as settled groups of people. Moreover the dictaphones used wax cylinders for recording; they were unreliable, and the shavers used to pare down the cylinders for re-use needed particularly frequent attention from a mechanic. One of the typists had seen modern electronic equipment at the

Business Efficiency Exhibition, and she and her colleagues felt that they had been given, and were expected to use, inferior tools. Moreover they felt that no special care was taken to instruct clients in the technique of using the dictaphone. A demonstration was given to some clients when the dictaphone was installed, without provision for following this up or instructing new users. Again, the typists inferred, from an apparent lack of attention, that their work was not regarded as important.

The information collected on typists' satisfactions was analyzed in terms of Chester Barnard's classification of incentives (1938). He distinguished between material and non-material incentives and between those personal and those offered to a collectivity of people. The full report on the study examined each of Barnard's detailed categories to see how far it related to the data collected. Here we can touch only on salient aspects. Notably, the idea that there could, or should, be positive satisfactions arising naturally from work, hardly entered the daily life of these typing pools. The rank and file as well as the Superintendents, and by inference the clients and administrators, appeared to act in accord with the stereotype view that work should be 'dull, colourless, drab, impersonal' (Balchin 1947). They all behaved consistently with the expectation that typists would not know, or need to know, the context or significance of their work. Compare, from a very different setting, Mosteller's (1972) observation in his foreword to a book: 'Perhaps the most heartening report on readability came from one of our authors, whose secretary told him after finishing the typing of a revision, that she enjoyed it enormously. When asked what she especially liked, she said that she had finally found out what the work of the office was all about.' There was generally a lack of vivid positive motive for working. What was missing was suggested by two exceptional pools: one because of the manifest importance of the work, the other because of strong personal devotion to the Superintendent. Both pools showed significantly low sickness absence.

Regarding Barnard's specific types of satisfaction, 'material inducements' such as pay were settled at an organizational level which effectively placed them outside the scope of the study. They turned up, however, in connection with perceived status. Several typists felt it unfair that a young colleague, recognized to be a fast worker, got less pay under the age-scale than someone older who did less. Of non-material rewards, prestige appeared not to be brought in as an incentive. There were three grades of typist, graded according to maximum speed achieved under test conditions. Superintendents were conscious of typists' grade, which affected pay. But status in the pool and expected work-performance did not seem to be related to grade. Indeed, typists often appeared to be unaware of their colleagues' grade. Pride in workmanship likewise seemed to be a neglected motive; such pride as appeared related chiefly to speed. Probe questions were asked about the signs of good work; answers concentrated on negative aspects, on freedom from faults. It was expected that a typist's work would have to be checked by someone else, even though typists who through exceptional circumstances checked their own work, expressed pleasure that they were trusted to do so. The report made suggestions for giving typists greater responsibility in such matters, suggestions not unlike those in the 1975 Typing Services Handbook (Civil Service Department 1975).

Applying Barnard's analysis to the practical situation, the distinction became blurred between social satisfactions experienced by the individual and those related to the collectivity in the way implied by the remark quoted earlier, 'just the atmosphere that keeps us going'. The investigator was surprised in one pool to find how acute were the resentful feelings of the typists, nearly all quite young, towards a Superintendent who insisted on old-fashioned total accuracy, achieved by retyping the whole sheet for an error. Their more realistic view was that neatly-corrected work should be accepted in a time of chronic overload. Yet these same typists also showed personal affection for their Superintendent, as well as respect for her skill as a typist. She on her own part was convinced that only duty should be a motivation at work; liking should not come into it. With hindsight, it might be thought that the Barnard categories, however useful, did not take account of a wholly feminine working situation and its peculiar ethos right up to quite recent times.

Acknowledgement

The author is grateful to the Department of the Environment, the successor to the Government Department in which the study was made, for permission to publish that report with a short explanatory introduction and minor editing to clarify local references. The Department is not, and the original Department was not, necessarily in agreement with the conclusions reached or the views expressed. This version (Stansfield 1977a), presented to the 1977 IEA/ES Conference on Job Satisfaction, is deposited with the British Library Lending Division, Boston Spa, Yorks. Shelf mark 78/1795.

Performance and job satisfaction in short-cycled repetitive work

A. Khaleque
Department of Psychology,
Catholic University of Leuven, Belgium

The relationship between performance and job satisfaction has been a matter of continued concern to the individuals connected with the world of work. Since an initial study by Kornhauser and Sharp (1932), investigators have been searching for relationships between these two parameters. Reviews of the literature in this field indicate that the relationship between performance and job satisfaction is still far from clear (Brayfield and Crockett, 1955; Herzberg, Mausner, Peterson and Campbell, 1957). However, a more recent review of the literature (Vroom, 1964) indicates that a low, but more or less consistent, relationship exists between performance and job satisfaction. Vroom reviewed 23 studies and these studies show a median correlation of $+.14$ between performance and satisfaction and out of these 23 studies the correlation between performance and job satisfaction was positive in 20 cases and negative in three cases. It is argued that the differences in the jobs studied and in the measuring instruments employed are two of the numerous causes of inconsistent findings (Locke *et al.*, 1964). To identify precise relationship between performance and job satisfaction in different jobs, there remains the need for more research to sample different types of jobs with multiple measuring instruments. The need for more than one method of measurement of job satisfaction is also advocated by Campbell *et al.* (1959) and Ewen (1964). But so far, few investigators have used multiple measures of job satisfaction in their studies and compared their subjects by standardized scales of job satisfaction.

Two instruments are of particular interest in this regard because of their repeated and extensive use by investigators in this field. The first of these is the Job Description Index (JDI) developed by Smith, Kendall and Hulin (1969) and the second is the Brayfield and Rothe Scale, developed by Brayfield and Rothe (1951).

The present investigation was designed:
1. to measure job satisfaction and find out relationships between performance and job satisfaction;
2. to find out relationships between performance and absenteeism on the one hand, and job satisfaction and absenteeism on the other hand; and

3.   to compare the results obtained by the Job Description Index (JDI) and
the Brayfield-Rothe Scale and to observe their intercorrelation.

Research setting and subjects

The research was conducted in a cigar factory. A total of 40 subjects, all
female, was taken in this study. The mean age of the subjects was 27.5 years
and the mean experience in the present job was 7.90 years. One half of the
subjects were randomly selected from the high performance group of workers
and the other half were randomly selected from the low performance group of
workers. The workers were divided into the high and the low performance
groups on the basis of the quantity and quality of their production. The mean
age and experience of the high performance subjects were 28.50 years and 9.25
years respectively: the mean age and experience of the low performance
subjects were 26.50 years and 6.55 years respectively. The educational qualification of the subjects of both the high and the low performance groups ranged
from primary school to lower secondary school level.

Task of the subjects

The task of the subjects consists in feeding machines with tobacco leaves
for wrapping and finishing cigars. The task is machine-paced, but the machine
can be stopped at any point by pressing a pedal. This short-cycled repetitive
work seems quite different from common assembly tasks in which the parts to
be assembled are always identical. Tobacco leaves, being biological products,
are quite variable and so at every cycle of the machine the workers have to
make a decision to place a tobacco leaf on the wrapper die in such a position
that as many cuttings as possible can be made from the leaf. Immediately after
placing a leaf on the die, the workers have to take away the hands and let the
cutting rollers pass over the die, and then they have to replace and readjust the
leaf on the die for the next cutting as soon as the cutting rollers have left the
die, and so on.

The workers have to remove the tobacco waste from the die, either
manually or by pressing aside the knee lever of the waste blowing device. They
have also to check the wrapped cigars, and either transfer them manually from
the bowl at the conveyor belt to the tray, or monitor the automatic cigar
transfer device. Thus within a brief work cycle of three seconds, the workers
have to check a tobacco leaf, to place it on the die in the proper position, to
remove their hands from the die, to let the cutting rollers pass over the die, to
check cutting and gluing, to inspect wrapped cigars, to remove waste of
tobacco leaves, to transfer wrapped cigars by hand or to inspect the automatic
transfer device, etc. The task appears to put heavy and continuous pressure on
the perceptual and mental faculties of the workers.

Measures of job satisfaction

The Brayfield-Rothe scale of Job Satisfaction was used to measure the
overall job satisfaction of the subjects. The Job Description Index (JDI)

was used to measure satisfaction of the subjects with the various facets of the job.

Results

The findings of the present investigation are shown in Tables 1 to 5. The subjects were divided into satisfied and dissatisfied groups on the basis of their scores on the Brayfield-Rothe scale of Job Satisfaction and according to the Brayfield-Rothe's criterion of division. The results of the Brayfield-Rothe scale showed that a significantly greater number of the subjects of the high performance group are satisfied with this job in comparison to the low performance group (see Table 1).

Table 1.   The relation between performance and satisfaction.

	Satisfied	Dissatisfied
High performance	16	4
Low performance	10	10
Total	26	14

Note: Z-test for differences between uncorrelated proportions shows that a significantly greater number of subjects of the high performance group are satisfied with their job than that of the low performance group.
($z = 2$; $p < .05$, two tailed test)

The results of the Brayfield-Rothe scale further revealed that the mean scores of job satisfaction of the high performance subjects are significantly higher than that of the low performance group (see Table 2).

Table 2.   Mean scores on Brayfield's job satisfaction scale of the subjects of the high and the low performance groups.

High performance group	Low performance group
Range of scores: 41 - 78	Range of scores: 36 - 76
M = 62.35	M = 56.50
S.D. = 8.92	S.D. = 8.89
N = 20	N = 20

Note: The mean score of the high performance subjects is significantly higher than that of the low performance subjects.
($t = 2.08$, d.f. = 38, $p < .05$, two tailed test)

In the present study, the Brayfield-Rothe scale of job satisfaction showed a significantly high internal consistency, with a correlation between odd-even split halves of 0.84, corrected to full length by the Spearman-Brown formula.

Job satisfaction scores obtained by the Job Description Index correlated significantly with the scores obtained by the Brayfield-Rothe scale (see Table 3). But the results showed that two JDI subscales (work and pay) out of five (work, pay, promotion, supervision and co-workers) neither correlated significantly with subscales of the same test (see Table 4) nor with the Brayfield-Rothe test (see Table 3). However, three other subscales (promotion, supervision and co-workers) correlated significantly with the Brayfield test and among them the two subscales (supervision and co-workers) correlated quite highly with this measure of overall job satisfaction (see Table 3).

Table 3.   Correlation between the Brayfield-Rothe scale and the JDI scale.

	JDI full scale		Subscales of JDI			
		work	pay	promotion	supervision	co-workers
Brayfield-Rothe scale	.63 ★★★	.25	.24	.35 ★	.64 ★★★	.51 ★★

Note: N = 40; ★ = p < .05; ★★ = p < .01; ★★★ = p < .001; the correlation coefficients without asterisk are not significant.

The findings of the present study about absenteeism showed that the incidence of absenteeism of low performance subjects was significantly greater than that of the high performance workers (n = 130; p .05 one-tailed). However the results showed no significant difference between the subjects of the satisfied and the dissatisfied group in the incidence of absenteeism.

Table 4.   Intercorrelations of JDI subscales based on the scores of the present study.

subscales	work	pay	promotion	supervision	co-workers
work	–				
pay	.21	–			
promotion	.28	.43★	–		
supervision	.02	.56★	.40★	–	
co-workers	.21	.22	.48★	.53★	–

Note: N = 40; ★ = p < .01 (two tailed test); the correlation coefficients without asterisk are not significant.

Analysis of the response distributions of some of the interesting items of the subscale 'work' of the Job Description Index has led to some striking findings. It has been found that a significantly greater number of the subjects, who consider their job as routine, are satisfied with their work and although they find the work to be routine they do not consider it boring or frustrating (see Table 5).

Response patterns of the subjects on another item, whether the work is simple or not, revealed that a significantly greater number of the subjects, who consider their work as simple, are satisfied with this work and although the work is simple to them still they get a sense of accomplishment in the work. (See Table 5.)

The response distribution of the subjects further revealed that a significantly greater number of the subjects, who consider their work both simple and routine, find their work satisfying and not boring. Similarly, a significantly greater number of the subjects, who consider their work as not challenging, do not find their work boring (see Table 5).

Table 5. JDI subscale · work: response distribution of the high and the low performance groups.

ROUTINE (N = 39)★	Yes	No	χ^2	p
Satisfying	30	9	11.31	<.001
Boring	3	36	27.31	<.001
Frustrating	7	32	16.02	<.001

SIMPLE (N = 20)★★	Yes	No	χ^2	p
Give sense of accomplishment	16	4	7.20	<.01
Satisfying	17	3	9.80	<.01

SIMPLE & ROUTINE (N = 20)	Yes	No	χ^2	p
Satisfying	17	3	9.80	<.01
Boring	1	19	16.20	<.001

NOT CHALLENGING (N = 32)★★★	Yes	No	χ^2	p
Boring	2	30	24.50	<.001

Note: ★ Among 40 subjects, 39 consider the work as routine and 1 subject considers the work as not routine;

★★ 20 subjects consider the work as simple and 19 consider the work as not simple, one subject is undecided;

★★★ 4 subjects consider the work as challenging, 32 consider the work as not challenging and 4 subjects are undecided.

Discussion

The present study provides evidence of a significant positive correlation between performance and job satisfaction in this repetitive job. Although two satisfaction measures, the Brayfield-Rothe scale and the JDI, were used in this study, the subjects were divided into the satisfied and the dissatisfied groups only on the basis of their scores on the Brayfield-Rothe scale. This was done considering the significantly high internal consistency of the Brayfield-Rothe scale and its significant correlation with the JDI scale in the present study (see Table 3). Moreover the results of the present study indicated that the JDI may not be an appropriate measure of job satisfaction in this case, since two of its subscales (work and pay) neither correlated significantly with other subscales of the same test (see Table 4) nor with the Brayfield-Rothe test (see Table 3). Non significant correlations of the two subscales of the JDI (i.e. work and pay), with its other subscales and with the Brayfield-Rothe scale, seemed due to the fact that some of the items of these two subscales were not quite meaningful in the context of the present job. For example, the item of the subscale 'work', as to whether the job is creative, did not seem to be appropriate for there was little creativity in this repetitive job. Similarly, the item of the subscale 'pay' concerning profit sharing was not relevant with the system of pay in the present case. Moreover, in this repetitive job, it seemed misleading to consider 'yes' response to items such as the job is routine, and simple, as the expression of dissatisfaction. Because, to a significantly greater number of the workers the work was satisfying even though they considered it simple and routine. However, two other subscales (i.e. supervision and co-workers) of the JDI correlated quite highly with the Brayfield-Rothe scale of overall job satisfaction. Thus the results indicate the importance of supervision and co-workers to overall satisfaction in this repetitive job.

The positive correlation between the two satisfaction scales, i.e. the JDI and the Brayfield-Rothe scale, should be interpreted with caution. Although, we cannot entirely rule out the probability of a partial Hawthorne effect on the positive correlation between the two satisfaction scales yet, it seems difficult to give a simple explanation of the Hawthorne effect, if there is any, on the positive correlation between the two satisfaction scales. In a field study like this, the probability that the response of the subjects may be influenced by a number of uncontrolled factors cannot be excluded. In the present study, although a significantly greater number of the subjects reported satisfaction with the job, nevertheless a number of them also reported dissatisfaction with the job. So it seems untenable to suppose that there is a Hawthorne effect for some workers and not for the other workers. It may be relevant here to mention the observation made by Cook (1967) and Diamond (1974) that despite widespread discussion of the Hawthorne effect, there is not much evidence of the Hawthorne effect in field experiments.

The present study provides evidence of a significantly greater rate of absenteeism of the low performance than of the high performance workers. But no significant difference in the incidence of absenteeism has been found between satisfied and dissatisfied subjects. Reviews of the literature in this field indicate that job satisfaction is not always strongly related to absenteeism (Brayfield and Crocket, 1955; Herzberg, Mausner, Peterson and Campbell, 1957; Schuh, 1967; Vroom, 1964). The result of the present study, as mentioned earlier, provides evidence that a significantly greater number of workers find satisfaction in this repetitive job and even though they consider the job as routine and simple yet they are neither bored nor frustrated with the job; rather they get a sense of accomplishment in performing it (see Table 5). The results of this study support the findings of Kilbridge (1960) that some workers like simple tasks.

These findings suggest the need to be cautious about the generality of some other findings in this field (Viteles, 1932; Walker and Guest, 1952), which indicated that boredom is more apt to occur in simple tasks than in complex tasks. The results of this study seem to support the findings of some studies (Smith, 1955; Roy, 1959) which indicated that boredom depends more on the characteristics of the workers than on the characteristics of the work. The findings of the present study further suggest the need to avoid overgeneralizing the importance of job enlargement in removing boredom and in providing job satisfaction in repetitive jobs.

In the light of available evidence, it may be concluded that as boredom appears to depend more on the characteristics of the workers than that of the work, so the solution of the problems of satisfaction and boredom in repetitive jobs seems to lie more in proper selection and placement of workers than in job enlargement.

The impact of repetitive work

T. Cox and C. J. Mackay
Stress Research,
Department of Psychology,
University of Nottingham, United Kingdom

Our modern consumer society has been made possible partly by the economic success of the different methods of mass production which were developed during the Industrial Revolution. However, while bestowing economic benefits, these methods have undoubtedly degraded work for many individuals, and have been attacked for this (for example, Braverman, 1974). Their use has almost always involved the *simplification* of jobs and the increased use of technology in the work process. With simpler jobs, relatively fewer skilled workers have needed to be employed, training has been reduced and greater flexibility in manpower planning has been achieved. These are among the obvious attractions of pursuing job simplification for the 'organization'. It is not surprising, therefore, that the simple job now appears to be an essential element in the profitable manufacture of consumer goods.

In its most extreme form this economically attractive element of work may consist of the continual repetition of a single unskilled act: the worker who carries it out having no control over the pace of that work, and little opportunity to decide how (s)he actually does it. These powers are often invested in the machines. The approach is 'production', and not 'person', orientated.

The development of management systems necessary for this approach was made easier by the advent of Frederick Taylor's Scientific Management movement (Taylor, 1911). Taylor laid out an approach to the management of the workforce and not as often believed, an approach to the development of work technology. That owes much to men like Henry Ford, who introduced the concept of the moving assembly line in 1914 (Chinoy, 1964). By comparison, Taylor addressed himself specifically to the problem of how to control the workforce in terms of buying and exploiting their labour. He believed it absolutely necessary for the 'organization' to be able to dictate to the worker the precise way in which their work was to be performed: scientific management gave some respectability to many of the harsher aspects of job simplification.

However, since the late 1960s, an intense debate has developed around the question of industrial work and the stress associated with it. Work stress, it is thought, can give rise to low job satisfaction, poor job performance and impaired physical and psychological well-being (health). Not surprisingly, simple repetitive work has given rise to much concern. It is now often described as 'boring or monotonous or meaningless', and has been cited as a major source of worker dissatisfaction and alienation (Gardell, 1973; Jessup, 1974; Swedish Employers' Federation, 1975). It is no coincidence that job improvement schemes are frequently designed to reduce simple repetition in work (Tripartite Steering Group on Job Satisfaction, 1975). There can be little doubt that this is now viewed as a probable source of occupational stress and a possible threat to individual well-being.

Stress research

In 1976, a special project grant was awarded to the Stress Research group in the Department of Psychology at Nottingham by the British Medical Research Council (MRC) with transferred funds from the Department of Employment: its aim to look at the psychophysiological correlates of repetitive work. A further grant from the United States Army's European Research Office (ERO) in 1978 allowed this interest to be expanded. The MRC project is partly concerned with the cost of exposure to repetitive work in terms of its effects on mood and general well-being, and partly with the relationship between the psychological and physiological responses to this source of stress. The ERO project is concerned with the exact nature of the demands inherent in repetitive work, and approaches this problem using Fleishman's (1975) 'abilities-requirements' method of producing task taxonomies. It also considers the cost of exposure to repetitive work. Glass's (1977) suggestion that the coronary-prone behaviour pattern (type A behaviour) is a strategy for coping with occupational stress is being examined. The projects are being carried out across two three-year periods (1976 to 1981) and, on their completion, will be followed by a series of recommendations for improving the quality of working life in relation to the practice of repetitive work.

Two members of Stress Research have developed a model of occupational stress which is being used to provide a framework for the group's research. This model was developed after an extensive review of the existing literature on stress (Cox, 1975, 1978; Mackay and Cox, 1977). The model is described in the following sections.

The psychological approach to stress

Stress is a highly individual phenomenon. It exists as a result of the person's appraisal of his involvement in his environments, both physical and psychosocial. This is the essence of the psychological approach: it emphasizes the importance of cognitive-perceptual processes. Stress, it has been suggested (Cox, 1975, 1978; Lazarus, 1966, 1976; McGrath, 1976) arises as a result of an imbalance between the person's perceptions of the demands made of him, and his perception of his ability to cope, when coping is seen as important. Demand can be externally generated and internally generated, reflecting needs and values, perhaps as described by Maslow (1970) or Locke (1976).

The transactional model of occupational stress

The person at work is faced with many different sources of demand reflecting the nature of his work environment, the tasks which go to make up his job and their organization, the psychosocial environment and his situation when not at work. What the person does outside work is both a determinant of his reaction to work, and at the same time affected by it. To some extent the sources of demand in the work situation, especially the more physical, can be identified and measured objectively. However, it is not actual demand so treated, which is important, but the person's perception of that demand, its psychological representation. It is suggested that the person actively and routinely assesses his work situation in relation to his own abilities. His needs and values are also taken into account during this process of cognitive appraisal. These can be viewed as internally generated demands. Furthermore, just as the work environment makes demands on the person, so it also supplies him with opportunities to meet and fulfil his needs. These 'supplies' are also taken into account during cognitive appraisal. The term cognitive appraisal was first used by Lazarus (1966, 1976) in the present context. When the person realizes that demands and needs are not 'balanced' by his ability to cope, or allowed for, then stress can be said to exist. One crucial aspect of this process of appraisal relates to the perceived consequences for the person of failing to cope. Perhaps stress only arises when failure to cope is important (Sells, 1970). Such failure in the work situation tends to leave the person's needs unfulfilled and this is probably a source of job dissatisfaction.

When stress arises, it is associated with a negative emotional experience and with both psychological (cognitive and behavioural) and physiological changes. Job dissatisfaction may be viewed as part of the 'cognitive' response to (occupational) stress, and may also be part of the development of alienation from work. It is possible that the physiological response has evolved as a preparatory or facilitory reaction for active behavioural coping. If coping is unsuccessful in reducing or eliminating the source of stress (and its experience) then abnormal activities may appear. The progression of cognitive and behavioural change in response to stress may thus be: first, an immediate response and the reorganization of the normal profile of behaviour, then the occurrence of abnormal activities, and finally a disorganization and disintegration of activity; a breakdown. All this will occur if the person thinks that coping with the source of stress is important.

The problem of stress is that its existence can pose a threat to psychological and physical health. It has been suggested, for example by Selye (1950) and by Levi (1972), that continual, repeated or severe exposure to stress is damaging. The responses to that stress can increase the rate of wear and tear on the body and its psychological processes, and that damage, increased vulnerability, breakdown and even death can occur as a result.

Repetitive work and the transactional model

The research currently being carried out at Nottingham into the problem of repetitive work is set within the framework of the transactional model of occupational stress. This research integrates two different approaches to the problem. First, an experimental workshop has been established in which the controlled study of simulated repetitive work can be conducted. This is run with the help of local industry. Second, an extensive field survey is being conducted of repetitive work and its effects on workers in the East Midlands of Britain. Again, this is very much dependent on the goodwill and co-operation of local industry. Both aspects of this research relate to unskilled and semi-skilled workers.

The experimental work seeks to manipulate certain of the demands inherent in repetitive work, such as the type of task to be repeated, the duration of the work period, the nature and level of pacing, and the method of payment. The effects of these manipulations are assessed against changes in the workers' mood, and in their performance on the job, and against their physiological state. In these experiments, the workers' abilities and needs are arguably kept constant and demand is altered. In later experiments, abilities will be assessed using standard psychometric tests, and this data will be related to performance on the job and to psychophysiological response.

The survey work seeks to understand and assess workers' perceptions of their work, and balance these against their individual characteristics and 'background' (biographical and social). This balance will then be related to those workers' state of health and current mood, and to their physiological state. This study on unskilled and semi-skilled workers' perceptions of their work provides an interesting contrast with studies on skilled, managerial and professional workers. For example, it tests the generality of the concept of 'job satisfaction' (see later). In certain of the planned studies existing measures of job satisfaction will be taken from the population under study, along with some measure of their behavioural response to stress (type A behaviour: Glass, 1977).

Most of the measures taken in the field survey and some of those used in the experimental work are based on questionnaires. Where this is so, the questionnaires have been developed at Nottingham on the particular population under study. This is held to be an important point, as many of the questionnaires currently available in occupational psychology are not appropriate for our present use. Three factors are thought to be involved:
(a) subcultural differences in the structure and use of every day language, possibly reflecting
(b) subcultural differences in the concept of work and its importance in life, and
(c) subcultural differences in the willingness and ability to complete questionnaires.

Six questionnaires have been, or are being, developed. First, mood is being successfully measured by the SACL (Stress-Arousal Checklist), which was the first of the Nottingham instruments to be developed (Cox, 1978; Mackay *et al*, 1978). This has been successfully used in a number of studies already published

(Bradley, 1978; Burrows *et al.*, 1977). Second, the workers' perceptions and descriptions of their jobs are being measured by the JDCL (Job Description Checklist). The development of this instrument is described later in this paper. Third, health is assessed in terms of a general well-being questionnaire and a medical history questionnaire. The former, it is hoped, will tap that area of health between complete fitness and presenting to a doctor with obvious illness. The medical history questionnaire examines the person's recent complaints and illnesses. The person's behavioural response to stress is to be measured on an instrument similar to the Jenkins Activity Survey (JAS). The JAS claims to measure various aspects of type A behaviour (coronary-prone behaviour) but was developed on an American population. A battery of questions similar to those asked by the JAS have been given to a British population and their responses are currently being analyzed.

Preliminary factor analysis (principle components) indicates a very complicated pattern of response, not at all like that claimed for the American JAS (Jenkins, 1971). Furthermore, it seems likely that the structured questionnaire used in the present study was as strong an influence on the responses obtained as were any characteristics of the population under study. Much more work is indicated for the development of this particular instrument. Last, the workers' biography, and social and leisure backgrounds are to be assessed using a simple form of enquiry, the Context to Work questionnaire.

The physiological measures being taken are based largely on the easily available body fluids; capillary blood, saliva and urine. Measures of heart rate are also being taken. From these measures a battery of physiological indicators of the stress response can be obtained: (a) blood glucose and cholesterol, (b) saliva flow rate, pH and sodium and potassium content, (c) urine volume, pH, ion content (see above), and catecholamine content, and (d) heart rate and regularity. Not all measures are being taken in any one study but, over the series of studies planned, a complete matrix of their inter-relationships should become apparent.

Perceptions and descriptions of repetitive work

Two major studies exist which go some way to describing workers' perceptions of repetitive work (Cox *et al.*, 1953; Caplan *et al.*, 1975). The first is a study conducted for the National Institute of Industrial Psychology (NIIP) in Britain, over 20 years ago, while the other, more recent, study was conducted for the National Institute of Occupational Safety and Health (NIOSH) in the United States.

Cox *et al* (1953) carried out detailed interviews with 160 women engaged in repetitive work in a variety of British industries. He identified three main areas of concern which were related to the impact of such work: these were freedom, security and creativity. Most of those interviewed disliked pacing, either by machine, conveyor belt or by others in their workgroup. Dissatisfaction was voiced, particularly where unnecessary constraints were imposed. On the other hand, changes in types of material worked upon, variations in working methods and job rotation were viewed positively and were regarded as ways of making time pass more quickly. Two points are of interest in this study. First, some workers mentioned that they preferred a 'moderate' level of pacing because this allowed them to earn a reasonable bonus at the end of the week; they feared that on self-paced work their rhythm and resolve to work quickly would soon dissipate, causing relatively less output and consequently lower wages. Second, large individual differences in what Cox referred to as 'attentional demand' (the extent to which the worker must give attention to the work process) were apparent from many interviews. Some liked tasks which demanded at least some of their attention, which it was said helped to pass the time, and also to reduce boredom; others liked tasks which could be performed automatically, allowing them to daydream or talk to their workmates. A recurrent theme throughout many of the interviews was the complaint of thwarting or under-utilization of skills. Many complained that the only skill required was the ability to work at a rapid pace for long stretches of time. Under-utilization of skill was one of the principal contributory factors in the aetiology of mental illness mentioned by Fraser (1947) in his study of engineering workers. It was particularly the case among female workers.

The NIOSH survey, carried out by the Institute for Social Research at the University of Michigan (Caplan *et al.*, 1975), investigated self-reported job demands in a variety of occupational groups ranging from unskilled to professional work. The survey was carried out using a long questionnaire administered at different organizations. The sample of several thousand consisted of male workers only. Results from this study indicated that individuals working on assembly line tasks (including some repetitive elements) suffer from high levels of stress in comparison with many other of the occupational groups investigated. Here, stress was measured in terms of self-reported under-utilization of skills, lack of participation and lack of adequate (preferred) job complexity. Moreover, these reported demands are associated with high levels of psychological strain, particularly boredom, anxiety and depression; a variety of somatic complaints was also mentioned. Some, more recently, reported work in the United States has also indicated that individuals from this occupational group have a much higher rate of admission to psychiatric clinics than do many other job types.

The job description checklist (JDCL)

Both the studies mentioned above are of obvious relevance to the study of repetitive work. However, for a number of reasons, a different approach to understanding workers' perception of work was taken in the present study. At the beginning of the previous section a number of constraints on the use of questionnaire techniques were outlined. These revolved around competence and performance in the use of every-day language. In addition to these, there were further constraints on the design and format of the job perception instrument for the population in the present studies. Briefly, these are as follows:

1. Because of the difficulties in reading and comprehension experienced by a reasonable proportion of those employed in unskilled and semi-skilled jobs, questionnaires need to be easy to read and interpret and simple to complete.

2. In order to fulfil the first requirement (1) it was thought necessary to avoid imposing an 'artificial' format or structure on the questions. The choice of material was guided to a certain extent by the task-qua-task taxonomy of stressors presented by Hackman (1970), but otherwise the approach was an empirical one; the final format was derived from the responses of the workers under investigation.

3. After discussion at shop-floor level it was obvious that the instrument should be confined primarily to task inherent factors, reflecting for example the physical constraints of the work, rather than areas normally associated with, say, clerical or managerial attitudes to work, such as promotion opportunities. This proved an advantage, as it was then possible to use the instrument in the laboratory simulation studies, where a person's experience of a job is measured in terms of days, or at the most weeks. This allowed a comparison of the two approaches to be made.

A decision was made to use a simple checklist approach based upon the use of job descriptive adjectives (JDCL). This technique has been widely used in personality research (Masterson, 1975), and mood research (Nowlis, 1965) as well as in the area of job satisfaction itself (Locke, 1976). Furthermore, this technique had already been used successfully in developing an inventory for the measurement of self-reported stress and arousal (Mackay, Cox, Burrows and Lazzarini, 1978).

The remainder of this paper describes the development of the JDCL together with some of the results so far obtained.

JDCL: detailed development

The checklist consisted of a simple set of instructions, a short series of questions about the worker and his job, and a list of 55 adjectives, each accompanied by a five-point frequency scale. The scale was as follows:

ALWAYS	4
OFTEN	3
SOMETIMES	2
RARELY	1
NEVER	0
CANNOT DECIDE	?

Workers were asked to use the list of adjectives together with the rating scale to describe as accurately as possible how they, as individuals, viewed their job. The list of adjectives was generated by a research committee, many with experience of research on the shop floor. Several hundred adjectives were initially put forward, but these were reduced within the constraints described earlier. Several lists were then taken to East Midlands factories and discussed with small groups of shopfloor workers. They were asked to indicate which words they might use, and which words they would never use, when talking about their jobs. They were also asked to suggest any words that they or others would use, but were not already listed. These alterations were studied within the overall plan and a list of 55 adjectives was arrived at. This list, took, on average, 10 minutes to complete.

Table 1.   Characteristics of work in participating companies

Company	A		B		C		
Factory	1	2	3	4	5	6	7
Type of industry	Light Engineering		Heavy Engineering		Pharmaceutical		
No. of employees	500	110	2000	194	550	454	696
No. subjects	43	32	52	64	89	98	50
Type of work	Assembly / Machine – Operation / Inspection	Press Operation / Soldering / Inspection	Machine – Operation / Inspection	Machine – Operation / Soap Moulding / Soap Packing	Machine – Operation / Confectionary Packing	Tablet Inspection / Packing	Conveyor Belt Operation / Packing
Shift system	3 Shift system / Dayshift / Twilight shift		Dayshift / Nightshift		Dayshift / Twilight shift		
Nature of work	Unskilled Repetitive	Unskilled Repetitive	Unskilled Repetitive / Semi-skilled Repetitive	Unskilled Repetitive	Unskilled Repetitive	Unskilled Repetitive	Unskilled Repetitive
Working week	40.00 hours		41.5 hours		40.00 hours		
Average overtime	4.00 hours		1.25 hours		4.00 hours		
Pay scheme	Flat Rate (Bonus Scheme)		Flat Rate (Bonus Sch.)		Flat Rate (Profit Earning Bonus Scheme)		
Length of training given	2 weeks	2 weeks	4-5 weeks	4-6 weeks	4-5 weeks	4-5 weeks	4 weeks
Ratio: females to males	M > F	F > M	M > F	F > M	F > M	F > M	F > M

The next stage involved administering the list to a large population of workers engaged in various forms of repetitive work. Three companies were involved in this study; a light engineering firm, a heavy engineering firm, and a pharmaceutical company. Over 500 workers from these companies participated in the research. The large majority of the participants were women. Most worked an eight-hour day shift, but some from the pharmaceutical company worked a 'twilight' shift (1700-2100 hrs). All subjects were informed volunteers. The general characteristics of the companies and the sample are described in Table 1.

Involvement with each company usually followed from discussions with both management and unions, and the interest shown by both groups was very encouraging. Most of the shopfloor workers approached appeared pleased to co-operate; only about 5% refused to fill in the checklist. Possibly this 5% would have been the most interesting group to study, but their right to refuse co-operation was not denied. Another 10% failed to complete the checklist correctly; many of these failures appeared to be due to reading difficulties, or to be simple errors. Since the majority of the repetitive jobs studied required constant attention, workers were usually allowed time off their jobs to fill out the checklist.

The coded responses to the list of adjectives were subsequently factor analysed. Principal components analysis was used; keeping unity in the diagonals of the inter-item correlation matrix. A rotated solution was adopted (varimax rotation). Initially, it was thought that four major factors existed, each displaying some degree of bipolarity. These were labelled: TEDIUM, PLEASANTNESS, PRESSURE, and DIFFICULTY. The results of the factor analyses carried out are shown in Table 2.

Table 2.   Results of factor analysis.

RELIABILITY OF FACTOR STRUCTURE:

Analysis	Number of variables	Number of subjects	Factors	Eigen values	Cumulative percentage of variance accounted for
1	67 (with traction adjectives)	301	1	10.08	14.6
			2	5.87	23.1
			3	4.39	29.5
			4	3.50	34.6
2	55	428	1	9.03	16.4
			2	5.00	25.5
			3	3.11	31.2
			4	2.85	36.3

FINAL ROTATED FACTOR STRUCTURE

Factor	Number of variables loading > 0.40		Typical variables
	+	−	
Pleasantness	19	0	Exciting, satisfying, great, enjoyable, fun
Tedium	7	2	Pointless, dreary, dull, boring, (worthwhile), (varied)
Pressure	10	1	Fast, tiring, demanding, pressured, (slow)
Difficulty	5	3	Difficult, complicated, worrying (easy), (simple), (easy to cope with)

These four factors were used to understand how the group of workers studied perceived and described their repetitive work. Three points were noted. First, the four different judgements were all independent. In particular, the judgement of PLEASANTNESS was independent of the other judgements. It was thus possible for workers to describe their jobs both as tedious (boring), pressured and difficult, but also pleasant. It was suggested that the pleasantness of a job depended heavily on social factors, while the other judgements related more directly to the task in hand. Second, no clearly defined 'job satisfaction' factor emerged, and the adjectives which might describe this feeling appeared to be incorporated in either the TEDIUM or the PLEASANTNESS factors. It therefore appeared that thoughts about 'satisfaction' were not foremost in the workers' descriptions of their jobs. It therefore follows that, if increasing job satisfaction is a key to improving the quality of working life, some shopfloor workers need first to be made more aware of what being 'satisfied' through work means and entails. Third, during the early part of the study 12 additional adjectives were added into some checklists. These described what Baldamus (1961) has called 'traction'—a pleasant feeling of being carried along by the natural rhythm of a repetitive job. However, no evidence was found in the present study for the concept of 'traction' in our workers' descriptions. The additional traction adjectives did not form an additional factor, nor did they substantially affect the other four factors. It therefore appeared that thoughts about 'traction' were not part of the workers' descriptions of their jobs, and thus not a redeeming feature of repetitive work (see also Turner and Miclette, 1962).

Each worker's score on the four factors was calculated, and multiple discriminant analysis was used to investigate differences between workers' descriptions according to the following criteria: company and factory, sex and work shift.

For the purposes of this analysis, information on the workers' age and length of time at the job (years) were used to help discriminate according to the above criteria. An overall analysis showed that the female workers in the light engineering company's two factories were older, and found their work less pressurised but more tedious (boring) than the workers in the other companies. It is possible that the increased pressure in the other factories offset boredom, possibly because the work in those factories demanded more attention. Looking at the pharmaceutical company's four factories it was possible to discriminate between female workers at factories 3 and 4. An age and pressure relationship was again found. Those at factory 3 were younger but felt more pressured. Perhaps as these workers enter their 'middle years' their increased experience of work may cause them to feel less pressured. Alternatively, those who found the pressure too great in the early years might tend to leave while relatively young (self-selection). Male and female workers at the heavy engineering factory were compared. Female workers were older but had spent less time (years) at their job, and they found it more pressured, more tedious but more pleasant. The differences in age and time at the job are explained by the fact that most of the women had returned to work after starting a family. They were therefore older but had not been working at the job for as long and thus felt more pressured.

The women probably found their work more tedious, because their jobs, compared with the men's, did not involve the same degree of variety. They did however work in a quieter part of the factory and were able to communicate more easily. 'Socializing' was thus easier. This may explain why they regarded their jobs as more pleasant. Shifts were compared at the pharmaceutical company. Female workers on the twilight shift were older, had spent less time (years) on the job, and found it less pressured, more pleasant but more difficult. Here again, the women workers had previously worked at the factory and had left to start a family. They returned to work the twilight shift until they were able to take up full-time employment. It was probably because they only worked a 4-hour shift that they found the work more pleasant and less pressured. The difficulty associated with the job may have been due to the fact that they had not been working on the job very long and were therefore still gaining experience.

The results of the multiple discriminant analysis show that the checklist is sensitive enough to distinguish between workers' descriptions of their work according to the criteria investigated. It is not possible to say with great certainty whether those descriptions reflect: (a) differences in worker characteristics, (b) differences in the structure of the workers' jobs, (c) differences in the work environment, or (d) other (social and organizational) factors. In assessing the importance of these factors it should be borne in mind that the workers participating in this study were of similar socio-economic and local background. They were randomly chosen from a wide variety of repetitive jobs, and the numbers studied were relatively large. Although the technical names for the jobs differed, several basically similar jobs were carried out in all seven factories. However, some of the differences in response observed were obviously due to the different characteristics of work and the workers involved. For example, women returning to work perceived their jobs in a different way to those who were not. However, not all the differences observed could be accounted for in terms of work or worker characteristics, and it was obvious from the anecdotal evidence gathered that social and organizational factors were very important in shaping the person's perception of their job. It is interesting to remember that a job could at the same time be described as pressured and difficult, and pleasant. Perhaps what occurred in such a situation was that two separate judgements were made. The job (task) itself was at an operational level, pressured and boring, but being at work was, for social reasons, pleasant.

Age, time at the job (years) and feelings of 'pressure' seemed in some cases to be interrelated in the present study. Perhaps the younger and less experienced worker feels 'pressured', until with increasing experience she has 'mastered' the job. This may occur after several years at work. Perhaps, as the worker becomes older still feelings of pressure return, as their capability fails to match the demands on them.

Conclusions

The present study on workers' perceptions of their work establishes three important points:

(a) that questionnaires used in occupational studies should be 'tailored' to the population of interest;
(b) that having done this for unskilled and semi-skilled workers, there is no evidence to show that the concept of 'job satisfaction' or 'traction' (Baldamus) is foremost in their descriptions of their repetitive work; and
(c) those descriptions can be adequately mapped in terms of four dimensions—pleasantness, tedium, pressure and difficulty.

Acknowledgement

The authors gratefully acknowledge the support of the British Medical Research Council and the US Army Research Institute (European Research Office).

A psychobiological approach to quality of working life: costs of adjustment to quantitative overload

Anita Rissler
Department of Psychology, University of Stockholm, Sweden

Long before the concept 'quality of working life' was introduced, hours of work were successively reduced by legislation. However, the 40-hour week does not apply to all professional groups even today. Unpaid overtime work is a common element in the career pattern of many white-collar professions as well as in many specialist occupations. Unwanted overtime was a component found to be an important factor contributing to dissatisfaction in a comprehensive study of job demands and worker health covering 23 occupations in the U.S.A. (Caplan, Cobb, French, Van Harrison and Pinneau, 1975).

Among aspects of work generally considered as contributing to job satisfaction and the quality of working life—such as challenging and meaningful tasks, autonomy, participation in decision making, growth opportunities and interaction with co-workers—hours of work, and balance between work and leisure time, are increasingly mentioned especially in countries with a large percentage of females in the work force, and with an active debate on work roles and family roles for both males and females.

In many occupations, challenging tasks require considerable investment of overtime work for extended periods. In other occupations, heavy overtime work is coupled with barren work tasks and double jobs enforced for financial reasons. Thus consequences of overtime work have to be studied in conjunction with the task content, when effects of overtime are evaluated. So far the impact of overtime work has been the focus for studies concerning quality of working life. Effects of extended hours at work in aviation have been examined (C. Cameron, 1973) in studies of fatigue. Fatigue has most commonly been studied using performance as the sole dependent variable and the results have been far from clear-cut. Mostly, performance decrements during continuous work have been sporadic, small and inconsistent due to the increased effort mobilized by the subject to counteract the effects of fatigue. Cameron (1973) has suggested that acute fatigue, that disappears with rest, should be separated from chronic fatigue requiring a longer time for recovery because of the preceding overload on the organism.

Overload and underload are useful concepts for studying and understanding consequences of work organization and working conditions in the whole arena of occupations (Frankenhaeuser and Gardell, 1976). Kahn (1973) has suggested a distinction between quantitative overload—i.e. having too much to do in too little time—and qualitative overload, implying difficult decisions, heavy responsibility etc. Underload describes work that is highly repetitive and monotonous, in which little use is made of the worker's skills.

Combinations of underload, quantitative overload and lack of personal control in saw-mill work has been shown as a threat to health and well-being (Johansson, Aronsson and Lindström, 1978). The joint impact of quantitative overload and low decision discretion has, in independent large Swedish and American samples, been convincingly related to mental strain symptoms and illness (Karasek, 1976). Time pressure, quantitative and qualitative overload also seem to be aspects of the work situation characteristic for persons with the type A-behaviour pattern which has been associated with increased risk of myocardial infarction (Rowland and Sokol, 1977).

Thus long-term, as well as acute, effects of work conditions, implying either underload or overload, are important to evaluate in respect of work motivation, job satisfaction and worker health. The present study of quantitative overload is part of a research project (Frankenhaeuser and Gardell, 1976) highlighting these themes by using both social psychological theory and psychophysiological methods.

Underload and overload are concepts emanating from arousal theory according to which the level of central nervous activation is important for performance and general well-being. Both too little and too much stimulation is non-optimal. In a series of experiments, Frankenhaeuser (1975) has shown that urinary adrenaline excretion is a sensitive indicator of activation level, induced by various environmental stressors, such as mental overload and underload, physical exertion, noise etc. Adrenaline is quickly mobilized in situations requiring active coping or passive flight (Cannon, 1914) and has consistently been related to self-reports of alertness, activation and mental strain in situations that have been cognitively appraised by the individual as having some emotional significance for performance or coping. Thus attitudes are important determiners of stress reactions on the physiological level, and serve as intervening mediators between the objective characteristics of the work situation and the physiological reactions to this environment (Lazarus, 1966).

After a period of increased effort and adrenaline mobilization, adrenaline levels decrease, but it has been shown that there are great interindividual differences in time of return to normal baselines (Johansson and Frankenhaeuser, 1973) implying that quick recovery is the more effective way to cope with acute stressors.

Adrenaline excretion can therefore be considered as a suitable measure of activation level and can be used in studies of job demands in working life, as urine samples are easily obtained without much interference with work. However, restrictions as to nicotine and caffeine consumption have to be reinforced to warrant valid activation measures.

Work tasks and overtime period

Acute psychophysiological reactions caused by demands from a circum-scribed period of heavy overtime were investigated during normal work. 'Carry-over effects' from work to leisure time were also obtained with psycho-physiological measurements late in the evenings. Further, long-term fatigue reactions were studied during the ensuing two months and cumulative effects were analyzed by studying time for recovery to baseline evening levels of adrenaline excretion (Rissler and Elgerot, 1978). The study was carried out at an insurance company. Fifteen female white-collar employees participated on a voluntary basis on 10 occasions spaced over a four-month time period. The distribution of work was very uneven at the division studied, with around 25% of the total amount of premiums per year arriving during the last fortnight in December each year. Immediate handling was a necessity which required a sizeable amount of overtime work during the first two months each year.

The tasks performed by these employees consisted of issuing insurance premiums. The work was described by the participants as rather standardized, the same type of tasks recurring, which could be solved according to given routines and tariffs. Autonomy was provided as to freedom to plan and carry out work tasks.

Job satisfaction

Questionnaire data disclosed that satisfaction with different aspects of work was high in the group studied. The participants described work as suffi-ciently interesting and independent, offering enough personal control and possibilities to apply skills. Opportunities for social interaction with colleagues were considered satisfactory. In all, work was described as rendering enough job satisfaction, not too much responsibility nor excessive mental strain.

Work motivation

Work was described as intrinsically motivating by this group of female employees with a mean work experience of 17 years in the same branch. Generally, the group valued a life filled with a meaningful job and work that was personally rewarding. As most important features at work were mentioned social interaction with colleagues, work tasks with variety, opportunities to learn something new, and authority to decide over own work tasks. Salary and responsibility were both considered less important in spite of a fairly low income level in the group.

Thus, this group of female employees definitely valued work that was intrinsically, rather than extrinsically, motivating besides home and family work, to which they still gave priority. They also seldom thought of job related problems at home. It should be mentioned that this group could be compared with several other groups in the same company of females and males having tasks implying both greater discretion and higher qualification (Elgerot and Rissler, 1978). Measures of work motivation and priorities did not distinguish this group from the others in any aspect questioned. Intrinsically motivating work tasks were thus as important for the female employees as for males, contrary to what is often claimed.

Psychophysiological reactions during overtime work

Subjective ratings of various aspects of work and of mood, as well as excretion of adrenaline and noradrenaline and heart rate measurements, were obtained one month before the overtime period, for comparison at weekly intervals during the most intense period of overload, and later at two-week intervals.

The number of hours overtime each week (Figure 1) was highest between Sessions 3 and 6 and consisted mainly of work at the weekends. Only during

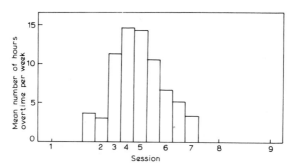

Figure 1.   Distribution in time and mean number of hours overtime work per week.

the most intense period was the work day extended up to one hour on an average. The period containing overtime work was rated as significantly more strenuous (Figure 2), chaotic, stressing and urgent as compared to periods

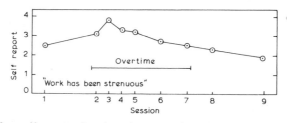

Figure 2.   Mean self-reports of work strain measured on nine occasions during a four-month period.

before and after. The excretion of adrenaline at work increased significantly as the amount of work was extended (Figure 3) and remained at a high level during the entire period of overload, after which period the excretion was lowered. Noradrenaline excretion was significantly raised over comparison level only towards the end of the overload period, and heart rate was consistently higher during the entire period.

The adrenaline level late in the evening (between 8 and 10 p.m.) was also significantly raised but the increase in level became progressively higher with time (Figure 3), thus not parallelling the actual amount of overtime at the end

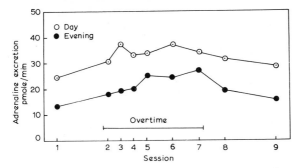

Figure 3. Mean excretion of adrenaline at work (empty circles) and during leisure time resting at home (filled circles) on nine occasions during a four-month period.

of the period. At Session 7, in spite of only three hours of extra work per week, the level of adrenaline excretion was as high late in the evening as during an ordinary workday.

Subjective mood ratings of increased strain and tiredness described the overload period at work, and increased tiredness, irritation and bad mood characterized the self-reports in the evening. Work efficiency was rated as progressively lowered over time but speed, precision and concentration were not judged as changed. Performance in a short concentration task was even improved during the latter part of the overload period.

Thus, the objective increase in work required was reflected in significant increases in subjective effort and strain as well as in physiological activation. Obviously, this increase in activation and mobilization of effort was instrumental in counteracting performance decrements. Especially noteworthy is the progressive increase of adrenaline excretion in the evening. The physiological mobilization needed at work apparently had after-effects implying a slower than normal return to physiological evening levels. Consequently, possibilities of using the reduced leisure time were diminished due to physiological over-activation and increased tiredness as a result of the overtime work.

Inter-individual differences

Thus, increased physiological and behavioural activation was observed to facilitate coping with the requirements during the period with extended working hours. In order to analyze demands put on the individual by this extra load, a separate analysis was made studying physiological recovery, thereby separating acute and chronic effects of fatigue. A criterion of adrenaline excretion was used to define physiological recovery. Half of the participants reached this criterion at various points in time during the overtime period, whereas the other half reached this criterion not until well after cessation of overtime work. Two groups were formed having shown fast and slow recovery respectively. When the two groups were compared, important differences were statistically ascertained. There were no differences between the groups in baseline adrenaline level before overtime work (Figure 4), but the group with slow recovery had a significantly higher adrenaline level at work during the

Satisfactions in work design

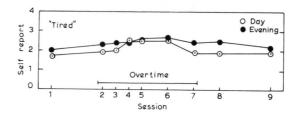

Figure 4.   Adrenaline excretion at work and at rest during a four-month period in two groups differing in rate of physiological recovery to baseline adrenaline evening levels after overtime work.

entire period and progressively increasing adrenaline excretion late in the evening during overtime as compared to the group with fast recovery. The evening levels of noradrenaline excretion and heart rate showed the same pattern of increasing activation for the group with slow recovery. Thus return to normal physiological resting levels in the evening was impaired for one of the groups. The remaining high activation in the evening in the group with slow return can be related to a group difference implying that this group slept worse and for a significantly shorter time during the overtime period.

The physiological group differences were not matched, however, with any differences in subjective strain, alertness or tiredness reported at the corresponding sessions. The physiological indices were thus possibly more sensitive indicators of overload than the subjective reports.

A careful analysis of the objective working conditions as well as of the family and leisure situation revealed no differerences between the two groups. Nor were there any group differences in amount of overtime work or age of the employees (median age 54 years).

However, when the overtime period afterwards was considered in a time perspective, it was obvious that the demands encountered at work had more serious implications for the group with slow recovery. Well after the overtime period a questionnaire was administered that contained health and mental strain indicators relating to symptoms experienced during the preceding year. A psychosomatic stress syndrome was isolated, implying that the subject had complained of all of the following problems during the preceding year—work experienced as mentally exacting, greater fatigue than the year before, stomach troubles, headaches and body tensions. This stress syndrome tended to be more frequent in the group with slow, as compared to fast, recovery (54% versus 14%). On reporting what they considered as causing mental strain, the group with slow recovery significantly more often reported strain from work pace and amount of work, i.e. quantitatively experienced overload. Thus, the increase in job demands had consequences for the group with slow recovery with respect to health and well-being.

Costs of adaptation

When considering acute reactions to this temporary increase in job demands, a picture of active coping is apparent, characterized by challenge to meet the demands and high motivation to carry out the extra duties by increase in effort and time spent at work. However, the standards of efficiency maintained by the employees required them to key themselves to a higher pitch of mental effort than usual. Viewed in a long-term perspective serious questions must be raised with regard to the potential harmfulness of these efficiency demands. The psychobiological approach used in this study indicated that the adaptational efforts, in the long run may bear a price, if the environmental demands are not matched in time with the psychophysiological state of the employees. This is most clearly shown by the gradual build-up of adrenaline excretion after work in the later sessions, when the actual period of overtime was almost over. This delay in time of physiological activation, with high activation when it was no longer needed, implies a misuse of resources for coping. Further, excessive lengths of environmental load during which behavioural efficiency is maintained may have its price by exhausting the adaptational resources, the consequences of which in the long run are not known. Costs of adaptation implying subjectively experienced overload and mental strain, impaired sleep and psychosomatic complaints were experienced by those with excessive activation and slow physiological recovery rates. It seems that duration of physiological recuperation can be used as a determinant of the harmfulness of the environmental load which may not be subjectively experienced at the moment of impact but may later show up as psychosomatic complaints. High work motivation cannot be taken as a guarantee for high quality of working life, if provisions for working are not keyed to psychobiological conditions for health.

This investigation was supported by a grant to Professors M. Frankenhaeuser and B. Gardell from the Swedish Work Environment Fund (project No 73/55). I am indebted to my co-worker, Anita Elgerot, M.A., with whom I carried out this study.

A study of quality of life and work in a professional group

P. Shipley
Department of Occupational Psychology,
Birkbeck College, University of London, United Kingdom

The ship's pilot is a well-qualified specialist navigator. Some pilots joined the service after a lengthy apprenticeship, but many came direct from the sea and in possession of a Master Mariner's ticket. There are about 1500 pilots in the United Kingdom, and about 500 fall under the jurisdiction of the most well-known pilotage district, Trinity House (London). Pilotage is an ancient institution; Trinity House received its Royal Charter from Henry VIII in the 16th century. It is a public service which involves 3 main groupings; shipowners and their agents, port authorities, and pilotage authorities. But the pilot's primary allegiance is to the ship and its Master.

The degree of pilots' involvement in management varies somewhat from district to district. There are some 70 different pilotage districts, and a variety of systems of work and operational procedures are practised mainly because of varying regional constraints. The number of pilots at these stations varies from one or two at small ports to 150 at the largest one. Some two thirds belong to a professional affiliation called the United Kingdom Pilots Association; the remaining third are members of a pilotage section of the Transport and General Workers Union. The pilot is, theoretically, self-employed. He has a medical examination on entry to the profession and there is little formal training. He builds up his pilotage skill and knowledge through years of practical experience. Most pilots go on piloting until aged 65, regardless of their level of fitness. Facilities for transfer to another district, or to another post within the profession which does not entail regular practical pilotage are limited.

Professional responsibility

The pilot carries a great responsibility for human life, and for material of high capital value, i.e. ships, their cargo, and shore installations. Although the Master is legally responsible for his ship even when the pilot is in control of its navigation, the shipowner may sue the pilot for negligence in the event of an incident. The pilotage authority has the power to take away his licence.

The essence of his job is familiarity, especially knowledge of his local district. When an incoming ship enters the limits of the district's pilotage waters, a pilot boards and navigates the ship inwards, unless the ship has a certificate of exemption. Pilots also take the ships outwards when leaving port. The pilot is familiar with the coastline and its landmarks, with the estuary or river, the port and harbour structure and its docks and berths. He knows the local tides, the prevailing winds, and the various hazards such as sandbanks and wreckage. There are various types of pilotage and a broad distinction may be drawn between sea and estuarial pilotage, and berthing or docking. These call on different qualities and abilities. It is a job characterized by intermittent stresses and fluctuating demands. For example, the pilot works irregular hours, and sometimes gets caught by chance in the unpopular 'night seam', a run of pilotage acts between 10 p.m. and 6 a.m.; an accident of the roster scheme or watch system in operation in his district. To some extent, the nature and constraints of the district and the kind of pilotage involved determine the kind of work system in operation.

Workload

The concept of 'workload' is a complex one in pilotage. Optimal systems of working are difficult to establish. 'Workload' in the sense of the distribution of number of pilotages, rest periods, and the sharing of work among a group of pilots, can be a bone of contention, rather than the demands made by the practical act of pilotage itself. For convenience, in our study we refer to the latter as 'direct workload', and this kind of workload does give rise to stress and strain on occasions. Our study is a survey of pilotage for stress problems with particular reference to the question of workload. Some pilots have worn portable cardiac monitors for us, and heart-rate discriminates rather well between different kinds of pilotage experience. We monitored pilots at work from both the mental and physical workload points of view. Boarding and disembarking with the use of a pilot boat can be a hazardous operation, especially in bad weather, and when the ship has a high freeboard. The decisions to be made in certain kinds of pilotage, such as manoeuvring a very large oil tanker (a 'supertanker') in marginal conditions, are another source of strain.

But for routine pilotage, the travelling door to door, especially getting home after a long sea pilotage at night, and the problem of getting adequate rest, are more commonplace considerations. The long periods of waiting on standby, and the uncertainty about when he is to be called, is also a potential source of strain on the pilot. We refer to these factors as 'indirect workload'. The pilotage service is theoretically available 365 days a year and 24 hours a day, and the pilot may be called at any time of day or night. Because ship loading and unloading takes place in normal working hours a pilot tends to be at work in what are called nowadays 'unsocial hours'. Sleep patterns and diet can be disturbed when there is little certainty or advanced warning built into the system, and the individual pilot has to cope with the effects of unexpected calls on his body rhythms, and on his domestic and social life. Such uncertainty of timetable is a strain which is difficult to measure in a scientific way. On the other hand, many pilots prefer this way of life to being at sea because of the domestic comforts they enjoy.

Forces of change

This lack of routine, and the constant variety of shipping and crews encountered, would suggest that the pilot is subject to constant daily change. But in the last half century pilotage has undergone many larger scale changes; commercial, political and technological. Although typically conservative in his views and working in an environment steeped in sea-faring tradition, the pilot needs sufficient flexibility and adaptive capacity to manage his rapidly changing world. In the United Kingdom pilotage operates under an array of rules and regulations. There is a single central piece of directly relevant legislation, the 1913 Pilotage Act, and a proliferating mass of local bye-laws which govern the operations which vary from district to district. The 1913 statute is widely recognised to be out-of-date in many respects, and a new pilotage bill is in preparation as part of a new Merchant Shipping Act.

Commercial changes have been significant in their impact, both nationally and locally. There was a post war trade boom up to the early 1960s when the demand for pilots was probably greater than their capacity to meet that demand comfortably. The world-wide trade recession has since left its mark, but so has industrial action. The viability of some ports has been substantially reduced, and the pilot is dependent on the prosperity of his port. But one port's decline is matched by another port's rise through major industrial change of another kind. Scottish oil ports are now in the ascendancy with the exploitation of North Sea oil ... until the oil runs out.

Important technological changes affecting pilotage have occurred in recent years. The declining number of ships piloted over the last decade or two is as much due to this factor as it is to trade fluctuation. Ships have grown bigger, and the ratio of large to small ships has radically altered with the consequence that there are fewer ships afloat. More minor technological changes in bridge design and shore aids have had effects on ships' pilots, but the increase in ship size is a far more challenging technological change. There are large container ships and bulk carriers afloat, and cargo is being carried in larger single units. It is the giant oil tanker, however, which looms largest in the mind of the pilot. This growth in ship size has been exponential. In the past 50 years the largest ships afloat increased nearly 100-fold from about 6,000 to 500,000 tons. A typical supertanker is over a quarter of a mile long, and is as wide as an 8-lane motorway. It can draw 60 ft of water, fully laden. Some of our ports are too small and our waterways too narrow, congested and confined for the comfortable accommodation of such monsters. There may be less than 6 in. clearance underkeel in a deep-dredged channel up to the berth. The sudden power failure leading to loss of steerage is an emergency when a large ship 'braked' at full speed could theoretically cover 2.5 nautical miles before coming to a stop. There are also special control problems in the berthing and manoeuvring of these ships. Damage to ship and shore can be most costly and there are grave pollution risks. The disaster to Torrey Canyon was a precursor of more recent dramas like the incident with the tanker Amoco Cadiz. Under difficult conditions of weather and spatial layout the pilot is operating at the limits of human skill. The equations of motion for these ships are largely unknown, and their slow-speed dynamics may result in a critical shortfall of vital information and feedback of control decisions. A pilot relies heavily on visual perception and is a keen judge of space, distance, velocity, acceleration, turn and swing rates. Yet should automation be a realistic possibility then the pilot will fear professional redundancy.

The effects of changes in manning levels and calibre of crew on board ship should not be disregarded. In 1967, the year of the Torrey Canyon disaster, there was an acute shortage of tanker crews, and attracting and retaining good calibre bridge staff is a continuing concern in the shipping world. It can thus happen that when the pilot has to take over he cannot find enough men to help with docking the ship. Spillages and near-collisions are not uncommon and about 10% of the world's incidents occur around the coasts of Britain. The majority of these occur in pilotage waters where the exposure to risk is naturally so much greater than on the high seas. Another significant change for the pilot has been a radical shift in the proportion of foreign to home trade ships in favour of the former. On some ships inferior manning, under-qualified bridge staff and language difficulties add to the problems of the job—as do 'rogue' ships of one kind or another which infringe mandatory shipping lane rules in the Dover Straits.

Professional strain and health

This study was set up as a result of earlier pilot initiatives, with a view to determining the health status of this occupational group. Some pilots suspected that a high incidence of cardiac mortality existed in the profession. Unusual levels of this class of disease in the 35 to 50 years age group were also suggested by our analyses of whatever limited records were available on pilots' deaths and sickness. The methodology was based on a conceptual model of sources of potential strain such as job factors, life style, personal variables and the forces of change. A mixture of methods was used, both objective and subjective. Pilot opinions and perceptions were collected informally, and more formally by means of carefully prepared questionnaires embodying rating scales and questions of the open and closed types.

The main questionnaire was made available to all pilots and it was possible by this means to assess pilot satisfaction with aspects of their work and personal lives. It was also used for identifying and gauging occupational strains as perceived by the pilots themselves. This 'stress-strain' component of the instrument was based on the person-role (person-environment) fit model developed by researchers at the Institute for Social Research at Michigan University (French, 1973 and Caplan *et al.*, 1975). Fig. 1 is a general model of stress, strain and health status adapted from the earlier Michigan work. 'Stress' is environmentally or situationally determined, according to this approach, whereas 'strain' is based on the individual and the individual's responses. By job 'misfit' is meant the degree to which job or role demands produce individual strain, and it was hypothesised that deficiencies as well as excesses of a given factor could give rise to job misfit as a particular class of strain. Misfit was predicted to correlate with dissatisfaction and other negative feelings such as anxiety, depression and hostility (Cooper and Marshall, 1978).

Role dimensions of interest included role conflict and ambiguity, role responsibility, status, workload, levels of skill utilization, and participation in decision-making. Discrepancies can be arrived at between what levels of a given factor people say they experience in their work and what they would prefer; and these can be combined into an index of strain. Reported health status, responses to a scale of psychological well-being and reports of lifestyle and behaviour outside work (smoking, drinking alcohol, sleeping, leisure habits), can be related to these job strain factors.

Predicted links were found in this study between strain variables and identified job stresses, in agreement with the Michigan findings. Also, like the Michigan researchers, we were less successful in relating stresses and strains to actual ill-health. The reason for this is multifold, and we suspect arose from the small numbers of reported illnesses, inherent weaknesses in subjective measures, and because of the more remote and tenuous nature of the actual stress-strain-health linkage process.

But the person-role fit approach proved to be a useful diagnostic tool, if only because it quantified the informally expressed views and opinions. (The quantified findings it was decided would carry weight and be more plausible). Our aggregated results showed the key job stresses were: uncertainty, frustration and physical hazard, in that order. Responsibility, status and variety produced the least job misfit. It is gratifying that men carrying such a burden of responsibility do in general feel they personally need a high degree of responsibility and feel able to meet the challenge posed by this particular job demand.

By means of a mood adjective checklist embedded in the questionnaire we were able to gauge the level of psychological health and well-being of this professional group. There is little evidence of emotional or mental ill-health, since 90% of the most frequently reported moods when on duty were of the positive kind. The remaining 10% refer to the sub-scales of negative feelings: anxiety, hostility and depression. As expected, those pilots with higher job misfit scores were more inclined to negative feelings, and expressed greater overall and specific dissatisfaction.

Professional satisfaction

As expected from our informal discussions and knowledge from other studies of similar occupational groups, pilots expressed a high degree of intrinsic job satisfaction, but grumbled about extrinsic factors. The biggest single source of satisfaction lay in the practical pilotage of ships; the ship-handling and the exercise of skill and knowledge. A sense of personal satisfaction, of self-esteem and pride, was derived from doing a difficult job well. There was also a high degree of interest and variety; no two ships or jobs are the same. Variety and interest also derive from the social aspects of practical pilotage, meeting different seafarers from other countries in particular. The pilot also enjoys a high measure of independence and the freedom to make his own decisions on the job. Professional independence was thought to be a pre-requisite for a safe and efficient pilotage service, but having no boss and being free from petty restrictions also form part of this treasured feeling of independence. Some pilots also expressed a liking for the irregularity of the

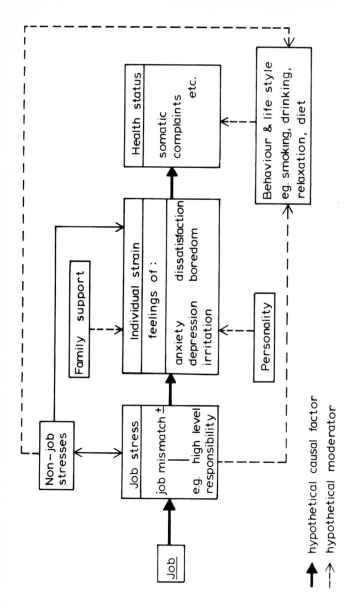

Figure 1.   General model of job stress, individual strain and health status.

work hours and enjoy time off during the day when other people are at work. Working with mariners and ships, but without the many disadvantages of sea life, was reckoned to be another major satisfaction. There is also a clearcut end to the job when the ship is safely tied up; the pilot does not take his work home in his briefcase.

In Fig. 2 this large measure of intrinsic job satisfaction is reflected in the high percentage of those surveyed who said they would make the same career choice if they could start again. The medical sample referred to in this figure was a carefully selected group of London pilots who volunteered to be investigated thoroughly medically so that a health profile of pilots drawn from a Master Mariner background could be established. Pilots in the medical sample consistently expressed greater dissatisfaction than the other pilots

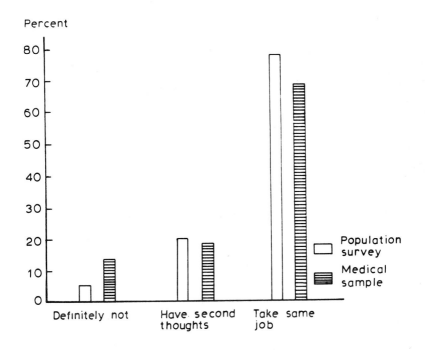

	Percent	
	Population survey	Medical sample
1. Definitely not	3.7	13.6
2. Have second thoughts	19.5	18.2
3. Take same job	76.8	68.2

Figure 2.   Percentage who would take same job again.

surveyed; which we think may reflect the special problems associated with London district pilotage. Sea pilotage in the London district involves a long pilotage act followed by a long and often awkward journey home in unsocial hours. Fig. 3 shows that pilots generally thought themselves to be better off than their counterparts at sea, but somewhat worse off than equivalent occupational groups ashore. (When asked to name similar shore groups pilots usually point to doctors, solicitors and other professionals who are providing a responsible service to the community after a long period of specialized training.)

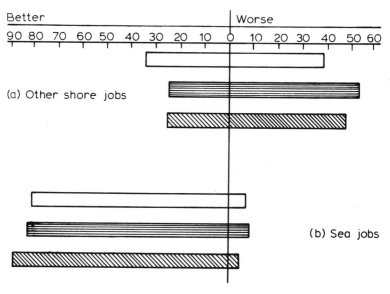

	(a) Other shore jobs		(b) Sea jobs	
	Better %	Worse %	Better %	Worse %
1. Population survey	35	38	81	7
2. Medical sample	25	53	83	8
3. Wives of medical sample	26	48	89	4

☐ Population survey
≡ Medical sample
▨ Wives of medical sample

Figure 3.   Comparisons with other jobs.

Professional dissatisfaction

Dissatisfactions centred broadly on conditions of work and on the organization and management of pilotage. The grumbles about the organization and its interpersonal relationships were to do with interference, either directly when the Master prefers to do his own pilotage and makes the pilot feel like a 'spare part', or indirectly with interference from 'outside sources' in pilotage matters. Under the heading 'conditions of work' the following represented the major dissatisfactions: turning out in bad weather and at night; getting on and off ships in bad weather; travelling home after long pilotage; the uncertain work hours and unpredictable nature of the work; disturbed sleep and meals and unsociable life style. Although we found high heart rates in conditions of high mental load during actual pilotage, and when a severe physical load was imposed getting on and off ships, another clue as to the origins of cardiac disease may lie more in the area of pilots' working hours and conditions and their adverse effects on lifestyle. These latter are a constant source of complaint and dissatisfaction in certain pilotage districts, especially long-haul districts.

The unpredictable nature of the working hours has an adverse effect, we surmised, on the body rhythms and cycles of those who are unable to adapt properly. But nearly all pilots mentioned the disrupting effects of such irregularity on other aspects of their personal lives, especially home life. Fig. 4 shows the generally high degree of global satisfaction with personal life, paralleling global job satisfaction findings. When this global factor is analyzed into facets a clearer picture emerges of where the problems lie. Notice that the London pilots in the medical sample showed substantially greater dissatisfaction with the quality of their home life than did the other pilots. This is surely a reflection of the working patterns associated with longer pilotage in this particular district.

In the questionnaire we explored the degree of perceived conflict between home and work. The frequent need to cancel plans and appointments stood out as a potential source of strain and frustration to the pilot and family, especially his wife. This may lead to family tensions and the pilot being deprived of a network of friends. Family and friends are the basis of that 'social support' which, according to the model in Fig. 1, will buffer and mitigate the stressful factors in the job.

In Fig. 5 the results are shown of further questions which explored specific work restraints on personal life. In order of importance the most prominent are: the limited opportunities for attending courses outside work; for developing outside commitments; for structuring free time; for sports and exercise; and for developing a wide social circle.

These findings at the crucial interface between personal and working life are somewhat ironic when compared with the motives pilots seemed to have had in joining the service. The majority of those who left the sea to become pilots seemed to have done so for the extrinsic reason of wanting 'a normal domestic life'. Conditions at sea are much better now. Ships' officers enjoy long spells of leave and, in some companies, wives can be accommodated on voyages. After coming ashore to enter the pilotage service, the mariner has had to adapt in many ways, but the adaptation required of his wife and family should not be disregarded.

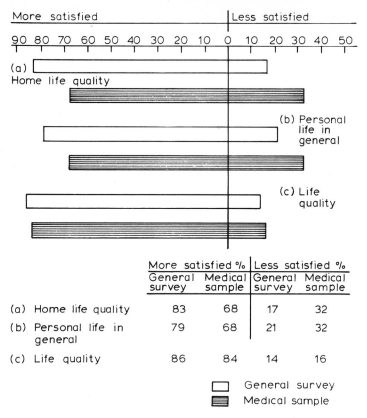

	More satisfied %		Less satisfied %	
	General survey	Medical sample	General survey	Medical sample
(a) Home life quality	83	68	17	32
(b) Personal life in general	79	68	21	32
(c) Life quality	86	84	14	16

Figure 4. Percentage satisfied/dissatisfied with quality of personal life.

Preferred improvements

We asked pilots what changes or improvements they would like to see. Many wanted more say in pilotage affairs and better rapport between themselves and the other protagonists in the system; ship-owners, port and pilotage authorities and government bodies of various kinds. More certainty and stability of workload is called for in terms of more predictable work periods and in terms of available work. Future security is clearly a concern and the need for guaranteed work, a stable income base and better pension rights was often expressed. There is also a strong call for earlier retirement, more in line with continental practice. Greater unity among pilots is a further desired change, and some showed an interest in a single national pilotage service, with a common standard of entry and a national training scheme. Pilots would also like port and ships authorities, and the general public, to develop an appreciation of the job they are doing and the conditions under which they work, which perhaps indicates the need for a pilotage public-relations function.

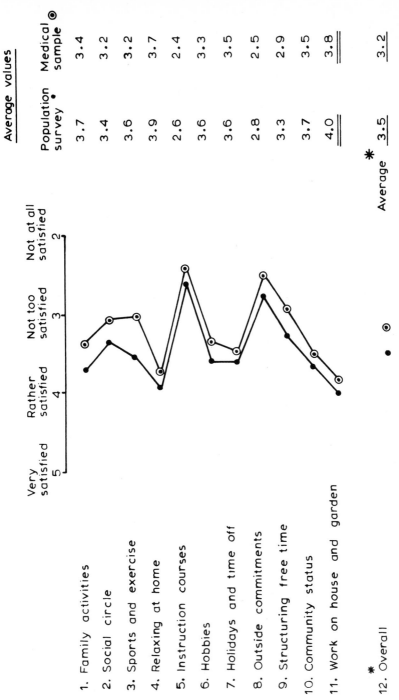

Figure 5.   Degree of satisfaction/dissatisfaction with restraints work has on personal life.

Other professional aspects

This project has been an inter-disciplinary effort with two broad goals. The paper has so far been confined to one goal: that of helping the client with his problems. The other goal is the more academic one of trying to contribute some insight into the problem of 'stress' and psychosomatic disease. This is reported elsewhere (Shipley and Cook, 1978) in the context of why some individuals are more vulnerable than others to occupational stress. By shifting the frame of reference from client to researcher other difficulties, dissatisfactions and questions emerge and new conflicts are spotlighted. There is the prime conflict between meeting the clients' needs and satisfying the more academic goals. There is the conflict inherent in the different interests represented among the various sponsors (pilots, government body, ports and shipowners). Indeed, identifying 'the client' pilot and his needs has been a continuous challenge and concern, because of the needs of the different districts. Of less importance, but a growing concern for modern research nonetheless, is that of bridging the gulfs between the disciplines represented around the research team's table. And lastly, different units and levels of analysis, from individual through groups to whole organizations present problems of cross-reference and require conceptual and methodological flexibility. Also, in the sensitive area of stress research, confidences can be given and personal information divulged which requires reciprocal attitudes of responsibility and accountability on the part of the researcher privileged with such information. This poses further difficulties when individual and organizational interests are in potential conflict. This project has thrown up a mixture of ethical, political, administrative, scientific and technical challenges to the researcher and the scientific and technical appeared often to be the easier to manage. (The researcher's formal training is, often, more or less exclusively confined to the latter.) How far should and can research and teaching institutions help those in the potential role of researcher and project leader to meet these role demands? In effect, to bridge the gap from social technician to social technologist?

Acknowledgement

This research was supported by a grant from the Department of Industry (Ship and Marine Technology Requirements Board), the National Ports Council, the Association of Pilotage Authorities of the United Kingdom, and the various pilotage professional associations and union bodies.

New forms of work organization: some Belgian case studies

S. H. Moors
Belgian Office of Productivity, Belgium

Semi-autonomous groups assembling electronic components

For reasons of social progress, a company, producing T.V. sets, wanted to experiment with the new organizational form of semi-autonomous groups. The reorganization took place in the department where tuners were assembled. A post factum evaluation of this reorganization (Moors *et al.*, 1975(a)) provided totally unexpected results conflicting with the intentions of those who had taken the initiative. This led to consideration of the more fundamental facts explaining why the new work situation was experienced in this way.

Change from the previous set-up to a newly organized production

In the original set-up, the assembling process of the tuners was split up in 15 consecutive operations: preparing coils (op.1), preparing cables (op.2), inserting components in section 1 of a small board (op.3), in section 2(op.4), in section 3 (op.5), in section 4 (op.6), soldering in automatic solderbath (op.7), visual control and repair of the inserting (op.8), visual control of the soldering and repair (op.9), ultrasonic cleaning (op.10), soldering the box around the board (op.11), fixing cables (op.12), mounting kernels (op.13), regulating the tuners (op.14) and repairing bad tuners by highly qualified technicians (op.15). Each of these operations was carried out by two to 10 workers. Each day every worker noted down the number of finished pieces. The salary was fixed with five different salary scales for the different tasks.

According to a rather vague conception of a semi-autonomous group, the new production flow is split up in 10 parallel groups, each sitting around a table where a complete tuner is assembled by six to eight persons. To aid materials handling and planning, workers at the beginning and end positions note down daily production. Instead of five there are now only two salary scales.

Results and discussion

As regards outputs, no changes in quantity appeared but quality scored

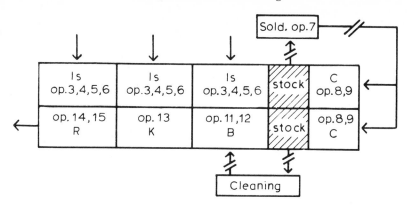

Figure 1.   The new set-up: a group of 6 to 8 workers sitting around a table. At every position the previous jobs now performed by one person are indicated. The preparatory work (op. 1, 2) is done by home workers.

higher. This improvement of quality is due to the fact that workers handling the product at the different phases sit next to one another so that information can be passed on immediately.

Concerning workers' satisfaction and the quality of working life, this new organizational scheme shows some positive elements. Job enlargement is obtained by increasing cycle-time and the task of the person who is adjusting is enriched by the highly qualified repairs she has to do. The worker has a better overall insight into the products he is putting together. There is greater equality in wages. There is more freedom. It does not feel like working at an assembly line.

The management hoped to have semi-autonomous groups which were able to function without a group leader, where all would be equal and group members would be motivated to deliver good products. The findings contradicted these intentions in three ways.

The status of the different positions is unequal. Lowest are the inserters (Is), next the controllers (C), then comes B and the highest is the regulator (R). The learning progression from Is to C to R leads to this while the lowest qualified task B has its relative high position from being physically near to R.

Although there is no formal leader, the worker R acts as the leader. She is not a leader because of her personal qualities but rather because of her position: she is the best qualified person, sits at the end of the production cycle and indirectly controls the work of the others, notes down the group results and therefore has to report to the departmental head.

In practice, job rotation almost never takes place: either training for every task is lacking, or the person does not know all the tasks thoroughly. Only for the unattractive kernels mounting does job rotation appear in each group spontaneously.

Analyzing the key problem

The 10 groups can be divided into two categories. Some think their group is good with good results and excellent interpersonal relations. Other groups have a negative image of themselves: results are poor and the tension and conflicts between the members of the group are frequent. It sometimes happens that workers sit at the same table without exchanging a word for several days. In the good groups the worker on the R position seems to be well accepted, whereas she is not at all accepted in the bad groups.

Our first idea for solving the interpersonal problem was to train the departmental head so that he could learn to cope with this sort of problem in group sessions. At an international meeting Emery proposed training two workers for the R position so that workers could select their own leader.

The problem only became clearer by looking at the way the interdependencies of the jobs in interaction with the personal capacities were creating work load problems. The products of Is are controlled by C and R. The more mistakes Is makes, the more work C gets. In case C has too many repairs to do, she can pass them on to R. Now, if R is very good at her job, she will do the extra work without complaining, so as not to increase the tension within the group. Moreover, she will not be easily overstressed so that she can comment in an agreeable way. On the other hand, a less able R worker cannot cope with her work and needs to complain. But the more she does, the more problems the others give her. So she prefers not to talk and silences prevail. Any approach needs to find a solution to this one-sided dependency.

Without realizing it a mini assembly line had been created without its normally built-in corrective mechanisms.

Work structuring and automated production machines

In this case study a production manager, feeling his job was threatened because of persistent poor production, tried and found the solution together with his production workers in work-structuring and group work. A post factum evaluation research (Moors *et al.*, 1976) revealed that, in respect of job satisfaction, a fundamental factor is work load. This factor is critical for work on automated production machines and it interacts with the form of work organization.

Problems of the previous organization and breakdown of the classical approach

Some 600 types of semi-manufactured electronic components, foil condensers, are produced in the department. The production process has 3 major phases. In the winding phase (W) coils are made by winding foil strips. These coils are flattened in the second phase (F-phase) and in the final phase the products are healed, measured and sorted according to value (M-phase). Each of the 3 major operations is performed by different automated machines. The workers have to bring in material, control the machines and take away the products. The 600 different types are constituted by the thickness and width of the foil, the thickness of the coils and their edges. For every major operation there are different types of machines.

The production was previously organized in sections corresponding to every major phase. The machines stood in rows next to each other and workers were individually responsible for four to six machines. Orders were distributed by the section leader. Control of quantity and quality was performed by controllers and this directly affected the bonus level. After every phase, coils went in temporary stock. At that time the department was confronted with several problems. The overall performance had been weak for several years. The demand of other departments could not be met and this caused serious problems. There was considerable tension between operators and controllers, especially since a certain amount of subjectivity exists in the quality evaluation. In addition, tension caused by quality problems was frequently noted between the section leaders. Finally the individual work gave rise to coordination problems between successive shifts. The management services department worked out a solution, particularly to meet the needs of other departments. In this solution the department would be split up and added to the finishing departments. This plan would have involved 25% higher investment costs and the head of the department would have lost his position. Therefore, the latter tried once again to draw on the resources of his own people.

A mixed work group reorganization and the results

A list of problems was drawn up by the leaders of the department and four work groups were set up to examine the method of operating the production machinery, rejects, machine operators, number of controllers and layout. Each work group had a heterogenous membership, i.e. a section leader, a machine operator and two workers. The workers taken were those known to be good workers and to have sufficient verbal capabilities to make an independent contribution. There was to be a weekly meeting. Any proposals were to be made on paper, accompanied by a summary of their advantages and disadvantages. The time between the meetings was also to be used for observations. In fact, we see that the work study methods and the tools of an organization service were being used here by the production workers in a simplified form, for example the taking of test samples, multi-snap-readings, etc.

In the layout work group, one worker made the suggestion that she would like to carry out all three phases herself. The department head took this up as the basic idea of the whole reorganization developed by the working groups. Not all operations would have to be carried out by the same person, but a few persons were trained in all phases so that they were ready to help each other and to perform the whole production cycle. The layout of the machinery was made in the form of a rectangle. The bonus was paid for group results and the results of both shifts were counted together in order to prevent coordination problems. Operators were to take responsibility for both quantity and quality. They planned their work themselves. Group after group was formed. The pace of the reorganization was dependent on the workers' readiness to help each other.

From an economic point of view, the same output is now being achieved by 49 persons instead of 60. There are 2 fewer foremen. The machine outputs have increased by 10% and rejects dropped by 50%. The production cycle is reduced to 2/3. Absenteeism has dropped. Overall performance is increased by 12%.

From a social point of view, the surplus staff could be taken up by expansion in other departments. Management support and training overcame the initial fears of the workers. Job content was enlarged and enriched. The opportunity was built in and the prerequisites fulfilled for mutual help, which could reduce stress at peak moments and give more scope for personal matters. The discussions and tensions between the workers and the controllers disappeared as well as the tensions between the sections. The workers received regular feedback on the results. Wage differentials between workers were eliminated and wages were raised because of flexibility. In fact a fixed wage resulted because the maximum bonus was easily earned. A new atmosphere was created by the feeling of working in an efficient department.

Work load: a very fundamental factor

This evaluation research was made three years later. The head of the department had already been promoted. A 56-item job satisfaction questionnaire was answered by the workers of the condenser department and a comparison group of workers who had individually organized assembly tasks. Almost all the condenser-workers preferred the new organization to the previous one. The overall job satisfaction was equal and highly positive (72% positive answers) in both groups. Nevertheless, the pattern is not the same. Findings confirmed some characteristics of the group work realized in this case: better interpersonal relations, a more positive reaction to leaders, more learning opportunities, more variation and smoother work flow.

One important exception appeared at that time: the condenser-workers felt a significantly higher work load. This finding was contrary to our expectations. The individual assembly work of the comparison group gave an impression of rush. In addition a more adequate operational training reduced the work in the condensers department and by means of group work the load at peak time could be levelled off. The puzzle became clear not from the comparison of group work versus individual work, but rather by analyzing the type of work itself. The comparison group has short cycle manual work. It requires higher physical efforts but once trained the rhythm is mastered. As compared with this, operating five automated machines gives moments of higher complexity and the feeling of not being able to cope with the problems arising. Theoretically we concluded that group work would be of no help if a permanent external factor was increasing pressure on all positions. In the questionnaire feedback sessions, which already had taken place, the workers cited one factor among others which corresponded to these criteria. The new head of the department, although not in agreement with our hypothesis, felt he had to do something on the basis of the report and solved the technical problem. Production increased by 54% and workers felt proud and less tired by their work.

Theory of the 'must' curve and the 'can' curve

Both cases showed the importance of the factor work load. Correlational studies too confirmed the highest negative numbers between job satisfaction and experience of work load (Moors *et al.*, 1975(b), 1976).

The 'can' curve and the 'must' curve vary over time

One can conceive the tasks and duties stated as work load potential. This work load potential, what 'must' be carried out, is not always the same at any given time. There may be quiet times, alternating with times of high physical demand or great mental complexity. One can present this variable in the form of a curve plotted with respect to time. When on the other hand one looks at the work load only as an average score, then one probably misses the most important characteristics of the work load (i.e. its variability) as far as it effects the experience of the work situation. There also is a 'can' curve. What one is capable of, also varies from one time to another. We are not always at all times equally capable with regard to all the aspects of the task which we have to carry out. Whenever the 'must' curve moves above the 'can' curve, this is the critical moment which can cause trouble in personal feelings and organization.

Interaction between 'can' and 'must'

The curves are not independent of one another. When one has been under too much pressure for some time, tiredness increases and one is capable of less achievement. If the organization of the work includes a recovery period when the pressure is less, capabilities again increase. If the type of task and the production process do not permit this, things get worse and worse and the feelings of powerlessness and excessive pressure increase. On the other hand, it is true that not enough pressure can also reduce capacity. It is known that sportsmen have to train a lot to achieve high physical performances. This also applies to intelligence: it does not develop without all-round practice. Conversely, 'can' also affects 'must'. When one cannot do a task at a particular time, the result is that even more has to be done afterwards, so that one gets even further behind. Perhaps operations are carried out incorrectly, which can make the confusion and the problems even worse.

The effect on personal experience

The relationship between 'can' and 'must' also affects personal experience. Whenever what must be done is slightly more than what can be done, a challenge is presented to the person to carry out his task in spite of this. When the increased tension and concentration lead to success, one obtains a feeling of growth and self-realization. If one continuously feels one cannot cope with the task, there is a feeling of powerlessness and loss of self-confidence. This is an unacceptable situation in which one becomes alienated from work and feels dissatisfied. Perhaps the person will seek positive experiences in aspects not connected with the task. If the work load is continuously too low, boredom and lack of interest follow. People will therefore look for positive experiences during the working hours in secondary activities. Feelings of uselessness may also arise.

The effect on relations with colleagues and management

When one cannot cope with the task at a certain moment, then one can endure less, the frustration tolerance level drops. One becomes touchy and more easily upset. One more readily reacts aggressively towards others. The counterreactions to this then usually make the situation worse. When one also has the impression that the source of the excessive pressure lies with a colleague, because he has for example carried out the previous operations badly, then this is the basis for a good many problems. If the cause of the increased work load lies in less than perfect tools, machinery or raw materials, then the resentment is aimed at the management. This affects the credibility of the management, it undermines readiness to make an effort and promotes the tendency to 'swing the lead'. It is clear that many interpersonal problems relate to the work design and are built into the organization structure reducing the likelihood of a good relationship between the 'can' curve and the 'must' curve.

Mechanisms of avoiding an unfavourable relationship between 'can' and 'must'

When tiredness is the cause of the feeling of no longer being able to cope with the task, people will, often in closely controlled situations, use stimulants which ultimately means exhaustion of the individual. The nature of many tasks allows limited effort and therefore maintains the feeling that things are all right. One can omit certain operations and carry out others more carelessly. The quality of the products is thus bound to drop, which sometimes in turn can increase the work load at later operations. There is also the danger that the machinery and installations are not kept so well and then this leads to a spiral of problems. One disturbance leads to another and the consequence is firstly a drop in quality and secondly an overload.

Many of the factors which increase pressure cannot be clearly recognized by the management or the fact that these factors are present is not noted; perhaps because the management itself is responsible for them. Many of these factors come up sporadically, and at the end of the day or week one forgets that they have arisen. In the face of these ups and downs and a negative evaluation by the management, the worker protects himself by keeping his output down to an equal minimum level which he can achieve under all circumstances. In addition, the management often goes along with this tendency as it simplifies planning, because a number of unpredictable factors are eliminated.

Methods which can have a favourable influence on the relationship

It is clear that job-oriented training increases the worker's capability as he learns a more suitable work strategy.

In addition a number of organizational measures can be taken to avoid situations with which he cannot cope:

First, where possible, one can let the worker fall into his own rhythm rather than let the machine control his rhythm for him. A worker can be capable of more and is usually willing to do this. He will in fact gain satisfaction in being able to do more. Perhaps the well-known phenomenon of 'traction' is linked with this.

Secondly, group work can have a peak reducing effect, but this is not necessarily so. The effect is in fact produced when the peaks do not occur for all the tasks at the same time.

Thirdly, one can also build in moments of rest after great tension to enable the workers to recuperate.

Finally, it is generally useful to carry out a detailed analysis of the interactions between technique and people. This can highlight a number of technical weaknesses which are a source of a good deal of pressure and which show the problems to be solved as a priority.

Consequences for the new forms of work organization

It would seem clear to us that each form of work organization, including the newer forms like job rotation, job enlargement, job enrichment, work structuring and semi-autonomous groups, should take into account work load. By this we mean not so much the pressure as such, but the relationship between the 'can' and the 'must' minute by minute in all situations. People want to take on other and new responsibilities only when they are capable of them. Learning is only attractive when one can cope with the pace. The many inconsistencies between the results of evaluation studies on these new forms of work organization can perhaps be explained by this factor. In fact, each of these forms brings with it its own difficulties. It always requires the learning of new tasks. Besides, job rotation requires changes in rhythm. Group work also means that one is dependent on the contribution of others: this is why the building in of interdependence is usually advised. Once there is a happy solution to the work load factor, which does not mean a minimum work load, such objectives as feelings of self-fulfilment and autonomy may be achieved.

Job satisfaction among chemical process operators

H. J. Foeken
University of Technology, Eindhoven, Holland

The research project described is aimed at the improvement of the working life of process operators. The aim is to understand better the relationship between job content and job satisfaction of this particular occupational group. The work of process operators differs considerably from many other industrial jobs. During a substantial part of their time they have to wait and watch but they must be prepared for swift and effective action in emergencies. They usually do 'mental work' but perform few physical activities. The number of process operators in industry is constantly increasing.

We have applied concepts about the humanization of work, job enlargement and job structuring to this type of work. The research is comparative in that we have studied jobs in different factories to assess the similarities and differences between job characteristics. By comparing job satisfaction scores from people holding these jobs we hope to evaluate the difference between more and less 'good' jobs and thus indicate how to improve them.

Before discussing the design of this study and the results obtained we shall very briefly describe the factory and the jobs we shall be considering. In the factory the product manufactured is a powder, which comes from the reaction of several fluids. After the reaction the raw product is purified, crystallized and dried. The whole process is fairly critical (things easily go wrong) and still in a more or less experimental phase. Compared to many other continuous chemical processes this one requires much vigilance, as the crystallization process and subsequent transport of slurry and powder frequently lead to pollution and/or obstruction of pipes, pumps and other machinery. The process is controlled by a team of 10 operators holding five different jobs.

The five jobs may be described briefly:

(a) cleaning filters and pipes according to a maintenance scheme;
(b) maintaining the crystallization part of the process, eg by maintaining correct physical conditions in vessels, cleaning pumps and pipes;
(c) managing the drying and transport of the final product: here there are clear-cut responsibilities; the operator is confronted directly and immediately with consequences of his actions;

(d) being responsible for the reactor, heating and pressure equipment, and a large amount of connected equipment, pipes and subprocesses: operators are only intermittently active, sometimes once a month; knowing and surveying the whole process; and

(e) control room operator, controlling the whole process and maintaining contact between supervision and the other operators.

Method

Much research on job satisfaction lacks a systematic way of dealing with factors like job characteristics, payment and organizational structure. When some of these factors have been changed, and the workers are more satisfied, the goal is reached and nobody knows precisely how this came about.

We tried to circumvent part of this problem by using a measuring device for task characteristics. A task is defined as that part of a process (in a broad sense) performed and/or supervised by an operator, and for which the operator is responsible. In this way satisfaction with task characteristics is intrinsic satisfaction and satisfaction with non-task job characteristics is extrinsic satisfaction. We support the emphasis laid on the enhancement of intrinsic satisfaction as a way of improving the quality of working life. Consequently, we think it is worthwhile to investigate the task characteristics of jobs. The focus of our research is the relationship between task characteristics and intrinsic job satisfaction. To eliminate as many as possible of the alternative explanations we also dealt with job characteristics which are not directly task-related.

Measuring instruments

(a) *task characteristics*

We restricted ourselves to the mental aspects of tasks, these being by far the most important in operators' jobs (Crossman, 1960). The instrument used is the 'Task Assessment Scales', a set of 21 scales, developed by Theologus *et al.* (1970), based upon extensive research projects by Guilford (1967), French (1951) and Fleishman (1967) who looked for a relatively stable set of abilities. Abilities are regarded as prerequisites for performance.

The TAS was successfully used to describe mental and psychomotor tasks (Theologus and Fleishman, 1971; Teichner and Whitehead, 1971). It consists of definitions of abilities, every definition being followed by a seven point 'thermometer'-scale with descriptive anchors at the high, low and midpoints. We translated and re-anchored 21 scales out of 50, discarding the psychomotor abilities. The labels of the scales we used are listed in Table 1. The TAS is a tool for describing technical characteristics of the work itself. We believe that implicitly a number of higher order aspects are measured as well.

A 'rich' job, for example, will have either high scores on some TAS-dimensions, or moderate scores on most of the dimensions. A 'poor' job on the other hand will have little or no high TAS-scores and moderate or low scores on many dimensions. Following this line of reasoning we used average

Table 1.   List of TAS-labels

1.	verbal comprehension	12.	category flexibility
2.	verbal expression	13.	spatial orientation
3.	ideational fluency	14.	visualisation
4.	originality	15.	speed of closure
5.	memorization	16.	flexibility of closure
6.	problem sensitivity	17.	selective attention
7.	problem solving	18.	time sharing
8.	number facility	19.	perceptual speed
9.	deductive reasoning	20.	choice reaction time
10.	inductive reasoning	21.	reaction time
11.	information ordering		

TAS-scores per task (scores per task per aspect summed and divided by 21) as an index of task-difficulty. As a way of validation of this meta-measure we calculated the number of TAS-dimensions on which a job was scored higher than 3.5. (midpoint). The five jobs studied were ranked according to their average TAS scores, and according to the number of TAS-dimensions exceeding the midpoint. These two rankings correlated perfectly.

The richness and poorness of jobs is in our view reflected in their TAS-scores. This holds particularly true for the aspects of autonomy, identity and variety.

(b) *job characteristics*

For each of the five jobs studied we formulated a job description, based on observation and instruction, interviews (with job incumbents, supervisors and staff members) and the study of any documents available. The job descriptions were discussed with the people mentioned, were revised and discussed again, etc.

(c) *satisfaction*

From the extensive literature on the subject it is clear that job satisfaction has several aspects. There is a difference between overall satisfaction and satisfaction with specific aspects; and there (probably) is a difference between satisfaction with the work itself and satisfaction with the job in general.

We searched for a common set of aspects, mentioned by many researchers. The set about which there seems to be fair agreement in producing satisfaction are skill variety (the number of different skills required to perform a task), task identity, task significance, autonomy (of the person performing a task), feedback (from the job itself and/or from other people, to a person performing a task) and dealing with others. These intrinsic aspects are measured in the Job Diagnostic Survey (Hackman and Oldham, 1974). Next to the work-intrinsic aspects mentioned, the JDS measures satisfaction with pay, security, contact with co-workers, supervision and growth opportunities.

In addition to its representativeness of the field, the JDS has two other advantages: it provides for repeated measurement in different formats; and its vocabulary and style seemed to fit the population we were interested in.

We translated a major part of the JDS and added some scales:

(a) a selection from the questionnaire used by Ford and Borgatta (1970). This was the list differing from the JDS most strongly in words, style and format that we could find.

(b) two questions using non-verbal responses. The respondents were asked to mark one of five faces all showing different expressions of pleasure (Kunin, 1955). Firstly the respondents were asked to express their satisfaction with the job in general. The second question was about satisfaction with the work itself, the things they had to do.

Procedure

Two operator teams were studied in a chemical factory. The researcher spent two weeks with each team, following the routine working hours in the late, and the night, shifts. The first week was used to achieve mutual acquaintance, and for gathering information upon which the job description could be based. In the second week, questionnaires were administered, job descriptions discussed and interviews held. The individual interviews with every operator were centred around satisfying and dissatisfying events and moments in the work.

The interviews were as free as possible. Responses were categorized afterwards. Eighteen out of 21 operators returned the questionnaires, either by reply-paid envelope or personally to the investigator. In the same period, two instructors described the five jobs in terms of the Task Assessment Scales. Their profiles (vectors of 21 dimensions) were averaged. The profiles were fairly similar, in that only 20% of the judgments by both instructors differed by more than one scale-point (eg job 1, scale 1 was rated 3 by instructor 1 and 5 by instructor 2).

The similarity between profiles can be described by the similarity coefficient (Cattell and Coulter, 1966), but this coefficient is meaningless when two profiles to be compared are not drawn from a large sample. In our case, the two profiles to be compared (eg, job 1 assessed by instructors 1 and 2) were drawn from the total set of 2 x 5 profiles. The values of the similarity coefficients obtained ranged from .22 to .47.

In the study two main questions were investigated:

(a) can a relation be found between characteristics of the work itself, and satisfaction with the job, or the work itself?; and

(b) to what degree (if any) is satisfaction with characteristics of the work itself related to satisfaction with the job in general?

These questions led us to a number of hypotheses, all having the form: on the average, operators holding jobs low on the TAS will report less satisfaction with aspect (j) than operators holding jobs with higher TAS scores.

The aspects (j) are the ones listed above. We assumed that the translated questionnaire items would measure the same factors they did in the original studies, and grouped the items from the two sources (Hackman and Oldham, Ford and Borgatta) into subsets per aspect. Before reporting the relationships found we give the TAS-scores of the jobs studied. In Table 2, the mean TAS core, number of TAS scores exceeding midpoint, number of respondents who completed the questionnaire and level of payment (and responsibility) are given. The jobs are described above.

Table 2.   Summary of the job characteristics and number of respondents per job.

Job	a	b	c	d	e
Mean TAS-score	1.7	2.7	2.7	3.3	3.8
Number of scores > 3.5	0	1	3	12	17
Number of respondents	2	4	2	3	6
Payment			low		high

We looked for differences between the means of the satisfaction aspect scores of operators, grouped by job. We also tested differences between the mean satisfaction scores of the operators in jobs a, b and c (low payment level) and those in d and e (high payment level). Because job c differed quite strongly from all other jobs with respect to its identity and feedback characteristics, the analysis procedure described above was also performed on the difference between (means of operators in job) a + b and d + e, on the difference between a + b and c, and on d + e and c.

Results

We discuss here only the significant findings (p 0.05).

For the aspects variety, feedback from job and feedback from others, groups (of operators in job) a + b are less satisfied than groups c + d + e, on nine out of 18 items.

One variable ('do you think your job is monotonous and always the same') showed differences in the predicted direction between all five group means.

With the aspect 'identity' (of the work), the operators in group b are less satisfied than the others. The same goes for autonomy (5 out of 10 items). All operators were less autonomous than they would like to be, but at the same time were content with the closeness and type of supervision. Apparently, something in the orders given to operators should be changed because the interviews gave some hints in this direction.

The aspect 'importance' reveals a difference between the operators in the three lower-paid jobs and those in the higher-paid jobs. On intrinsic aspects of the job (eg, do you find the work itself interesting?, is doing your work satisfying to you? etc) for seven out of 10 variables no differences were found between the mean scores of operators in the different jobs, or combinations of them. Only three out of 10 items showed a difference between groups a + b and c + d + e.

Overall satisfaction with the work itself, and with the job in general, is shown in Fig. 1. (The responses were given by marking one of five faces differing in expression.)

As can be seen, the operators in low TAS-jobs tend to have a higher satisfaction with the job than with the work, whereas operators in higher TAS-jobs tend to the opposite. The differences between groups are not statistically significant. From the interviews we found some possible explanations of the

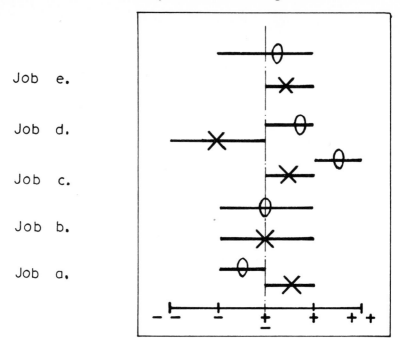

Figure 1.   Ranges and means of satisfaction scores per group of operators holding the same job.
X = mean score of satisfaction with the job in general
O = mean score of satisfaction with the work itself.

differences which seem to exist: people in low jobs have few other opportunities, and are relatively well-paid; people in higher jobs like the work, but are
less content with physical inconveniences. No differences were found between
group means of satisfaction with pay, security, contact with colleagues and
growth opportunities. This suggests that differences in global satisfaction are
related to intrinsic factors. There were no differences between the group mean
scores on a growth need strength measure. The correlation between satisfaction with the work itself and satisfaction with the job in general (non-verbal
measures) was .03. Only 'contact with colleagues' and 'payment' showed a
significant correlation with the non-verbal satisfaction with the job in general.
With respect to the non-verbal score of satisfaction with the work itself 14
variables showed a significant correlation. The aspects measured by those
variables could be divided into four groups:
(a)   measurements of satisfaction with identity,
(b)   measurements of satisfaction with feedback,
(c)   measurements of satisfaction with variety, and
(d)   measurements of satisfaction with autonomy.
From the interviews we hoped to get specific information referring to sources of
satisfaction, causal relationships and the role of individual (person related) factors. After summarizing and categorizing the interviews two things became clear:
(i)   almost all factors and events contributing to satisfaction were related to
the work itself; and

(ii) from the factors contributing to dissatisfaction, a smaller part is related to the work itself, and a bigger part to the job in general (mainly physical conditions, shiftwork and information from supervision and staff).

These findings support Herzberg's (1966) theory.

Evaluation and conclusion

This study supports the hypothesis that operators derive satisfaction and dissatisfaction in their work from two clearly distinguishable sources:

(a) the job in general, important aspects of which are payment and contacts with colleagues; and

(b) the work itself, relevant aspects of it being autonomy, identity, variety and feedback.

It seems that the TAS is a useful tool in describing some, but not all relevant characteristics of the work itself. From other sources (Theologus, Romashko and Fleishman, 1970 and experiments now being conducted by this author) it is clear that the TAS scores can be refined by increasing the number of judges using it in describing a job. It seems that the instruments used (TAS, questionnaire and interviews) are sufficient to describe and diagnose differences between operators and jobs, both in the same factory and in different factories. From the comparison of these differences suggestions for improvement can follow. Other field studies using this approach are in preparation.

Work structuring and safety

J. T. Saari and J. S. Lahtela
Institute of Occupational Health, Helsinki, Finland

One of the principles of production design is breaking of the manufacturing process into a chain of brief operations. This practice has advantages as far as efficiency and cost minimization are concerned. But it also has drawbacks. For instance, because of monotony of the work, job satisfaction (Hackman and Lawler 1971, Seybolt and Gruenfeld 1976) and worker motivation (Lawler 1969, Brief and Aldag 1975) may be reduced.

Because of the need to improve working conditions, a demand to restructure work has arisen. Researchers have suggested that an optimal job is characterized by such factors as variety and autonomy (Lawler 1969, Hackman and Lawler 1971, Sims and Szilagyi 1976, Rousseau 1977, Hacker and Macher 1977).

In the literature, these dimensions are generally considered in a positive light, but no consideration seems to be given to the amount of these various factors a job should be allowed to contain. On the contrary, when principles are given for job design, it is recommended that new and different tasks be added, that the cycle time be increased, and that auxiliary and preparatory tasks be added (Wild 1975, p. 58). No upper limits of the cycle time or number of new tasks etc are suggested. Intuitively, one can predict that both ends of these dimensions are less desirable. Particularly from the point of view of safety, the 'positive' extreme may lead to adverse effects. Jobs that are too variable and autonomous may be unsafe.

As an illustration of this assumption, a brief description of a recent Finnish study in the light metal industry follows.

Method

In the study nine factories were involved. They were selected from companies located in the eastern and western parts of Helsinki. Five of the companies were selected because their annual accident frequency was significantly higher than the company average in this industry in the Helsinki area (group 1). In the other four companies the annual frequency of accidents was lower than the average (group 2). Therefore, the accident frequency of group 1 was high and that of group 2 low during the two years prior to the investigation.

In all the companies studied the maximum weight of the articles produced was 100 kg. The degree of mechanization was about the same; the number of workers in each was more than 100.

From each company every sixth worker was selected for the study. Each subject was interviewed and his work was observed for 45 minutes. Observations were made by one of the authors (J.L.). Among other things, the type of products, machines and other technical devices used, the production lay-out and the job structure were all recorded.

The number of workers observed in group 1 was 131. The average frequency of reported accidents was 262.4 accidents/10^6 man hours for this group (1975). The number of observations made in group 2 was 115, and the average frequency of reported accidents was 118.3 accidents/10^6 man hours. The total number of workers in both groups was 1962. No fatal or permanently disabling accidents had occurred in either group during the previous year. The ratio of the frequencies of accidents with an absence of more than three days was 2:1 for the two groups.

Results

Such technical factors as unguarded parts of machines, obstacles on the floor, slippery floor etc were more prevalent in group 1, but these factors could not completely explain the differences in the accident frequencies (Saari and Lahtela, to be published). A discriminant analysis based on such technical variables correctly classified only two-thirds of the work places observed.

Personal protective devices—gloves, goggles, and ear protectors—were more often used by the workers in group 1.

The workers' job experience and length of service in the respective company (Fig. 1) were similar in both groups. The workers in group 2 were, on the average, two years younger and there were more females. The average length of vocational training was shorter in this group.

More distinct differences between the groups were found in the structure and type of jobs. Fig. 2 illustrates one aspect of these differences. In group 1 the jobs consisted of more tasks. A total of 14 different tasks were included: among them were machining, product packing, reading of drawings, repair work, maintenance, clean-up, fetching of tools and materials, product inspection, etc. The median number of tasks belonging to the job was 4.97 in group 1 and 2.76 in group 2. In the former the jobs commonly involved maintenance, the fetching of tools and materials, clean-up and other irregularly appearing subsidiary tasks in addition to the main task.

Also, the number of different tasks performed during the observation period was higher in group 1. The average was 2.6 (maximum 5) in group 1 and 1.9 (maximum 4) in group 2.

Machining was the task that was performed in both groups during the major part of the observation period (Table 1). It was followed by the preparing of machines for production, product inspection, manual transport and

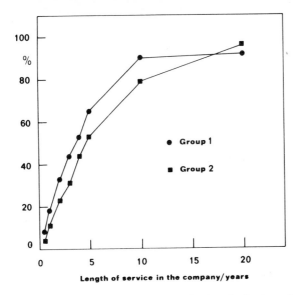

Figure 1.   Cumulative distributions of the length of service in respective companies.

clean-up. Table 1 confirms the results shown in Fig. 2.

The classifications used so far are based on the technical aspects of production. Table 2 indicates that the tasks performed during the observation period differed in character. The observer assessed the dissimilarity of the

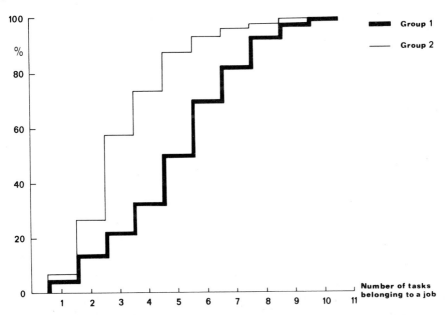

Figure 2.   Cumulative distributions of the number of tasks belonging to a job.

Table 1. Proportion of observation period used for a particular task.

Task	Group	Proportion of time used for observation period						Total		χ^2	p
		0%		1-90%		>90%					
Machining	1	29	22%	75	57%	27	21%	131	100%	26.9	<0.001
	2	29	25%	31	27%	55	48%	115	100%		
Preparing machines for production	1	91	69%	39	30%	1	1%	131	100%	10.8^X	<0.01
	2	100	87%	10	9%	5	4%	115	100%		
Products inspection	1	75	57%	56	43%	–	–	131	100%	5.2^X	<0.05
	2	82	71%	29	25%	4	4%	115	100%		
Manual transport	1	92	70%	39	30%	–	–	131	100%	18.8^X	<0.001
	2	106	92%	8	7%	1	1%	115	100%		

^{X} Observations in columns 1-90% and >90% were counted together in the χ^2 testing.

various tasks. This assessment not only concerned inter-task dissimilarity but also intra-task dissimilarity. The assessment was based on a number of examples. It took into account: (a) information processing, (b) decision-making and (c) types of movements.

Table 2. Amount of dissimilarity between the tasks performed during the observation period.

Amount of dissimilarities	Group 1		Group 2	
	n	%	n	%
None	10	7.7	34	29.6
Little	89	67.9	65	56.5
Some	29	22.1	14	12.2
Much	3	2.3	2	1.7
TOTAL	131	100.0	115	100.0

$\chi^2 = 21.3$
p <0.001

There were also differences in the degree of autonomy between the groups. Four aspects of autonomy were assessed, i.e. the workers freedom of (a) scheduling various tasks, (b) selecting the method to be used (movements, tools etc), (c) determining working speed and (d) determining time and length of rest break. Although the four aspects were assessed separately, they have been presented in Table 3 in a combined form. When autonomy is determined in this manner, group 1 had a greater degree of autonomy than group 2. Even when the four aspects are assessed separately, there exists a significant differ-ence between the groups in the same direction.

It was also found that in the companies with a high accident frequency (group 1) the tasks observed occurred more infrequently and the cycle times of the tasks were longer.

Foremen, safety officers, workers' labour protection representatives, and shop stewards of the companies in both groups were interviewed without prior notice. The objective was to determine their attitudes and opinions towards safety and preventive measures.

Table 3. Degree of autonomy when the four aspects of autonomy are combined.

Degree of autonomy	Group 1		Group 2	
	n	%	n	%
None	123	23.4	166	36.1
Some	200	38.2	116	25.2
Complete	201	38.4	178	38.7
TOTAL	524	100.0	460	100.0

$\chi^2 = 26.2$
$p < 0.001$

No major differences were revealed between the two groups, although there was a tendency to estimate the annual accident frequency as lower than it actually was in group 1 and higher in group 2.

The only difference between the groups which might have influenced the accident frequency of the respective companies is presented in Table 4. The foremen in group 1 tended to shift the main responsibility for safety to management, while the foremen in group 2 accepted it more readily. As to opinions about means of accident prevention no differences existed.

Table 4. Foremen's replies to the question: "Who is mainly responsible for accident prevention?"

Responsible party	Group 1		Group 2	
	n	%	n	%
Management	17	53	4	17
Foremen	4	13	10	42
Workers	2	6	2	8
Safety officer	2	6	3	12
Someone outside the company	7	22	5	21
TOTAL	32	100	24	100

Discussion

There are both advantages and disadvantages with the research design used in this investigation. Normally, accidents cannot be observed directly without enormous costs. The data must, therefore, be gathered through interviews of eyewitnesses and victims. But in dramatic incidents like accidents, the subject's memory may easily be distorted, especially if questions of responsibility are likely to interfere. In this study direct observations could be made. On the other hand, both groups worked at job stations with built-in potential for accidents. Therefore, the differences may be weak.

The results indicate that jobs in the companies with a high frequency of accidents are more variable and autonomous than in the companies with a low frequency of accidents. In other words, the jobs in group 1 often included the kind of tasks that are used to increase variety and autonomy. Other studies have proved that many accidents really occur in subsidiary tasks like the fetching of tools and materials, the cleaning of the work place, maintenance, repair etc. (Saari 1977, Saari and Rinne, 1977). Variety and autonomy may thus increase the probability of accidents, and a conflict between the different goals of work design may arise.

The mechanism behind this phenomenon is complex. Indeed more than one mechanism exists. This finding is difficult to explain in terms of the accident-proneness theory or the energy-involvement theory. But in terms of the information-flow theory (Surry 1969, Hale and Hale 1970, Singleton 1976) the results can be understood. In a variable job, a worker cannot develop a set of routines that are performed automatically. He has to work in a stimulus-response mode which is too slow for many tasks. Therefore man's capacity to handle information may be exceeded. Autonomy, on the other hand, reserves a part of the information handling capacity for planning and decision-making. If enough time has not been allocated, a risk may arise. More simply speaking, in variable jobs the worker cannot thoroughly learn all the dangers and hazards involved in the working environment.

The other possible mechanism may be found in the technical aspect of production. If autonomy characterizes the wrong phases, all benefits of mass production cannot be utilized. For instance, the tools selected may be inappropriate.

In conclusion, it seems that variety and autonomy may increase the probability of accidents. Obviously, this is not an unavoidable phenomenon. The means of avoidance are the careful planning of jobs and the adequate training of workers. The workers should be thoroughly trained to do any additional tasks that occur as well as to handle efficiently autonomous jobs that demand planning and decision-making. In addition, the work design must be done very carefully.

Job redesign in the bindery: a case study

Brian Peacock
Department of Industrial Engineering, University of Hong Kong

The reason for the study

A situation had arisen in the bindery attached to the University of Hong Kong library where there was a large backlog of periodicals and soft covered books waiting to be bound. Preliminary enquiries indicated unreasonable criticisms, inefficient procedures and low morale. The pressure for changes was coming from all quarters. The users wanted better access to readable material. The administration were faced with dealing with increased demands on the bindery and, as they were constrained by budgets, their ideas turned to higher productivity. The book binders felt disgruntled about salary and status in comparison to other junior members of the library staff, and so were prepared to accept that changes resulting in higher productivity could be a means to achieve their ends. The librarian and senior book binder were concerned with ways and means of satisfying all concerned.

The complex problem presented by the bindery, like many job restructuring projects (Butteriss and Murdock 1975, 1976), was one not suited to the methods of traditional scientific experimentation. Rather it was one where, after careful examination, a combination of established remedies could be applied. Evaluation of which changes had which effects could follow only from an impartial observation of the continuing situation.

The binding process

The work of the bindery involves putting hard covers on journals, books and theses, and making book repairs. This process consists of removing the original covers, making a new cover of paper, card and cloth, lettering this cover with title and other reference information, and finally assembling the pages and cover with various sewing and glueing operations (Table 1). In addition to this full binding process the bindery puts hard covers on newly purchased paper backed books by 'laminated', 'flush' and 'perfect' binding processes. These processes may make use of the original cover in which case the lettering stage is not required. Furthermore in the 'flush' binding process the pages are not rounded prior to assembly. 'Perfect' binding is a process that avoids the time-consuming sewing of individual leaves. It is estimated that, on average, full binding takes twice as much time per item as these less complicated methods. The decision to use full binding or a less time-consuming process is dependent on the value of the book, although all journals are fully bound.

The binding process lends itself to batch work because of the economics of time in the use of the guillotine and the book press, and the requirement for the glue to dry. It is also common for a number of volumes of the same shape and size to be bound at the same time. However, at the time of the investigation, batching was only used within stages; the general process involving a continuous flow of materials between the stages.

Table 1.   The binding process.

Section	Tasks	Equipment
Documentation	Preparing binding instructions	Bench
Sewing	Removing existing covers Sewing sets of pages	Bench Sewing machine
Forwarding	Assembling and trimming the pages Cutting cards, cloth and end papers Assembling the backs	Press, saw, guillotine Round and backing machine Bench
Lettering	Making up lettering blocks Labling covers with gold leaf	Lettering press
Casing in	Assembling backs and pages	Press, bench
Checking	Inspection and documentation of finished product	Bench

Availability of library material

As far as the user was concerned, the binding process started long before the removal of the original covers. When the last issue of a volume had been on the current shelves for a short time the whole volume was taken, for reasons of space limitations and security, to the periodicals department for documentation. If the volume was incomplete, for example if there were missing issues or the index had not arrived, it was stored in an alphabetical order on shelves in the periodicals department. After documentation, complete volumes were placed on a trolley, which holds about 60 volumes, and when the trolley was full it was pushed into the bindery. A similar procedure was practised in the accessions department with paper-backed books. Thus library material was bound in an approximately chronological order although a 'flexible priority system' was superimposed depending on the persuasive powers of different users.

It was common to find six or seven full trolleys in the bindery, and others in the periodicals and accessions department. Access to the readable material that had been 'removed for binding' involved a time-consuming search through various shelves and trolleys by the senior book binder, a member of the periodicals department and the would-be user. Although no records were kept it was estimated that a journal might have been virtually inaccessible for six or more months due to factors unrelated to the actual binding process.

The bindery

In general the bindery appeared to be very congested. The senior book binder's desk was surrounded by trolleys with incoming material and bound work waiting for inspection. There were also work-in-progress queues of varying size at each binding stage. There was congestion at the book press which was used in two stages of the binding process. The layout of equipment was historical rather than functional thus leading to unnecessary movement of people and material around the bindery. This congestion presented problems of safe lifting and transporting of heavy loads of work in progress.

Observation of the workplace indicated common environmental problems. The windows were blanked off with paper to prevent entry of the afternoon sun during the winter months. This, although reducing the radiant heat load and glare, caused variable lighting conditions, particularly at the lettering stage. The noise of a portable circular saw used in perfect binding was an occasional nuisance—particularly to the adjacent library departments.

The book binders

The bindery had 10 members of staff—a senior book binder (with more than 20 years experience) in charge, five book binders and four assistant book binders. The senior book binder was responsible for all aspects of production control and supervision within the bindery, including documentation, preparation of binding instructions and inspection of completed work. The other members of the bindery staff had specialized activities within an established skill hierarchy. Lettering was at the top of the skill list and was performed by two of the more experienced book binders. Most of the book binders, however, had some experience in all stages although there was no planned rotation. The salary structure and status of the bindery staff was such that they were the 'poor technical relations' in a professional/clerical environment. However to put their situation in the broader context of Hong Kong, where the trade of book-binding has relatively low status (Quinn, 1977) they had comparatively good working conditions, security and salaries. Thus labour turnover had never been a problem.

Productivity

The work of the bindery has traditionally been reported monthly by the senior book binder as a count of items in various categories. However the total item count was generally regarded by the administration as the most useful index of productivity. This index does not give a true reflection of bindery capacity due to fluctuations in the proportion of full binding work. Furthermore the standard reporting format did not take into account the number of days in a particular month nor absence due to sickness or annual leave. As productivity was going to be a key issue in the implementation of changes, a detailed analysis of production figures was instituted. Table 2 indicates that, whereas there had been a decrease in the annual item count over the three years before the investigation, the demands on the bindery for periodicals binding had been increasing.

Table 2.   Annual production figures. (The reporting year ends in July.) A fully bound item is
assumed to take, on average, twice the time of a paper back.

Category	Before the changes			After
	1973/74	1974/75	1975/76	1976/77
Periodicals	5397	5800	6446	8649
Other fully bound items	1715	1515	860	381
Repairs, paper backs, etc.	4005	3171	1843	2373
Total items	11117	10486	9149	11403
Full binding equivalent	7112	8900	8288	10217

The changes

A series of discussions with library and bindery staff indicated the following objectives:
1.   Readable material should be made readily accessible.
2.   The time taken for the physical process of binding should be reduced to a
minimum practical level. This in turn indicated a need for better production control.
3.   The backlog of material waiting to be bound should be reduced.
4.   Efforts had to be made to improve the lot of the book binders.
It was decided therefore to implement in January 1976 a variety of changes
including:
1.   Procedures for storing periodicals waiting to be bound.
2.   A small batch system of working in the bindery integrated with job
rotation.
3.   Purchase and relocation of equipment and a general uplift of the working
environment.
4.   A review of salary and status structure.
5.   The use of subcontractors to perform the less skilful work of binding
paper backs.
As with any exercise of this nature it was necessary to manage carefully the
transition period so that all concerned would be familiar with the purposes and
details of the proposed changes.

Equipment, workplace and materials

The layout of the bindery was reorganized to provide a unidirectional flow
of periodicals and books. Raw materials were stored next to the appropriate
process component. A band saw and a second book press were purchased to
eliminate a major equipment conflict. In these ways, time and effort expended
in non-productive transport of materials were reduced. In addition to these
workplace changes, the new batch system effected a considerable reduction of
the congestion caused by work in progress.

Batches of journals awaiting binding are now stored on shelves in the main
library area adjacent to the bindery and rapid access to them was arranged
through a 'cardex' reference system.

The lighting situation was improved by lowering all the fluorescent tubes
from the high ceiling and by providing venetian blinds for the windows. In

this way a higher and more consistent light level was achieved—250 lux for the general work surfaces and 500 lux in the lettering area. The use of venetian blinds also had the effect of removing glare in the afternoons of the winter months and reducing the radiant heat load on some of the work stations.

Job redesign

A system was introduced in which bindery staff were grouped into three teams each consisting of a team leader and two other book binders. Each team was responsible for the whole binding process on a particular batch within a five day period.

In the month prior to the change some rotation of jobs had been introduced so that the book binders would acquire the speed skills necessary for their new jobs. The teams were chosen to cover the necessary range of skills and some specialization was necessary during the first weeks of the system. However it is intended that all jobs should eventually become interchangeable.

The introduction of the batch system inevitably imposed some problems of work organization to avoid conflict of equipment requirements and bottle-necks. The binding process was therefore broken into three stages—'sewing', 'forwarding' and 'lettering and casing in'. Batches were chosen so that each of the first two stages took one and a half days. The duration of the lettering stage was about two days for periodicals but only about one day for paper backs. The activities of the teams were staggered with each team carrying a buffer of odd jobs which were normally performed during the wait for the lettering stage.

After about nine months under this system a further change was introduced with one team staying on a particular stage for three weeks. A batch was still processed within a week but the enlargement concept of each team being responsible for the whole binding process on a batch was lost. This change was at the request of the book binders who felt that the rapid rotation of activities caused 'too much pressure' and that the change-over periods wasted time.

The batch and team system produced a great improvement in production control. Under this system the senior book binder could plan the work of the bindery up to two or three months ahead. Furthermore the output of the bindery becomes predictable. These advantages, however, were offset by the disadvantage that there was a greater amount of overt control over the activities of the book binders. Previously they had been paced only informally by the size of the pile of journals at their station. Under the new system, however, it was clear to everyone concerned how hard a team or an individual was working.

Six months after the initial changes the senior book binder was redesignated as chief book binder and the assistant book binders, in view of their experience, were all promoted to the book binder category. The team leaders were promoted to the senior book binder grade 18 months after the initial changes.

A variety of other workplace and organizational changes and observations were made which, although having face validity, complicated the evaluation.

Evaluation

Some of the changes had obvious immediate beneficial effects. Periodicals awaiting binding became readily accessible. Periodicals are now only inaccessible during the physical process of binding which takes about one week. The problem of the backlog and matching demand with bindery capacity was partially solved by subcontracting for the binding of paper backs. The flow of materials and production planning and control are more streamlined than before and the bindery has a much tidier appearance.

In order to put this productivity index in perspective a detailed analysis of the work of the bindery was made. Productivity analysis took into account the actual man days worked and the relative difficulty of the full and partial binding. These two variables were shown to have a large effect on productivity measures in this labour intensive process, although the overall item count or the periodicals count will continue to be the basic index.

As the book binders became more familiar with the new system the batch size was gradually increased to about 70 volumes depending on the specific difficulty of a batch (size of journal, amount of lettering etc). Sixteen months after the introduction of the changes the backlog of periodicals had virtually disappeared and the potential annual capacity of the bindery has increased to more than 10,000 (full binding equivalent) items.

The subjective reports from the book binders and chief book binder were mainly positive with regard to the new way of working, but this may have been due to Herzberg's (1968) 'extrinsic' factors or simply the expected response to the attention that had been paid to them.

Conclusion

If evaluation of this exercise is related to the usefulness of the available techniques then it is clear that a systematic study of the methods followed by a rationalization of procedures can result in marked improvements in productivity. What is also clear is that the predominence of issues related to salary and productivity indicated that the motivational effects of job intrinsic factors had greater credibility among the administrators of the changes than among the book binders themselves.

The administration of the changes was in itself an informative exercise. There was no doubt that pressure for change was coming from all sides, but there were different, and sometimes conflicting, objectives that had to be resolved. Commonly, in situations of this nature the key issue is that all concerned must be fully informed and must participate in the decisions as far as possible. In this instance, the book binders were involved in the discussions but it was clear that the most significant ideas came from the managers of the changes. The apparent contribution of job restructuring in this case may have been due to the continued systematic attention to the situation rather than any intrinsic enrichment.

Managerial learning needs for effective employee participation

L. Damodaran
Human Sciences and Advanced Technology (HUSAT),
University of Technology, Loughborough

The relationship between employee participation and job satisfaction is complex and unclear. Despite the lack of clarity there are powerful implicit and explicit assumptions and expectations concerning this association which underlies the current interest and experimentation in employee participation. It is the first concern of this paper to distinguish between the motivations which give rise to experiments in employee participation and the psychological functions served by participation. It must be emphasized that this paper is concerned only with the processes of immediate participation, that is, direct involvement of all members of the work force in decision-making, as distinct from participation of elected representatives as envisaged in the recommendations of the Report of the Committee of Inquiry on Industrial Democracy (Bullock, 1977). (This committee was appointed to advise on questions relating to representation at board level in the private sector.)

The specific motives behind attempts at employee participation are perhaps as numerous as the experiments. Participation is commonly used in an effort to resolve a problem which defies resolution in other ways, for instance, persisting high labour turnover and absenteeism or poor quality standards. The precise way in which the participation process is expected to have beneficial effects on the solution of such problems is rarely made explicit and this can confound attempts at evaluating the impact of participation. Other more long-term objectives may include a desire to be highly competitive in attracting the best new recruits from the labour market, or to lead the way in innovative working methods.

A number of research projects conducted by members of the HUSAT Research team at Loughborough University have examined aspects of participation in design processes. The findings suggest that the psychological value of participation at the individual level lies in the opportunity it offers for people to function as integrated mature human beings rather than as Tayloristic adjuncts to machines. A realistic model of 'typical' human behaviour based upon observations of how people actually behave in non-work situations would include expressions and manifestations of, for example, individual differences, preferences, choices, responsibility, discretion, creativity, problem-solving, variety seeking and risk-taking. A comparison of this 'non-work model of man' with a model of man in his formal work role would reveal the former to be far more varied and complex. Many manifestations of mature adult behaviour have no legitimate place in formal work roles on the factory shop floor or in the office (although expressions of creativity, problem-solving and risk-taking etc may well be revealed in informal practices, some quite at variance with overall organizational objectives). In such circumstances the fundamental contribution which employee participation offers to individuals is the opportunity to exhibit in a legitimate, institutionally-approved way, the varied and complex behaviour patterns which characterize the adult human. The increased scope for mature adult behaviour on the part of every member of the work force is a potential reward of participation for the individual as well as for the whole organization (Argyris, 1964).

The effective participation process allows each individual to contribute freely his knowledge and expertise to influence decisions relevant to his work role. This simply-stated condition for effective participation belies the magnitude of change required in most British organizations before such a process can occur. Some of the organizational and managerial problems which inhibit transition to such a climate are the subject of this paper.

Factors inhibiting change

Magnitude of changes

While considerable behavioural change is required for the rank-and-file to become 'participative', even more dramatic changes are required for managers at all levels to adopt a more participative approach to decision-making. Since it is largely managers who create the organizational climate, it is their responsibility to take the initiative in changing prevailing practices and conditions. To achieve these changes demands that the manager modifies his behaviour in his interpersonal interactions at work, and that he changes the performance appraisal and reward systems he applies to his subordinates. Furthermore he needs to change his problem-solving procedures to incorporate contributions from his subordinates. Such fundamental changes in managerial role are far from easy to achieve and some of the specific difficulties which arise are discussed below.

Lack of experience of participation

Even where there is genuine commitment to the idea of participation, it is not easy to take the first step since there is a lack of experience of participative processes and a lack of knowledge of how to proceed. The confusion concerning objectives of participation merely adds to the uncertainty on how to proceed. Expectations, hopes and fears of participation differ widely. First line and middle management may interpret any prospects of devolution of power as a personal loss of control and authority while senior management may sometimes regard it as but one step from anarchy. With such ambivalence and lack of clarity surrounding the whole issue of participation it is not surprising that there is considerable confusion and many misconceptions about how to proceed. Where fears of the process and of the outcome of participation characterize managerial response, there may be overt reluctance to attempt to be participative.

Participation mechanisms

In the absence of clear guidance on how to proceed towards greater participation, a variety of ad hoc mechanisms have been used to attempt to start the participative process. Project committees, participation groups, problem-solving groups and task groups are some of the mechanisms utilized to begin dialogue between management and work force. In utilizing these mechanisms there is frequently uncertainty as to the terms of reference of these groups and confusion about objectives. While the specific composition of these mechanisms varies, typically it includes members of management and of the rank-and-file. Often a trade union shop steward belongs to the group and, in some cases, a change agent with expertise in organizational change is also included.

One of the few common features of the various mechanisms is that the participants will meet together as a group or as sub-groups. The modus operandi of these groups can differ widely. Some groups elect chairmen, some have a self-appointed managerial chairman, some attempt to operate without a formal leader. The degree of formality, the size, type of venue and frequency of the meetings also vary. Some groups spend considerable time defining their terms of reference and classifying their role vis-a-vis other established institutionalized mechanisms. Others launch themselves immediately into tackling the presenting problems which initially led to the experiment in participation.

Generally the meetings will be concerned with organizational problems of varying specificity. The nature of the problems can range from, for example, working out the details of a scheme for flexible working hours, to a very general issue such as how the organization can become more participative.

Patterns of managerial behaviour

Given the wide variation in scope and application of the different participation mechanisms, it is not surprising that the effectiveness of these mechamisms also varies considerably. A systematic appraisal of the relative influence that various factors exert on success in participation has yet to be conducted, but three patterns of managerial behaviour which emerge in 'participation meetings' have already been identified.

Constructive adaptation

This response occurs where management and work force co-operate in an atmosphere of goodwill and trust to ensure that the participation mechanisms operate in a positive way from the early stages.

Characteristically, constructive adaptation occurs in organizations with a history of good employee relations and, in particular, with a good communication system. It appears that ready availability of information, and a work force accustomed to having access to considerable information, may be a precondition for effective participation.

Typically, managers exhibiting a constructive adaptation response begin the early interactions in the selected participation mechanisms by acknowledging their own dilemma and uncertainty concerning the processes and likely outcomes of participation. However, they also express their enthusiasm and invite other participants to take part in a joint co-operative exploration of the possibilities of mutual gain from the participative process.

Overt expression of their lack of knowledge and experience of participation by management allows the other participants to realise that their own ignorance of the process does not place them at a disadvantage. This shared experience allows the group to proceed to establish objectives, to work out a viable mode of operation and to re-define their roles to permit constructive changes to be identified and implemented.

Reversion to status quo

This response arises where the lack of guidance and knowledge on how to proceed causes such intolerable discomfort and embarrassment to managerial participants that they resort to more familiar behaviour patterns. For instance, in one recent case study, project committee meetings were intended to provide a supportive, collaborative venue for resolution of specific persistent problems. These meetings were very quickly rendered ineffective by a senior manager who could not change his behaviour in order to share problems and to discuss possible solutions in an open-ended way. Instead, he devoted his energies to employing the same behavioural patterns he used in works council meetings; namely, explaining the external causes of the problems and the reasons why any attempts at amelioration were impossible. The essential problem where this kind of response occurs is that the manager uses well-tried, familiar modes of behaviour of established institutions in a new environment which demands a different pattern of behaviour. To dismiss issues voiced through a participation mechanism as being beyond control is to deny the participants any possibility to effect a solution. In a venture which purports to seek problem-solving and participative problem-solving such a response represents a complete contradiction of stated and actual intent on the part of the manager. The net result is that participants quickly become sceptical of any likelihood of being allowed influence over decision-making in areas of concern to them. The whole 'participation' process becomes meaningless in these circumstances.

To avoid 'reversion to status quo' requires managers to exhibit behaviour consistent with their avowed intent to gain employee participation. However, it is extremely stressful for some managers to attempt to experiment with new behaviour in the presence of either their peers or their subordinates. To be seen to be in a learning situation can be very threatening to the manager who feels he must always appear competent and proficient in the eyes of other members of the organization. Carefully-structured learning experiences in a protected environment using such techniques as role-playing may be necessary for some managers to begin to develop 'participative behaviour'.

Adoption of a laissez-faire style

Confusion about the nature of participation leads some managers to believe that participation is tantamount to handing over all initiative to their subordinates and expecting them to take the lead. This belief is manifested by the manager failing to provide any direction or structure in his 'participative' interactions. He merely exhorts those who are present in a meeting 'to participate'. While such behaviour may appear entirely appropriate in the abstract, it completely ignores the learning which is required for people to make the transition from operating in a passive role under tight controls to working with a high degree of autonomy. The transition has to be guided and gradual while allowing participants to influence the degree and rate of change. In the absence of such guidance, the discomfort experienced by participants can be so acute that further meetings are avoided or abandoned. Far from requiring a laissez-faire approach, the early efforts at gaining participation need to be carefully structured to fulfil an educational role and to provide opportunities for new behaviour to be practised.

The manager's learning needs

Achieving effective interaction

It is essential for successful management-worker interaction, first that all members of the work force should feel their views are valued and, second, that they should feel sufficiently at ease to state these views in the chosen participation mechanism. Past experience of interaction with management will determine whether the rank-and-file feel their opinions are valued. The ease with which the rank-and-file feel they can express their views in meetings will also be influenced by their prevailing relationship with management but will also be affected by the way the meetings are operated. Managers who are accustomed to speaking in formal meetings may not be sufficiently sensitive to the inhibitions which their subordinates may experience in voicing their views. unfamiliarity with the setting of a meeting, uncertainty concerning their role and awareness of subordinate status can effectively silence prospective participants. The manager may need guidance to help him to manage meetings aimed at gaining participation. Knowledge of the potential effects of such factors as size of the group, respective status and seating arrangements on interaction is needed to assist him. Application of such knowledge alone may not be sufficient to ensure rewarding interactions. Part of the problem may lie in the difficulty some managers experience in empathising with the work force. Here the need is for more knowledge of the worker's total life-style, value system and style of communication. Without a degree of insight into the worker's perceptions it will be difficult for a manager to arrive at a structure conducive to effective interaction.

Another requirement to promote effective interaction is for help in arriving at a 'contract' between the various participants which delineates the kinds of contribution which are expected, acceptable and appropriate, and which establishes possible objectives, tasks and problems for the work of the group.

This latter step can do much to reduce the fear of 'speaking out-of-turn' and to air the inevitable confusions and uncertainties concerning the whole mission.

Accepting help

Joint problem-solving by management and workers is both a vehicle for participation and an objective of it. Since there is an assumption, established and supported by tradition, that it is the managerial function to solve problems it is often very hard for managers genuinely to invite and to welcome assistance from the work force in problem-solving. The ethos of many organizations will promote the view that to share a problem is to acknowledge either that an effective solution has not been identified or that such a solution has not been implemented. Since both these possibilities are likely to be regarded as 'failings' by a traditional management it is not easy to admit to them. This is a primary reason why many 'participation meetings' do not achieve problem-sharing but are devoted to explaining and justifying continued manifestation of the problem. Many individuals feel safer endorsing the status quo and feel it to be safer to do what has always been done rather than to adopt new procedures with uncertain outcomes.

Losing control

Managers can often be reluctant to permit participation of their subordinates in issues of any real significance, since they fear that any devolution of power and influence will undermine their own position. These fears only arise where managers have a concept of a finite amount of power existing in an organization. Such a concept promotes the view that more power in decision-making by the workers directly implies a loss of power for the manager. This is a popular managerial view of the outcome of employee participation. It holds true only if the manager perceives participation being restricted to the boundaries of the sub-system within which he operates. Yet the mission of participation is to allow all members of the organization to increase their exercise of discretion and autonomy at work. For the manager, this means divesting himself of many control activities within his work area and concerning himself more with conditions at the boundary of his department or managerial function. Improving transactions between his department and others, engaging in more forward planning, providing guidance and information laterally and vertically are some of the ways of increasing his control over his work environment while permitting his subordinates to expand their horizons. The progressive and effective manager is more likely to perceive greater autonomy of his subordinates as a liberation for himself, permitting him to attend to wider and longer-term issues. The more limited individual will need guidance and help to enlarge his sphere of influence and level of competence.

Appraisal and reward systems

A powerful constraint upon the manager who succeeds in promoting participation of his subordinates is that the traditional reward system in the organization is likely to be perpetuated. This means that his performance will be assessed and rewarded on criteria relating to his personal technical expertise or on specific output levels rather than upon overall effectiveness, stability and commitment of his team. This problem requires that the reward system of an organization be modified to include criteria for assessing and rewarding the benefits of participation. Without formal rewards for the processes and results of worker participation the organization will not become significantly more 'participative'.

Conclusion

Managerial difficulties in making the transition to a participative mode of behaviour are serious potential obstacles to achieving greater organizational effectiveness and more rewarding work roles for all members of the work force. The difficulties faced are by no means insurmountable, and the following are some of the measures which can facilitate the learning process demanded of managers embarking on the new modes of behaviour:

(a) Guidance from an external or internal change agent with expertise in the technology of implementation of change.
(b) Modification of reward systems, performance appraisal schemes, job evaluation procedures, etc, to be compatible with the principles and objectives of participation.
(c) Provision of effective communication networks and mechanisms to promote lateral and vertical communication.
(d) Allowance of extensive periods of time for learning and changes to occur before evaluating and discontinuing experiments in participation.

To return to the opening remarks concerning the relationship between job satisfaction and employee participation, it is important that steps are taken to ensure that participation schemes have a positive effect upon the level of job satisfaction experienced by managers. The degree of behavioural change required of managers can threaten their overall job satisfaction unless adequate organizational support is provided, particularly during the initial learning period. Paradoxically, devolution of considerable routine decision-making to his subordinates can make more, rather than fewer, demands upon managerial skills. This occurs because a greater proportion of the manager's load becomes concerned with forward planning, problem-solving and with issues at the periphery of his managerial function. Gaining the opportunity to develop these managerial skills can be an important source of reward for the manager provided that the pace of learning and change is self-regulated. The essential point is that employee participation schemes should present opportunities for all employees, not just shop-floor level operatives, to expand their horizons and to develop and utilize their skills. Managerial commitment to participation cannot be gained unless there are rewards for such commitment. Furthermore, long-term major organizational change cannot be achieved if certain levels of the hierarchy regard themselves exempt from the participation process. Board level directives to senior managers requiring that they adopt a participative management style is an unreal and valueless exhortation unless the relationship between senior managers and members of the Board also becomes more participative. The same principle applies throughout the organizational hierarchy. At each level, the devolution of influence to one's subordinates must be compensated by an increased scope for the exercise of discretion and autonomy in another sphere. Finally, it should be remembered that managers are also employees and their role in employee participation is a crucial one for the long-term success of the organization.

Acknowledgements

The survey research on which part of the paper was based was funded by a grant from the S.S.R.C. awarded to K.D. Eason, Loughborough University. Action research currently in progress is supported by the Work Research Unit, Department of Employment and by a number of industrial organizations in the U.K. The author wishes to thank Professor B. Shackel, K.D. Eason, T.F.M. Stewart, C.P. Ide, Loughborough University, Dr. Lisl Klein, Jennie Blake, The Tavistock Institute of Human Relations, Dr. R. Halford, Pilkington Brothers Limited, for their support and contributions to the research programme.

Computer assistance and the air traffic controller's job satisfaction

R. Crawley and P. Spurgeon
University of Aston in Birmingham, United Kingdom

Only in the last 40 years have technological developments in aircraft design and manufacture, and a parallel growth in demand for civil flights, necessitated the setting up of a ground-based air traffic control (ATC) service. The form and extent of that service have changed considerably to keep pace with developments in air traffic, and consequently the civil air traffic controller's job has been subject to frequent change.

Few people outside ATC realise that the largest part of ATC is performed in buildings physically separate from the major airports and by controllers who never look at 'real' aircraft in the course of their job. The only controllers who observe aircraft directly are those operating in the Visual Control Room at airports. The remainder, who work in Approach, Terminal, En Route or Oceanic control, either observe radar displays or flight data displays.

The stipulated objectives of ATC are to provide a safe, expeditious and orderly flow of traffic. ATC in the United Kingdom, as in much of Europe, presents special problems to the controller. The first of these is the considerable limitation on 'controlled' airspace, due to military and private aviation requirements, which means that most civil aircraft must adhere to a few airways while in U.K. airspace. Secondly, U.K. airports are only a few hundred miles from the main continental airports. Since jet aircraft operate most economically when cruising at high altitudes, European flights spend a considerable time climbing or descending, both of which they prefer to do as quickly as possible. In some ATC sectors, most aircraft under control can be climbing or descending, thereby increasing the controller's workload since the probability of conflict increases under those conditions.

Impact of technological change on controllers

Despite the controller's reliance on numerous technical aids, in particular radar and telecommunications, he is still very active in the system and has complete control over conflict prediction, resolution and other forms of decision-making. The advent of radar control has, if anything, increased his involvement in the control of aircraft, certainly with respect to tactical control. The only opposing trend in the UK has been the increase in strategic planning; for example by standardizing procedures, which has reduced the flexibility of operation for many controllers.

There are indications, however, that the fundamental nature of the controller's job may undergo considerable change before the end of the century as a result of the introduction of sophisticated computer-aided systems. Up till now, computer systems in UK air traffic control have served as an information storage and retrieval facility, additionally performing simple calculations concerned with time estimates. Although these systems have altered the controller's job peripherally, the executive functions have remained fully under his control.

However, the present ATC system in the UK is unlikely to be able to cope with projected increases in air traffic movements beyond the end of the century (Department of Industry, 1977). Additionally, airlines and governments are likely to demand more economical trajectories in the future in response to the pressure of rising fuel prices. For these reasons alone, some form of more sophisticated computer-assistance is envisaged in the UK and other parts of the world. In the UK, preliminary research has been carried out for an ATC system in which the computer assists the controller to predict conflicts. (Ruffell-Smith, Ord and Whitfield, 1977). In the USA, proposals have been advanced for a system in which the computer performs both conflict prediction and resolution, and the controller 'manages by exception'. (Jenney and Lawrence, 1974.)

It is in this context that the Civil Aviation Authority and Ministry of Defence have jointly sponsored a four-year contract to investigate the implications of controller attitudes and reactions to computer assistance for system design. The objectives of the contract are:

(a)   to predict the likely reactions of controllers to various degrees of computer assistance;
(b)   to evaluate the likely 'costs' of such reactions to organizational and system effectiveness; and
(c)   to suggest guidelines for the allocation of tasks between controller and computer in the light of (a) and (b).

Air traffic controllers' attitudes and motivations

The nature of the controller's job has made it a popular subject for psychological research for many years, but only in the last decade have the attitudes and motivations of the controller been studied systematically in a number of countries.

All studies of controllers have found that they are about as satisfied with their job as a whole as other occupational groups are on average. About 91% of a group of 792 controllers in the USA stated that they were satisfied or very satisfied with their profession (Smith, 1973). This compares with an average figure of 80% for other occupational groups, although this latter figure was adjusted downwards to allow for some tendency to exaggerate the degree of actual satisfaction (Blauner, 1963). A survey of 203 controllers at Frankfurt

Airport reported that about 79% declared their job to be satisfying (Singer and Rutenfranz, 1971) although it should be noted that the survey was carried out immediately before industrial action commenced. Broadly similar findings have been reported in both Switzerland (Grandjean, Witzka and Kretzschmar, 1968) and Sweden (Kennholt and Bergstedt, 1971). A later study by Singer and Rutenfranz (1972) reveals a close relationship between expressed job dissatisfaction and job related health disturbances, independent of the age and experience of the controller.

A feature of these studies, and indeed of studies in other occupational fields, is the apparent paradox between a high frequency of reported satisfaction with the job as a whole, and specific responses indicating considerable dissatisfaction with parts of the job. Singer and Rutenfranz (1972) suggest that many employees misunderstand the general question concerning 'satisfaction with the job' to mean satisfaction with the work content rather than with the job as a whole. In our view, this is but one example of a persistent ambiguity in job satisfaction research commonly caused by lack of conceptual and methodological definition and one which has been reported in the literature for many years (Brayfield and Crockett, 1955; Muchinsky, 1977; Singleton, 1977).

The job satisfaction research in the USA (Smith, Cobb and Collins, 1971; Smith, 1973) has used similar methodology to that of Herzberg (1966). Smith asked controllers to cite three aspects of their work which they liked best and three they liked least. In the positive response category, controllers most frequently mentioned Job Challenge and Job Tasks. These were two of the nine response categories used by Smith on the basis of individual response 'clusters'. 'Job Challenge' included statements referring to traffic complexity, accomplishment, decision-making freedom and responsibility. 'Job Tasks' included use of radar, procedures, types of position operated, and amount of traffic. The negative response categories mostly referred to Management, Equipment and Work Schedule.

These findings, as Smith notes, are very similar to the factors listed by Herzberg in his Two-Factor Theory of Motivation. Since Smith uses similar methodology to Herzberg's this is not surprising, for there is substantial evidence to show that studies using his methodology tend to produce similar results. Those job variables related by respondents to satisfaction are intrinsic or job content variables, while the dissatisfiers are extrinsic or job contextual. If a different methodology is used this dichotomy does not occur and Herzberg's 'satisfiers' tend to be related to both satisfaction and dissatisfaction to a greater degree than the 'hygiene' factors (Ewen, 1964; Vroom, 1964; Dunnette, Campbell and Hakel, 1967; Warr and Wall, 1975). This phenomenon is discussed by Farr (1977) in the context of attributional artifact. Taking an overall view of controllers, Smith (1974) comments that they 'tend to be intolerant of routine, demanding of opportunities to participate actively in decision-making processes, and capable of providing sophisticated input concerning the structure and management of the ATC system'. (p. 6) Elsewhere (Smith, 1973) he notes the distinct possibility that automation may make the controllers' job more routine and less challenging, thereby reducing their morale and efficiency, and so counteracting the advantages of automation. It is this risk that provides the starting point for our research.

Involvement of behavioural scientists in systems design

However interesting these job satisfaction studies may be, they do not provide the sort of data that facilitate socio-technical systems design, which is the main objective of the present study. In particular, they do not study task characteristics in any detail.

A number of writers have pointed out the need to take into account social values and employee needs when designing work systems (Jordan, 1963; Sackman, 1967; Hedberg and Mumford, 1975). It is only recently that engineering courses have included social science aspects of systems design, and many computer science courses still omit these aspects. As a result, system designers have tended to operate primarily within a technically-oriented framework, viewing technology as the principal means for achieving organizational goals (Mumford, 1971). In Mumford's view, this approach can lead to 'undesired ends and to inefficient solutions—in particular to a form of systems design which excludes any consideration of human needs as variables which should be catered for in the system'. (1971, p. 10.) The solution is threefold: to educate and train engineers and computer scientists to incorporate social values in their system design; to include behavioural scientists on the design team; and to obtain input into the design stage from system users.

There are two levels of involvement for behavioural scientists, conceptually distinct but in practice interdependent. At the higher level, system design provides a moderately detailed framework for system operations, but does not necessarily provide a detailed 'modus operandi' for individuals within the system. The lower level of job design provides this greater detail at the individual job level. While jobs may be redesigned without fundamentally affecting system design, the reverse is generally not true. The critical importance for behavioural scientists of becoming involved at the earlier system design stage is that system designers may impose constraints on individual jobs which make the adherence to social values and employee needs impossible later on. An example in ATC might be a decision at the system design stage to allocate certain decision-making functions to the computer. In this event, it would prove extremely difficult to compensate for the critical loss of responsibility suffered by the controller.

Impact of systems design on employees

It is legitimate to question the basis of behavioural science involvement in systems and job design. Where is the evidence for Mumford's earlier assertion that technically-oriented systems design leads to 'undesired ends'? The bulk of the evidence comes from the supposed indirect effect on employee attitudes and behaviour caused by changes to the job content.

As a reaction against the all-pervading influence of Calvanism in the nineteenth century, there has been a tendency for social science to emphasize the limitations of the importance of work in people's lives (Dubin, 1956; Worsley, 1970). Nevertheless, there is a consensus that work is an important aspect of many people's lives in advanced industrial societies, although the reasons may differ between individuals (Worsley, 1970; Abrams, 1973). Klein (1976) states that 'work plays such an important part in the life of individuals and of society that changing the nature of work implies nothing less than a culture change.'

Since work is of such importance, it is to be expected that changes to its content due to systems design will influence employee attitudes and behaviour. At a general level, there is evidence to suggest that any change in people's lives may affect their physical and mental wellbeing (Rahe, McKean and Arthur, 1967; Toffler, 1970). At a specific level, it has been suspected for a number of years that job content causally influences employee behaviour. On the one hand there are reported cases of poor job design causing job dissatisfaction, absenteeism, turnover, and low morale and motivation (Walker and Guest, 1952; Brayfield and Crockett, 1955; Herzberg, 1966); and on the other, action programmes for job redesign in the form of job enrichment to remedy the aforementioned ills (Biganne and Stewart, 1963; Herzberg, 1966; Paul and Robertson, 1970). In fact, the relationship between job content and employee behaviour is far from clear because of the variable level of methodological rigour in many of the studies. (For a review of this problem see Hulin and Blood, 1968; Hackman and Lawler, 1971.) A further explanation for the paucity of knowledge about the effects of job design is our limited capability to measure the effects (Hackman and Oldham, 1975). Previous studies of job enrichment programmes have used comparatively insensitive measures of the effects of job change, involving 'before-and-after' attitude and job satisfaction surveys, and occasionally work outcome measures such as work quality, output levels, absenteeism and turnover. However, these measures have not directly examined the employees' perception of the change.

Justification for socio-technical systems design

However, justification for the inclusion of employee needs in systems design does not rest solely on the relationship between work content and employee behaviour. There is a strong case for improving the quality of working life per se, regardless of any effects on organizational output and effectiveness (Maslow, 1968; Cherns, 1973, 1975; Jackson, 1973; Warr, 1973). For example, it is unacceptable for employees to be alienated from their work by automated systems that reduce their autonomy, and engender feelings of meaninglessness and powerlessness. The classical research in this area reveals that automation reduces alienation (Blauner, 1964). However, these findings are typically obtained in cases where blue-collar workers in manual systems performing fragmented work become semi-skilled white-collar workers responsible for the monitoring of complete segments of work. In Air Traffic Control, the controllers already experience autonomy, responsibility and a sense of meaning in their work. There is a real danger that automation will alienate them unless carefully designed. Changing expectations and values among school leavers and employees may have their effect too. Davis (1971) writes:

'The seeming ease with which new (automated) technology satisfies material needs, coupled with the provision of subsistence-level support for its citizens by society, has stimulated a growing concern on the part of the individual over his relationship to work, its meaningfulness and its value—ie a concern for the quality of work life. (...) It appears that people may no longer let themselves be used; they wish to see some relationship between their own work and the social life around them, and they wish some desirable future for themselves in their continuing relationship with organisations.'

In Air Traffic Control there is an equally strong case for maintaining the intrinsic motivation of controllers in their work, whether or not there is clear evidence of a relationship between job content and employee behaviour among employees in general. One suspects that most air travellers would prefer motivated controllers on the ground, however slim the evidence. If, as seems likely, controllers continue to provide the best possible service to aircraft while they remain at their post, no matter how dissatisfied they might be with the job, one might ask in what ways their behaviour will change as a result of changes to their job.

Before we can contribute to the design of ATC systems from the point of view of controllers' needs, we require a theoretical model. In addition, the systems design team from the Royal Signals and Radar Establishment at Malvern with whom we shall be working are primarily concerned with allocation of tasks between controller and computer, rather than the wider aspects of system design. Recently, a relevant theoretical model has been developed by Hackman and Oldham (1974) following earlier work by Hackman and Lawler (1971). The model is presented in Fig. 1. The model proposes that 'Personal and Work Outcomes' (such as high internal work motivation, high satisfaction with the work, low absenteeism and turnover) are a function of three 'critical psychological states' (experienced meaningfulness of the work, experienced responsibility for work outcomes, knowledge of results). The theory proposes that these psychological states are created by the existence of five core job dimensions as shown in the diagram.

An important supplement to the model is the moderating effect of an individual difference characteristic they call 'Individual Growth Need Strength' which may be defined as the strength of the person's desire to self-actualize. Thus only people who have a high desire for personal growth will tend to respond positively to a job which is high on the core job dimensions. People low on growth need strength may experience anxiety when faced with a job high in motivation potential.

Methodology

Since the principal objective of the research is to develop guidelines for system designers in terms of the controllers' needs from the job, it is important that we present the guidelines in a form that can be used by any designers, whether they have behavioural science training or not, and at the earliest possible stage in the design process. The fundamental drawback to the current models and theories is that there is no self-evident or stipulated bridge that relates tasks and skills to the 'core job dimensions'. How is the designer supposed to know whether a particular system design has reduced Skill

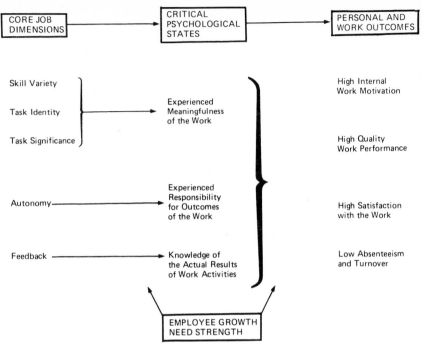

Figure 1.   A theoretical model relating the core job dimensions, the critical psychological states, and on-the-job outcomes (as moderated by employee growth need strength). From Hackman & Oldham (1975).

Variety or Physical Variety? Furthermore, it is quite probable that different tasks and skills have differential value attached to their performance by employees. This is certainly a logical conclusion that may be drawn from Instrumentality-Expectancy Theory (Lawler and Porter, 1967). Thus before being able to predict the relationship between a specific level or pattern of Skill Variety and Personal and Work Outcomes it is necessary to know the value attached to the skills involved. Theoretically, if not practically, it would be possible to reduce skill variety without fundamentally affecting employee reaction. From a system design point of view, we are interested in those skills which are widely valued amongst the work force over a prolonged period of time.

It may be useful at this point to clarify our use of the terms 'task' and 'skill', since there is such a diversity of definition in the literature. A task is defined as 'a major element of work or a combination of elements of work by means of which a specific result is achieved' (Stammers and Patrick, 1975). The same authors define a skill as 'an organized and co-ordinated pattern of mental and/or physical activity in relation to an object or other display of information, usually involving both receptor and effector processes.'

Before deciding on the methodology, two particular questions needed to be considered. First, should the job content be described objectively (for example by consulting management, training manuals and by 'naive' observation) or subjectively by determining the controllers' view of what they are doing? The implications of different methods of task description are discussed by Weick (1965) and Hackman and Lawler (1971). For our purposes, there is clearly a case for determining subjective task descriptions since one might expect a closer relationship between subjective tasks and employee reactions than would be the case with objective task descriptions. On the other hand, in order to compare the task allocation for different systems the task descriptions must bear a fairly close resemblance to objectively arrived at descriptions. Secondly, is it sufficient to describe the job content at a fairly general level, in the manner of Hackman and Oldham (1975), or is there a need to be more specific and move down to the task level?

The decision was made to conduct a task analysis of a selection of functional positions occupied by controllers at two main units: the London Air Traffic Control Centre (LATCC) at West Drayton, and Heathrow Airport. In particular those positions involving executive control of aircraft would be studied. The task analysis is to be written primarily in ATC 'language' so that it may provide a first line of discussion with controllers. Subsequently, the task analysis is to be translated into a Skills Analysis expressed in information processing terminology after Miller (1974). It is hoped to define an appropriate methodology for examining controller reactions to changes in tasks and skills. The research will involve frequent changes to the level of analysis and discussion; for example, moving from the specific task level when discussing particular aspects of job content with the controller, to the more general level of broad skill descriptors for comparison between systems.

For a full appreciation of the work content, it is important to consult the system users for detailed information on all aspects of their work role. Damodaran (1977) cites several examples of such information. For example: (a) non-routine events, (b) 'bottlenecks' and interruptions to the work flow, (c) human interactions in the work process, (d) procedures/techniques/ special skills, (e) documents/reference books/equipment used, and (f) task interdependencies.

The Task Analysis, which commenced at LATCC in February 1978, is based on a technique of hierarchical task analysis and tabular format by Shepherd (1976), which in its turn was based on a technique by Annett, Duncan, Stammers and Gray (1971). Although the analysis is still in progress, an extract from the preliminary hierarchical diagram is shown in Fig. 2. The data were mainly collected by the following methods: observation whilst sitting next to the controller; listening to all forms of communication involving the controller; informal on-the-job questioning; and informal off-the-job questioning.

A vital part of the analysis has been the continual checking of data with the controllers. Thus there is undoubtedly a significant subjective element to the data collected. Preliminary indications are that this will not affect adversely the use of the task analysis for between-system comparisons.

Subsequent to the task and skills analyses, small group experiments and exercises will take place to establish the relationship between work content and controller motivation and reactions. The proposed methods include group and individual interviews, questionnaires, and small-scale computer simulation exercises. Amongst specific techniques that are being considered are an

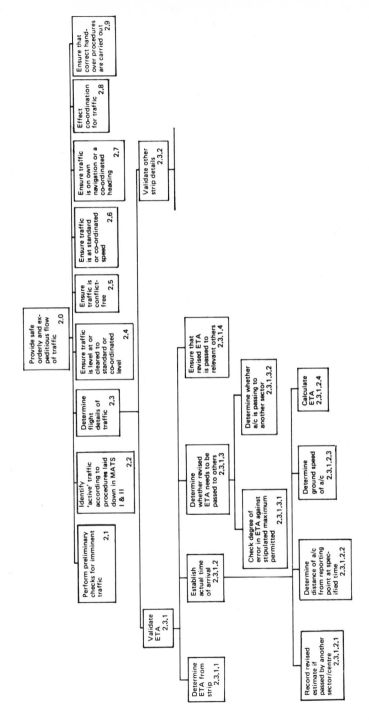

Figure 2.   An extract from preliminary Task Analysis diagram representing tasks of sector radar controller at the London Air Traffic Control Centre.

adaptation of Hackman and Oldham's (1975) Job Diagnostic Survey, and Standing's (1973) Work Grid. Consideration is also being given to Mumford's approach in particular with reference to her recommendations for evaluating employees' attitudes to change both general and specific; their rigidity or flexibility in attitudes or behaviour when presented with change; and their perceived ability to influence the situation.

The research as described is not expected, either by the contract sponsors or the researchers, to provide clear and complete answers to all the questions raised by the research objectives. A characteristic problem is the scarcity of both general research into the effects of automation on comparable occupational groups (eg Hofmann, 1971) and of relevant research in the field of ATC. (Davis, Kerle, Silvestro and Wallace, 1960; Older and Cameron, 1972; Nealey, Thornton, Maynard and Lindell, 1975; Colouris, Tashker and Penick, 1978). Moreover, there is uncertainty as to the degree of relevance of findings based on controllers today to a situation 15-30 years hence, this being the likely delay before full system implementation of the type discussed earlier. It is difficult to assess the impact that a new generation of controllers with possibly different expectations, living in an uncertain socio-economic environment, might have on the situation then.

Acknowledgement

This report was prepared in connection with research being carried out under M.O.D. agreement, No. AT/2097/026 ASA funded by the Civil Aviation Authority and Air Travel & Transport Industry Training Board.

The relevance of personnel assessment

G. Arends
Department of Industrial Psychology,
N.V. Philips Gloeilampenfabrieken, Eindhoven, The Netherlands.

Information about a man's capacities has always been an important contributory factor in the selection and placement of applicants. In the past, this was based on the experience that performance mainly depended on the abilities a man possessed. Nowadays this relation is no longer so obvious. At least as valuable as having the necessary abilities for the work, is a man's willingness to use them in the proper way. It has proved important to match people's expectations and capacities to the job content and to the internal industrial climate in which they have to work; and this makes it necessary to have a thorough understanding of what motivates them to perform and often requires adjustments within the organization.

Changes in production systems, in the working environment, in methods of communication, etc. are developments in organizational settings which are frequently stimulated by the way workers function, and by their changing styles of behaviour.

The object of the present paper is to demonstrate the relevance of test research in the process of enhancing job satisfaction. It is shown that the analysis of testing procedures not only provides a means of evaluating both tests and workers, but also of assessing weak points in the organization of the work.

The main findings presented here are by-products from investigations of the predictive value of our selection test series in some Latin American countries. The companies concerned regarded these data as a kind of X-ray picture of the local management policy, revealing the strong and weak points in the organization. To put the results collected from four different Philips' plants into perspective we have placed them against the background of our recent experience in Holland.

Trends in our research findings

The rapid industrial developments which took place after World War I led the Philips company to start using tests for the selection of various categories of workers. Most of the tests stemmed from existing series and were adapted to the specific requirements for training in, and working on, the large variety of activities involved in the manufacture of our electro-technical products.

The predictive value of the tests was checked regularly by comparing applicants' test scores with their performance at the workplace. In those early stages, we learned that the relation between test scores of a number of apprentices and the results in various training situations (eg 3 years for a skilled worker) was adversely influenced by the lack of interest demonstrated. In contrast to these findings, no motivational factors were reported from the industrial area to upset the relation between the scores of the selection tests and the performance data (ratings by superiors). In fact very satisfying validation coefficients were found there. The explanation may be that before 1940, and particularly in the pre-war years when unemployment was high, the close relation between the quality and quantity of performance and the amount of income stimulated workers to work to their full potential. For economic reasons the workers had to adapt to the requirements of the job.

However, when our selection battery for semi-skilled workers was again tested in the 1950s, in the period of full employment, we found for the first time that the predictive validity was disappointingly low. Detailed analyses demonstrated that the correlation between what a person can do (his ability) and what he actually does in his daily work was strongly influenced by his will to perform. We then found a trend of curvilinear relationships: the higher the persons' test scores were, the better the ratings of their performances. Above a certain level of ability, however, this increase stopped and sometimes even declined.

This led us to the assumption that underutilization—i.e. having more capacity than is strictly necessary for the work—causes lower output via diminishing involvement in the work. Probably the way they performed and their behaviour were now used by workers as a means of expressing any dissatisfaction they may have felt with their work, their working conditions and so on.

Strangely, this phenomenon was mainly noticed in male workers. Female operators who, according to our standards, were working far below their ability level, performed well. They were satisfied, and liked the simple work that enabled them, for example, to carry on a lively conversation with their fellow workers, or so they claimed. That was what we noticed in the early 1950s.

The dislike of working in industry which males have—and to an increasing extent females now also have—can be attributed to a variety of reasons. As clearly expressed in attitude surveys, some aspects as product organization (van Beek, 1964), payment schemes, health complaints etc had a negative influence on the individual's satisfaction in the work. Much attention has recently been paid to the organization of the work, to the layout of the workplace and the working environment, seen from an ergonomic point of view (Kelderman *et al.*, 1963). The importance of motivation as a factor capable of stimulating or inhibiting performance in the factory was again underlined by a number of analyses of absence rates and of labour turnover data. In the 1960s we noticed, on various occasions, that both these forms of expressing dissatisfaction with the existing situation were related to the relative level of difficulty of the work. Uneasiness that followed from unused abilities, frequently found an outlet in workers' behaviour (Arends 1974). This kind of research led to more critical discussions about the Tayloristic basis of the production organization. New approaches in job enrichment, job enlargement, participative decision making and job re-design, etc resulted from that (den Hertog 1977).

We were impressed by two main findings of our investigations. First, the difference between the abilities available and those which were either used or unused not only proved to be a disturbing factor in the work attitude in West European culture, but its influence was also demonstrated in comparable ways in Philips' production units elsewhere. Sometimes the lack of satisfaction resulted in a high labour turnover or absence rates, in other situations it was reflected in the quality and quantity of the performance and in relationships with management.

Secondly, our main experience to date has been obtained at the level of the semi-skilled worker. However, the same phenomenon of dissatisfaction related to one's ability for the work has also been noticed recently in some groups at the middle and higher management levels (Arends *et al.*, 1978). This time, the feelings of unease were not so sharply expressed as in labour turnover, but more often in the desire for more growth and development, for better communication with management about work, for better performance prospects, and for more autonomy.

At the moment we have a strong feeling that the relative importance to the individual of his expectations (based on his views on various factors such as income, spare time, security, growth, status, etc) as compared with his evaluations of those factors in reality is very central to the process whereby he decides whether or not to do things and how to do them. For example, some people consider their capacities too great for the job to be performed. If that is true and their expectations for growth and development, if any, are not met by the company, this discrepancy will influence their behaviour with regard to output, absence, and leaving. Where capacities fall short, or have been over-estimated, the result may be a low work tempo, stress, feelings of nervousness and absence from work.

It is clear that both the expectations and the evaluation of reality are very subjective and therefore hard to measure. We are familiar with the accusations that attitude surveys and interviews are not very reliable. But we know, too, that their results at least indicate trends which have proved valid and helpful in practice.

Abilities and performances: some recent findings

As an illustration of the above we will briefly mention the main results of some investigations in a number of Latin American countries at the level of semi-skilled factory work. They were carried out as part of a check on the predictive value of our test series for semi-skilled workers.

Workers' abilities and selection tests

The series consists of nine tests (partly manual performance tests, partly paper-and-pencil tests), examples of which are printed in Fig. 1.

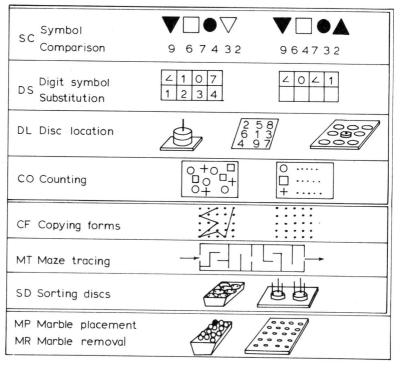

Figure 1.   Basic sub tests forming part of the Philips language-free test battery.

Layout, instruction and scoring are kept strictly uniform by careful training of the test administrators and by regular checks on their work. We therefore assume that the results collected in various countries can be considered as belonging to one total group, and we can ignore existing differences in culture, in way of thinking, and in level of education (Arends 1975). (The raw scores from various National Organizations have been made 'comparable' by converting them by means of local norm scales.)

Workers' performance

The difficulty in situations like this is to find reliable criteria for testing the tests. Having learned from previous experience, we always ask not only for criteria such as performance data but also for ratings for behavioural data (interest, contacts with supervisors, absence, labour turnover, etc) and ratings for the possible influence of intrinsic and conceptual factors on the worker's motivation to perform.

In all the organizations concerned, the ratings were given by a local committee consisting of at least the plant manager, the head of the relevant department and the personnel officer. In order to get reliable and comparable data they were all informed and trained by our industrial psychologist for Latin America before the start of the investigation.

The tables presented here refer to the overall data from four National Organizations: Argentina, Peru, Venezuela, Uruguay. (Further investigations in eight plants in Mexico and Brazil, involving 300 personnel confirms the same trends.) The entire data relate to over 200 semi-skilled workers, operators, assemblers, inspectors, etc doing various levels of factory work, spread over the Latin American continent and rated by non-professionals.

In Fig. 2 workers' performances and behaviour as rated by their chiefs are presented in percentages!

From a rough inspection we observe: the speed of learning of the workers involved is very acceptable; the performance, however, is of a lower level; the quality and quantity produced by about one-quarter is 'below normal'; and about 40% of the workers are rated as 'not interested' in the work (i.e. in the job as it exists now).

It is easy to deduce that supervisors' contacts with the workers cannot be entirely smooth since they have to stimulate members of their group who are not interested.

Test scores and performance ratings

This investigation started as a check on the validity of the tests. We were therefore interested to learn about the relation between the individual test scores and speed of learning and performance in terms of quality and quantity. The correlation coefficients between the total test score for the test series and various ratings from each of the four countries are indicated in Fig. 3.

There were a number of conclusions:

The performance i.e. the quality and quantity of the work, is what every plant manager is interested in. Sad to relate, the relations between the test scores and performances were not only low, but in two countries even negative (33, -07, 19, -32).

Fortunately, the speed of learning demonstrates a more favourable result: the correlations between the test scores—collected in the selection procedure—and the speed of learning the factory work are significant and quite high.

Taking into account the negative correlations with interest in the work in three of the four countries, we may very cautiously suggest that the more capable the workers were (higher test score), the better they could learn their jobs, but the less often they were interested in their work. The result was that their performance had no relation with their abilities.

A comparable trend is that the higher the abilities of workers are, the lower the rating for smooth contacts with the supervisors.

In the following figures the comparisons of test levels and performance ratings, and of test levels and the rating for speed of learning are presented in graphic form.

The level of the persons' test scores does not demonstrate a worthwhile relationship with the quality of their performance.

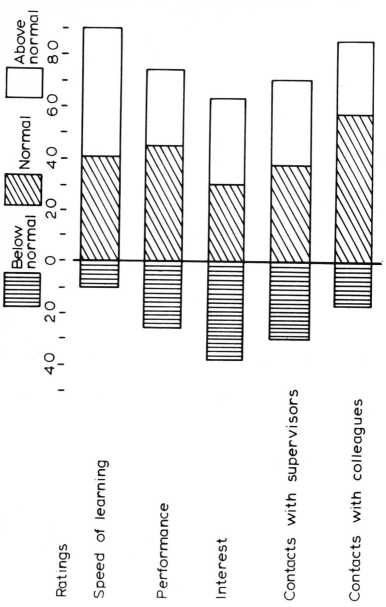

Figure 2.   Frequency distributions of ratings (in percentages).

	Ratings for :			
	Performance	Speed of learning	Interest in the work	Contact with supervisors
Total Test Score	33 -07	84 68	-32 -10	01 -08
	19 -32	90 83	-27 16	-36 -02

Figure 3.   Test scores × various ratings (correlation coefficients × 100, abridged from the investigations in four separate countries). A square around a co-efficient means that the correlation is highly significant (1%); a minus signifies that the correlation is negative.

However, the fact that tests have substantial links with the abilities for semi-skilled work in a factory is demonstrated by Fig. 5. The bosses' ratings for the speed of learning factory work were highest for the persons who yielded the highest results on the tests.

For those interested in our validity problem we can also show in a graph that, if a person has certain capacities, then the more interested he is in the work the better his performance will be. (As mentioned above in semi-skilled factory work there is a range of jobs of differing complexity for which different test levels are more adequate. To facilitate presentation we have neglected that aspect here.)

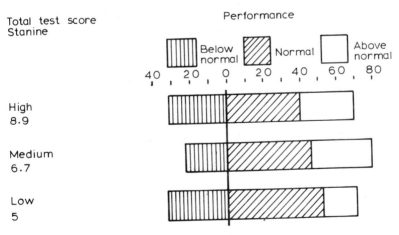

Figure 4.   Test scores × performance rating (in percentages).

In Fig. 6 we notice that within each ability level the more interested people were in their work, the better their performance; and comparing the levels of ability we see that the lower the test level, the lower the performance level. Interest apparently cannot compensate for a lack of ability.

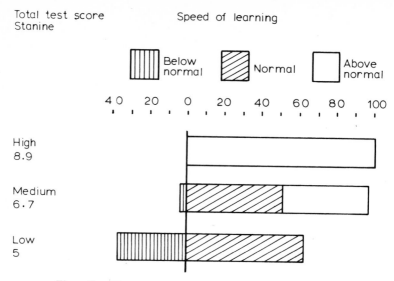

Figure 5.   Test scores × speed of learning (in percentages).

Still more explicit is the influence of 'interest in the work' found in relation with the ratings for 'the speed of learning the job' and the level of ability, as indicated by the total test score in the installed procedure about one year later (not illustrated here).

There we noticed that whether they were interested or not, all workers with high test levels learned the job at above-normal speed; and the lower the capacities, the greater the correlation between the degree of interest in the work and the speed of learning.

Some further analyses of 'interest in the work' showed that the quality and quantity of their workers' performance is of vital importance for every company. Fig. 7 gives another illustration of how the ratings for 'interest in the work' and for 'performance' are interrelated.

We did not calculate the extent to which contamination may have influenced these results. Of course this investigation can only indicate relationships between 'interest' and other work aspects, not causality. Nevertheless, it is still very convincing that the managements in the four countries considered 'interest' to be so highly related to the way the workers do their daily jobs.

If we could therefore detect the influences which are expressed in 'interest' we might: either find tools by which the working conditions can be adjusted, if required and if possible (aspects of ergonomics, psychology, sociology, medicine, organizational design, etc); or adapt our selection policy or training system in order to get a more appropriate type or worker; or do both.

The big problem now is to find out what positive and negative aspects influence that dynamic force 'motivation' that we have called 'interest in the work' here.

Below we give two examples which demonstrate how the various ratings were interrelated and how they were reported to the management team in the National Organization concerned. The findings should be treated with

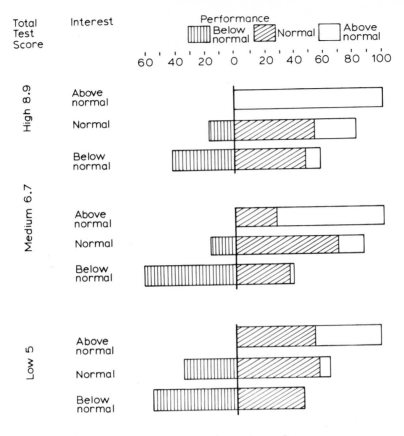

Figure 6.   (Test scores × interest) × performance.

caution. These results are only indications and must be seen as trends. They are intended (and used) as starting points for internal discussions between management and workers.

The first example is 'interest' related to under-utilization of capacities. In Fig. 8 a comparison is given between what we will call over/under-utilization of capacities and the rating for interest in the work. We know by experience what the best fitting test scores are for each of the work levels (semi-skilled jobs). The workers can thus be grouped into the following categories: 'under-utilization': greater capacities are available than are needed for the work they perform; and 'well placed': capacities are exactly right for their jobs (owing to the situation on the labour market no 'over-utilization' workers have been hired in these countries; but there were in the 8 plants in Mexico and Brazil).

The relationship with interest is illustrated in Fig. 8.

Example A: capacities available related to capacities needed × interest
It is clear that in the group of workers with more capacities than they need for their work, people who are rated as 'below average interest in the work', occur relatively more frequently.

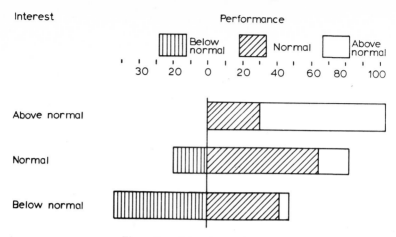

Figure 7.   Interest × performance.

Example B: 'interest' related to the 'need for using one's abilities'. The questionnaire asked ratings for the extent to which a number of factors might have influenced the individual worker's performance positively or negatively. Here we assume that a positive influence on the work performance—resulting, for example, from work in keeping with the worker's capacities and interest, and/or the possibility of growth, etc (according to the raters)—mainly occurs if such a possibility has been realised or is seen by the worker to be within reach. We have simply added those three ratings which the factor analysis showed to be the most important for 'Performance':
• work in keeping with the interest and capacities of the worker,
• the possibility of development and training,
• the possibility of growth and promotion.
They all range from very negative (1 point) up to very positive (5 points).

In the next graph (Fig. 9) we compare interest on a 5-point scale and classified into 3 groups.

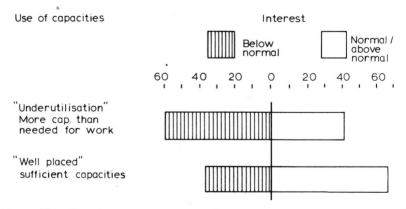

Figure 8.   Capacities available related to capacities needed × interest.

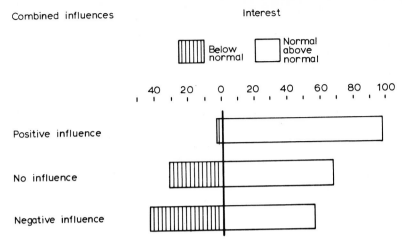

Figure 9. Three main influences on performance x interest:
- work according to interest and capacities
- possibility of development
- possibility of growth.

influences: positive = the sum of 3 ratings is 10 points or more.
 neutral = the sum of 3 ratings is 8 or 9 points.
 negative = the sum of 3 ratings is 7 points or less.
The greater the positive influence of the three intrinsic factors mentioned above, the higher the interest was.

Negative influence (work offers no possibilities at all for 'self-realisation') coincides with a strong negative interest. The stimulating effect of these factors on the job, however, is not related to interest in the work in every case. Interest in the work still has roots other than the three factors under consideration (correlation coefficient for three influences x interest is: 0.65).

In tables and comparisons not reported here—because for example the samples were rather small—we also found there was a trend towards the relation between interest and performance, ratings becoming still clearer if the capacities/growth/development influences were taken into account.

A consideration of our experiences

Some general conclusions may be drawn from our investigations.

Man's capacities are essential for his work performance.

In practice we find indications that the worker is not always motivated to use his full abilities.

Dissatisfaction with work can be expressed in different ways: in the quality and quantity of the products, in absence rates and labour turnover data, etc.

The reasons why workers are not inclined to make the most of their abilities differ in nature and often strongly depend on the specific aspects of the organization concerned.

The challenging aspects of the job, working environment, information and communication, etc. all seemed to be related to the way people acted in their work situation.

There are implications in the findings for organization design and working conditions. It is important for each company to learn what factors influence their workers' behaviour.

It is clear that in many situations money is losing its key function as the only or main 'motivation to work'. It may be that it still influences the quantity of a person's performance, but, it will often only be an indirect stimulus to his natural attitude to quality. Obviously the company's need for higher quality in work performance is closely related to the worker's demand for higher quality in working life.

Once income and job security are more or less guaranteed (by the companies' rules, by law, etc) workers' claims evolve towards other aspects.

The simplest way to know the directions these take is to ask people themselves.

Not all the investigations mentioned above are of a high scientific standard, but the results of a simple survey which is well prepared and carefully carried out, besides being adapted to the needs of the area, can also be an eye-opener and provide a basis for fruitful internal discussions.

Cautiously extrapolating the trends which we have found in the past years, further developments can be expected in the direction of a working climate in which topics such as those mentioned below will become still more central than in the past.

(1) Work layout, maintenance of tools, working environment:

These mostly ergonomic factors are not only directly related to physical health but were often seen by the interviewees as a reflection of a manager's esteem for his workers; eg when the quality of tools and machinery 'unnecessarily' hampered performance, or when the workplaces and canteen were dirty etc.

(2) Work content and its organization:

We frequently read about the need for challenging work, for work according to abilities, in which a person can maintain his self respect (and others respect). In some experiments with small autonomous groups at operators' level, and lately with skilled workers in engineering works (Wester, 1978), involving changes from process to product groups, the workers' attitudes and performance increased.

In view of the directions of people's reactions, we consider 'capacities' as a critical topic. In our opinion the process of the growing awareness of one's own abilities, and at the same time of the need (and the feeling that it is 'a human right') to explore them, might become a very central force in an individual's attitude towards work.

(3) Information communication:

We noticed a great need for information and some kind of security (knowing where you are, what you are, and what the company can offer for your personal growth). Communication concerning changes in work situations, on individual performance, and on possibilities for future developments, were frequently mentioned as important influences on motivation, both at semi-skilled level and in surveys amongst middle and senior staff executives.

The central idea behind all the findings mentioned in this paper is that involvement in an activity can only be expected if a man is interested in it, if it is in line with what he thinks is important for him. Then he will be motivated to devote his full attention and abilities to that work.

Of late, selection tests have been receiving increasing negative attention in the press and in political discussions. They are described as scientific instruments, invented by large organizations to manipulate people in such a way that the labour force available yields optimum returns. In this paper we have tried to show that the same data can also be used in another way, to indicate how jobs can be fitted to the workers. By appealing to their needs for such things as growth and development, mutual interests can be served.

Acknowledgement

The main body of this study is a result of close collaboration with Dr. A. Simeone, Argentina, Philips industrial psychologist for Latin America.

References

Abrams, M., 1973, Subjective social indicators. *Social Trends*, 3, 35-50. (London: HMSO).

Adams, J.S., 1963, Wages inequities, productivity and work quality. *Industrial Relations*, 3, 9-16.

Aertssen, Erna, 1975, Determinants of work satisfaction in nursing personnel of a psychiatric hospital. (Dissertation for a master's degree in psychology, stencilled, in Dutch). (Leuven: Catholic University of Leuven).

Agurén, Hansson, Karlsson, 1976, The Volvo Kalmar Plant. Rationalization Council SAF-LO, Stockholm.

Andrisani, P.J. and Miljus, R.C., 1977, Individual differences in preference for intrinsic versus extrinsic aspects of work. *Journal of Vocational Behavior,* 11, 14-30.

Annett, J., Duncan, K.D., Stammers, R.B. and Gray, M.J., 1971, Task Analysis. Department of Employment *Training Information Paper No. 6.* (London: HMSO).

Arbeitsstättenverordnung, 1975, Verordnung über Arbeitstätten. Bundesgesetzblatt Nr. 32, Seite 729-742, ausgegeben zu Bonn am 25.3.1975.

Arends, G., 1974, Labour Turnover, summary of findings in the Philips Concern, pp. 2-9, (Eindhoven: Philips Industrial Psychology Department).

Arends, G., 1975, Experience with selection tests in various countries. In: *Ethnic variables in Human Factors Engineering* (Edited by Alphonse Chapanis) (Baltimore: Johns Hopkins University Press). pp. 261-269.

Arends, G., Simeone, A., O'Farrell, M., 1978, Investigation into the human resources and the motivational climate of the executive level of the Peruvian Philips Organisation. Internal memorandum. (Eindhoven: Philips).

Argyris, C., 1964, *Integrating the Individual and the Organisation.* New York: Wiley, 1964).

Argyris, C., 1970, *Intervention Theory and Method—a Behavioural Science View.* (London: Addison Wesley).

Balchin, Nigel, 1947, Satisfactions in work. *Occupational Psychology*, 21, 125-134; 22 (1948), 16.

Baldamus, W., 1961, *Efficiency and Effort.* (London: Tavistock Publications).

Barnard, Chester, 1938, *The Functions of the Executive.* (Cambridge, Massachusetts: Harvard University Press).

Becker-Biskaborn, G.-U., 1975, Ergonomische Erkenntnissammlung für den Arbeitsschutz mit Informations-system. Forschungsbericht Nr. 142, Band I und II, der Bundesanstalt für Arbeitsschutz und Unfallforschung Dortmund; Wirtschaftsverlag NW GmbH, Bremerhaven 1975.

Beddoes, Thomas, 1801, *Hygëia.* (Bristol: J. Mills).

Beek, H. van, 1964, The influence of assembly line organisation on output, quality and morale. In: *Occupational Psychology*, 38 (3), pp. 161-172.

Biesheuvel, S., 1975, 'One more time, how do we motivate the Herzberg theory?' *Psychologica Africana*, 16, 33-34.

Biganne, J.F. and Stewart, P.A., 1963, Job Enlargement: A case study. *Research Series No. 25.* (State University of Iowa, Bureau of Labour and Management).

Björk, 1976, Individuals, Groups and Parties involved in Change Work. In Swedish, PA-Council, Stockholm.

Blauner, R., 1963, Extent of satisfaction: A review of general research. In: *Psychology in Administration* (edited by T.W. Costello and S. Zalkind) (Englewood Cliffs, New Jersey: Prentice-Hall).

Blauner, R., 1964, *Alienation and Freedom*. (University of Chicago Press).

Blum, M.L. and Naylor, J.C., 1968, *Industrial Psychology*. (New York: Harper and Row).

Bowles, M.L., 1976, Job satisfaction: Measurement and Meaning. (Unpublished University of Wales Ph.D. thesis Uwist: Cardiff).

Bradley, C., 1978, Psychophysiological effects of stress in diabetic patients, ischaemic heart disease patients and healthy subjects. Ph.D. Thesis, University of Nottingham.

Braverman, H., 1974, Labour amd monopoly capital. (*Monthly Review Press*: London).

Brayfield, A.H. and Rothe, H.F., 1951, An Index of Job Satisfaction. *Journal of Applied Psychology*, vol. 35, No. 5, 307-311.

Brayfield, A.H. and Crockett, W.H., 1955, Employee attitudes and employee performance. *Psychological Bulletin*, 52, pp. 396-424.

Brief, A.P. and Aldag, R.J., 1975, Employee reactions to job characteristics: a constructive replication. *Journal of Applied Psychology* 60 (2) 182-186.

Brophy, A.L., 1959, Self, role and satisfaction. *Genetics Psychology Monographs*, 59, 263-308.

Burrows, G.C., Cox, T. and Simpson, G.C., 1977, The measurement of stress in a sales training situation. *Occupational Psychology*, 50, 45-51.

Burt, C. and Banks, C., 1947, A factor analysis of body measurements for British males. *Annals of Eugenics*, 13, 238-256.

Butteriss, M., 1975, The quality of working life: the expanding international scene. *Work Research Unit Paper No. 5*. Department of Employment, United Kingdom.

Butteriss, M., 1975, A strategy for job enrichment: a summary of Hackman and Oldham reports. *Work Research Unit Paper, No. 6*. Department of Employment, United Kingdom.

Butteriss, M. and Murdock, R.U., 1975, Work Restructuring Projects and Experiments in the United Kingdom. *Work Research Unit, Report No. 2*. Department of Employment, United Kingdom.

Butteriss, M. and Murdock, R.U., 1976, Work Restructuring Projects and Experiments in the United States of America. *Work Research Unit, Report No. 3*. Department of Employment, United Kingdom.

Cameron, C., 1973, A theory of fatigue. *Ergonomics*, 16, 633-648.

Cameron, S., 1973, Job Satisfaction. The concept and its measurement. *Work Research Unit Report*. Department of Employment, United Kingdom.

Campbell, D.T. and Fiske, D.W., 1959, Convergent and discriminant validation by the multitrait-multimethod matrix. *Psychological Bulletin*, 56, 81-105.

Campbell, D.T. and Stanley, J.C., 1963, *Experimental and Quasi-Experimental Designs for Research*. (Chicago: Rand McNally).

Cannon, W.B., 1914, The emergency function of the adrenal medulla in pain and the major emotions. American Journal of Physiology, 33, 356-372.

Caplan, R.D., Cobb, S., French, J.R.P. Jr., Van Harrison, R. and Pinneau, S.R. Jr., 1975, Job Demands and Worker Health. (Washington: *National Institute for Occupational Safety and Health, Publication No. 75-160* (NIOSH). U.S. Department of Health, Education and Welfare).

Cattell, R.B., 1952, *Factor Analysis*. (New York: Harper).

Cattell, R.B. and Coulter, M.A., 1966, Principles of behavioural taxonomy and the mathematical basis of the taxonomic computer program. *British Journal of Mathematical and Statistical Psychology*, 19 (2), 237-269.

Centers, R. and Bugenthal, D.E., 1966, Intrinsic and extrinsic job motivations among different segments of the working population. *Journal of Applied Psychology*, 50, 193-197.

de Charms, R., 1968, *Personal Causation: The Internal Affective Determinants of Behavior*. (New York: Academic Press).

Cherns, A.B., 1973, Better working lives: a social scientist's view. *Journal of Occupational Psychology*, 47, 23-28.

Cherns, A.B., 1975, Perspectives on the quality of working life. *Journal of Occupational Psychology*, 48, 155-167.

Cherns, A.B., 1976, The principles of socio-technical design. *Human Relations* 29 (8) 783-792.

Chinoy, E., 1964, Manning the machine—the assembly line worker. In: Berger, P.L. (Ed.), *The Human Shape of Work: Studies in Occupational Sociology.* (New York: Macmillan).

Civil Service Department, 1975, Management Services Handbook: Typing Services. (London: Civil Service Department, E.125).

Colouris, G.J., Tashker, M.G. and Penick, M.C., 1978, Policy impacts of ATC automation: Human factors considerations. U.S. Department of Transportation FAA-AVP-78-1.

Cook, D., 1967, The impact of the Hawthorne effect in experimental designs in education research. Washington, D.C. U.S. Office of Education, No. 0726. Reported in: *Handbook of Industrial and Organizational Psychology.* (Edited by M.D. Dunnette) (Chicago: Rand McNally, 1976).

Cooper, C. and Marshall, J., 1978, *Understanding Executive Stress.* (London: Mcmillan).

Corlett, E.N., 1974, Work organisation and performance on the shop floor. Paper read at Annual Conference of British Psychological Society, Nottingham.

Cox, D., Dyce Sharp, K.M. and Irvine, D.H., 1953, Women's attitudes to repetitive work. (London: NIIP Report No. 9).

Cox, T., 1975, The nature and management of stress. *New Behaviour,* 2, 493-495.

Cox, T., 1978, *Stress.* (London: Macmillan).

Cross, D., 1973, The worker opinion survey: A measure of shop floor satisfaction. *Journal of Occupational Psychology,* 47, 193-208.

Crossman, E.R.F.W., 1960, *Automation and Skill.* (London: HMSO).

Dalziel, Stuart, J. and Klein, Lisl, 1960, The human implications of Work Study: the case of 'Pakitt Ltd.' (Stevenage, Hertfordshire: Warren Spring Laboratory, Department of Scientific and Industrial Research).

Damodaran, L., Stewart, T.F.M. and Eason, K.D., 1974, Socio-technical Ramifications of Forms of Man-Computer Interaction. Paper to Altorg Conference, Gothenburg, July.

Damodaran, L., 1976, User Involvement in System Design: Why? and How? Proceedings of Conference on 'Computing and People '76', Leicester Polytechnica, December.

Damodaran, L., 1977, Work Research in Action. *HUSAT Memorandum No. 138,* Department of Human Sciences, Loughborough University of Technology.

Davis, C.G., Kerle, R., Silvestrom, A.W. and Wallace, W.H., 1960, An activity analysis of the positions in a high activity Air Traffic Control Tower. (Philadelphia, Pennsylvania: Courtney & Co. Inc., Report 39, FAA-BRD-40).

Davis, L.E., 1971, The coming crisis for production management: technology and organization. *International Journal of Production Research,* 9, 65-82.

Davis, L.E. and Cherns, A.B. and Associates (Eds.), 1975, *The Quality of Working Life.* (New York: The Free Press).

Davis, L.E., 1977, Evolving alternative organisation designs—*Human Relations,* Vol. 30, No. 3, pp. 261-273.

Department of Trade and Industry, 1977, *Report of the committee of inquiry on industrial democracy,* Chairman Lord Bullock (London, HMSO).

Department of Trade and Industry, 1977, *Preliminary Study of long-term Air Traffic Systems in Europe. Volume I.* (London: HMSO).

Diamond, S.S., 1974, Hawthorne effects: Another look. Unpublished manuscript. University of Illinois at Chicago. Reported in: *Handbook of Industrial and Organizational Psychology.* (Edited by M.D. Dunnette). (Chicago: Rand McNally, 1976).

Dubin, R., 1956, Industrial workers' worlds: a study of the 'central life interests' of industrial workers. *Social Problems,* 3, 131-142.

Duncan, D.B., 1955, Multiple range and multiple F tests. *Biometrics,* 11, 1-42.

Dunnette, M.D., Campbell, J.P. and Hakel, M.D., 1967, Factors contributing to job satisfaction and job dissatisfaction in six occupational groups. *Organisational Behaviour and Human Performance,* 2, 143-174.

Eason, K.D., Damodaran, L. and Stewart, T.F.M., 1974, 'MICA Survey'. Report of a Survey of Man-Computer Interaction in Commercial Applications. SSRC Project Report on Grant No. HR 1844/1.

Edwards, A.L., 1972, Experimental design in psychological research 4th edition. (New York: Holt, Rinehart and Winston).

Elgerot, A. and Rissler, A., 1978, *Omställning till arbete i kontorslandskap.* (*Adjustment to work in open plan office*). Department of Psychology, University of Stockholm, Rapporter. (In press).

196 *Satisfactions in work design*

Elliott, D., 1976, Conference review: Issues of value. In: Warr, P. (ed). *Personal Goals and Work Design*. (London: Wiley).

Emery, F.E., 1967, The Democratisation of the Workplace. *Manpower and Applied Psychology*, 1, 118-129.

Enzel, M.E., Hansen, R.D. and Lowe, C.A., 1975, Causal attribution in the mixed motive game: Effects of facilitatory and inhibitory environmental forces. *Journal of Personality and Social Psychology*, 31, 50-54.

Evans, M.G., 1972, Relations among weighted and non-weighted measures of job satisfaction. *Studies in Personnel Psychology*, 4, 45-54.

Evans, M.G., 1973, The moderating effects of internal versus external control on the relationship between various aspects of job satisfaction. *Studies in Personnel Psychology*, 5, 37-45.

Ewen, R.B., 1964, Some Determinants of Job Satisfaction: a study of the Generality of Herzberg's Theory. *Journal of Applied Psychology*, 48, 161-163.

Fachnormenausschuss Ergonomie im Verein Deutscher Ingenieure Verschiedene ergonomische Normen.

Farr, R.M., 1977, On the nature of attributional artifacts in qualitative research: Herzberg's 2-factor theory of work motivation. *Journal of Occupational Psychology*, 50 (1), 3-14.

Faunce, W.A. and Dubin R., 1975, Individual investment in working and living. In: *the Quality of Working Life* (edited by L.E. Davis and A.B. Cherns), Vol. 1, pp.299-316 (The Free Press).

Fein, M., 1974, Job enrichment: a re-evaluation—*Sloan Management Review*, 15 (2) 69-88.

Fleishman, E.A., 1967, Development of a behaviour taxonomy for describing human tasks: a correlational-experimental approach. *Journal of Applied Psychology*, 51 (1), 1-10.

Fleishman, E.A., 1975, Toward a taxonomy of human performance. *American Psychologist*, December, 1127-1149.

Ford, R.N. and Borgatta, E.F., 1970, Satisfaction with the work itself. *Journal of Applied Psychology*, 54 (2), 128-134.

Fossum, J.A., 1973/74, Urban-rural differences in job satisfaction. *Industrial and Labor Relations Review*, 27, 3, 405-409.

Frank, L.L. and Hackman, J.R., 1975, A failure of job enrichment—the case of the change that wasn't. *Journal of Applied Behavioural Science*, 413-436.

Frankenhaeuser, M., 1975, Sympathetic-adrenomedullary activity, behaviour and the psychosocial environment. In: P. H. Venables, M.J. Christie (Eds.) *Research in Psychophysiology* Chapter 4, pp. 71-94. (New York: Wiley and Sons.)

Frankenhaeuser, M. and Gardell, B., 1976, Underload and overload in working life: Outline of a multidisciplinary approach. *Journal of Human Stress*, 2, 35-46.

Fraser, R., 1947, The incidence of neurosis among factory workers. Industrial Health Research Board of The Medical Research Council. Report No. 90. (London: HMSO).

French, J.W., 1951, The description of aptitude and achievement tests in terms of rotated factors. *Psychometric Monographs, No. 5.*

French, J., 1973, Person-Role Fit. *Occupational Mental Health* 3, 1.

Galbraith, J.K., 1967, *The New Industrial State*. (Boston: Houghton Mifflin).

Gardell, B., 1973, Quality of work and non-work activities and rewards in affluent societies. Reports from the Psychological Laboratories, University of Stockholm, No. 403.

General Household Survey, 1975, 1978. (London: HMSO).

Ginzberg, E., 1975, Work structuring and manpower realities. In: L.E. Davis and A.B. Cherns (eds), *The Quality of Working Life, Vol. 1*. (New York: The Free Press).

Glaser, D., 1976, *Productivity Gains Through Work Life Improvement*. (New York: Harcourt Brace Jovanovich).

Glass, D.C., 1977, Stress, behaviour patterns and coronary disease. *American Scientist*, December, 1109-1116.

Goldthorpe, J.H., Lockwood, D., Bechhofer, F. and Platt, J., 1970, *The Affluent Worker: Industrial Attitudes and Behaviour*. (Cambridge: CUP).

Grandjean, E., Wotzka, G. and Kretzschmar, H., 1968, Psychophysiologic investigations into professional stress on air traffic control officers at the Zürich-Kloten and Geneva-Cointrin airports. (Unpublished manuscript, Swiss Confederate College of Technology at Zürich).

Guilford, J.P., 1967, *The Nature of Human Intelligence*. (New York: McGraw-Hill).

Gurin, G., Veroff, J. and Feld, S., 1960, *Americans View Their Mental Health*. (New York: Basic Books).

Hacker, W. and Macher, F., 1977, Psychologische Beiträge zur effektiven und persönlichkeits-förderlichen Arbeitsgestaltung in der Industrie. Socialistische Arbeitswissenschaft 21: 3, 207-210.

Hackman, R.J., 1970, Tasks and task performance in research on stress. In: McGrath, J.E. (ed.), *Social and Psychological Factors in Stress*. (New York: Holt, Rinehart and Wilson).

Hackman, J.R. and Lawler, E.E., 1971, Employee Reactions to Job Characteristics. *Journal of Applied Psychology Monograph*, 55 (3), 259-286.

Hackman, J.R. and Oldham, G.R., 1974, Motivation through the design of work: Test of a theory. *Technical Report No. 6*. (Department of Administrative Sciences, Yale University).

Hackman, J.R. and Oldham, G.R., 1974, The Job Diagnostic Survey: An instrument for the diagnosis of jobs and the evaluation of job redesign projects. *Technical Report No. 4*, Department of Administrative Sciences: Yale.

Hackman, J.R., 1975, On the coming demise of job enrichment. In: E.L. Cass and F.G. Zimmer (ed.), *Man and Work in Society*. (New York: Van Rostrand Reinhold).

Hackman, J.R. and Oldham, G.R., 1975, Development of the Job Diagnostic Survey. *Journal of Applied Psychology*, 60 (2), 159-170.

Hale, A.R. and Hale, M., 1970, Accidents in perspective. *Journal of Occupational Psychology* 44 (2), 115-121.

Harshbarger, T.R., 1977, *Introductory Statistics: A Decision Map* (2nd edition). (New York: Macmillan).

Hedberg, B. and Mumford, E., 1975, The Design of Computer Systems: Man's vision of man as an integral part of the system design process. In: *Human Choice and Computers*. (Edited by E. Mumford and H. Sackman). (Amsterdam: North Holland).

Heron, W., 1961, Cognitive and physiological effects of perceptual isolation. In: P. Soloman *et al.* (Editors). *Sensory Deprivation*. (Harvard University Press). pp. 6-31.

Hertog, F. den, 1977, The search for new leads in job design: the Philips case. *Journal of Contemporary Business*, 6 (2).

Herzberg, F., 1968, One more time: How do you motivate employees? *Harvard Business Review* 46, 53-62. In: Davis, L.E. and Taylor, J.C. (1972). *Design of Jobs*. (Penguin).

Herzberg, F., Mausner, B., Peterson, R.O. and Capwell, D., 1957, Job attitudes: Review of research and opinion. (Pittsburg: Psychological Service Pittsburg).

Herzberg, F., Mausner, B. and Snyderman, B.B., 1959, *The Motivation to Work*. (New York: Wiley).

Herzberg, F., 1966, *Work and the Nature of Man*. (Cleveland: World Publishing Co.).

Hill, A.B., 1975, Work variety and differences in occupational boredom. *Journal of Applied Psychology*, 60, 121-131.

Hofmann, P.B., 1971, Meeting Resistance to Hospital Automation. *Hospital Progress*, April, 45-60.

Hulin, C.L., and Blood, M.R., 1968, Job enlargement, individual differences and worker responses. *Psychological Bulletin*, 69 (1), 41-55.

Jackson, P., 1973, Better working lives: an organisational consultant's view. *Journal of Occupational Psychology*, 47, 29-31.

Jenkins, C.D., 1971, Psychological and social precursors of coronary disease. *New England Journal of Medicine*, 284, 244-255 and 307-317.

Jenney, L.L. and Lawrence, K.A., 1974, Implications of automation for operating and staffing an Advanced Air Traffic Management System (AATMS). (Cambridge, Massachusetts: U.S. Department of Transportation. Report No. DOT-TSC-OST-74-14.111).

Jessup, G., 1974, Job satisfaction and job design. *Work Research Unit Paper No. 1*. Department of Employment, United Kingdom.

Jessup, G., 1977, The case for shop floor participation. *Department of Employment Gazette*, 85 (6), 575-577. (London: HMSO).

Johansson, G., Aronsson, G. and Lindström, B.O., 1978, Social psychological and neuro-endocrine stress reactions in highly mechanized work. *Ergonomics*. (In press).

Johansson, G., Frankenhaeuser, M., 1973, Temporal factors in sympathoadrenomedullary activity following acute behavioral activation. *Journal of Biological Psychology*, (1), 67-77.

de Jong, J.R., 1973, The Humanisation of work. Occasional paper. (Utrecht: Berenschot).

de Jong, J.R., 1974, Tendenzen zue Partizipation. Erweiterung der Arbeitsinhalte und ihre Beziehung zu Prozessen beruflicher Bildung. (Hannover: Hermann Schroedel Verlag).

Jordan, N., 1963, Allocation of functions between man and machines in automated systems. *Journal of Applied Psychology*, 47, 161-165.

Kahn, R.L., 1973, Conflict, ambiguity and overload: Three elements in job stress. *Occupational Mental Health*, 3, 2-9.

Karasek, R.A., Jr., 1976, The impact of the work environment on life outside the job. Ph.D. thesis, unpublished, Institute for Social Research, University of Stockholm.

Kelderman, F., Wely, P. van, Willems, P., 1963, *Vademecum Ergonomics in Industry*. (Eindhoven: Philips Technical Library).

Kelley, H.H., 1971, *Attribution in Social Interaction*. (New York: General Learning Press).

Kennholt, I. and Bergstedt, M., 1971, Attitudes towards the work and working conditions among Air Traffic Control Personnel in the Aviation Administration. (Stockholm: Swedish Personnel Administrative Council).

Kilbridge, N.D., 1960, Do Workers prefer larger Jobs? *Personnel*, 37, 45-48.

Kirkland, J., 1976, Interest—Phoenix in Psychology. *Bulletin British Psychological Society*. 29, 33-41.

Klein, Lisl, 1976(a), *A Social Scientist in Industry*. (Epping, Essex: Gower Press).

Klein, L., 1976(b), *New Forms of Work Organization*. (Cambridge University Press).

Konings, V., 1974, Intrinsic and extrinsic work motivation in automobile workers. (Dissertation for a master's degree in psychology, stencilled, in Dutch). Leuven: Catholic University of Leuven).

Kornhauser, A. and Sharp, A., 1932, Employee Attitudes: suggestions from a study in a factory. *Personnel Journal*, X, 393-401.

Kornhauser, A., 1965, *Mental Health of the Industrial Worker*. (New York: Wiley).

Kunin, T., 1955, The construction of a new type of attitude measure. *Personnel Psychology*, 8, 65-78.

Lachter, L.E., 1971, Are you considering a second career? *Administrative Management*, April, 28-32.

Lawler, E.E., 1969, Job design and employee motivation. *Personnel Psychology* 22 (4), 426-435.

Lawler, E.E. III, 1976, Conference review: Issues of understanding. In: Warr, P. (ed.) *Personal Goals and Work Design*. (London: Wiley).

Lawler, E.E. and Porter, L.W., 1967, Antecedent attitudes of effective managerial performance. *Organizational Behaviour and Human Performance*, 2, 122-142.

Lazarus, R.S., 1966, *Psychological Stress and the Coping Process*. (New York: McGraw-Hill).

Lazarus, R.S., 1976, *Adjustment*. (New York: McGraw-Hill).

Lemke, E. and Wiersma, W., 1976, *Principles of Psychological Measurement*. (Chicago: Rand McNally).

Levi, L., 1972, Stress and distress in response to psychosocial stimuli: Laboratory and real-life studies on sympathoadrenalmedullary and related reactions. *Acta Medica Scandanavica*. Supplement 528.

Lindholm, 1977, Towards a more Human Engineering. Paper delivered at the EAPM Conference in Madrid, June 1977. (Stockholm: SAF).

Lindon, L.D., 1978, Self-referent, job-referent and orientation to work. Paper presented to the Department of Occupational Psychology, Birkbeck College (unpublished).

Locke, E.A., 1976, The Nature and Causes of Job Satisfaction. In: *Handbook of Industrial and Organizational Psychology*. (Edited by M.D. Dunnette) (Chicago: Rand McNally).

Locke, E.A. and Whiting, R.J., 1974, Sources of satisfaction and dissatisfaction among solid waste management employees. *Journal of Applied Psychology*, 59, 145-156.

Locke, E.A., Smith, P.C., Kendall, L.M., Hulin, C.L. and Miller, A.M., 1964, Convergent and Discriminant Validity for Areas and Methods of Rating Job Satisfaction. *Journal of Applied Psychology*, 48 (5), 313-319.

Mace, C.A., 1948, Satisfactions in work, *Journal of Occupational Psychology*, 22, 5-16.

Mackay, C.J., and Cox, T., 1977, Transactional model of occupational stress. Paper presented at III Promstra seminar, Department of Engineering Production, Birmingham. (*Stress Research Report 4,* Department of Psychology, University of Nottingham).

Mackay, C.J., Cox, T., Burrows, G.C. and Lazzerini, A.J., 1978, An inventory for the measurement of arousal and stress through self-report. *British Journal of Social and Clinical Psychology* (In press).

Madge, C., 1948, Payment and incentives, *Journal of Occupational Psychology*, 22, 39-45.

References

Maslow, A.H., 1970, *Motivation and Personality*. (New York: Harper & Rowe (2nd edition)).

Maslow, A.H., 1968, *Toward a Psychology of Being* (2nd edition. Van Nostrand).

Masterson, S., 1975, The adjective checklist technique: A review and critique. In: McReynolds, P. (ed.), *Advances in Psychological Assessment*. (San Francisco: Jossey-Bass).

McClelland, D.C., 1961, *The Achieving Society*. (Princeton: Van Nostrand).

McGrath, J.E., 1976, Stress and behaviour in organisations. In: M. Dunnette (ed.), *Handbook of Industrial and Organizational Psychology*. (Chicago: Rand McNally).

Meissner, N., 1971, The long arm of the job: a study of work and leisure. *Industrial Relations*, 10, 239-260.

Miller, R.B., 1974, A method for determining task strategies (U.S. Government Report No. AD-783-847).

Moors, S., Vansina, L. and Verborgh, E., 1975(a), Etude de groupes semiautonomes dans une entreprise d'électronique (Brussels: OBAP).

Moors, S., Vansina, L. and Verborgh, E., 1975(b), Travail en groupe et satisfaction au travail dans un atelier de confection (Brussels: OBAP).

Moors, S., Vansina, L. and Verborgh, E., 1976, Restructuration des tâches et machines automatiques de production (Brussels: OBAP).

Morse, N.C., 1953, Satisfaction in the white collar job. Ann Arbor Survey Research Centre, Institute for Social Research, University of Michigan.

Mosteller, Frederick, 1972, In: *Statistics: A Guide to the Unknown*. Tanur, Judith M. *et al.* (San Francisco: Holden-Day). Foreword, p. ix.

Muchinsky, P.M., 1977, Employee Absenteeism: A review of the literature. *Journal of Vocational Behaviour*, 10 (3), 316-340.

Mumford, E., 1971, Economic evaluation of computer-based systems. Book 3: Systems design for people. (National Computing Centre Ltd).

Mustafa, H. and Sylvia, R.D., 1976, A factor analysis approach to job satisfaction. *Public Personnel Management*, 4, 165-172.

Nealey, S.M., Thornton, G.C., Maynard, W.S. and Lindell, M.K., 1975, Defining research needs to insure continued job motivation of Air Traffic Controllers in future Air Traffic Control Systems (Report No. DOT-FA74WA1-499). (Seattle, Washington: Battelle, Human Affairs Research Centers).

Nicholson, N., Brown, C.A. and Chadwick-Jones, T.K., 1976, Absence from work and job satisfaction. *Journal of Applied Psychology*, 61, 6, 728-737.

Nowlis, V., 1965, Research with the MACL. In: Tomkins, S.S. and Izard, C.E., (eds.), *Affect, Cognition and Personality*. (New York: Springer).

Nunally, J., 1970, *Introduction to Psychological Measurement*. (New York: McGraw-Hill).

Older, H.J. and Cameron, B.J., 1972, Human Factors Aspects of Air Traffic Control. NASA Report No. CR-1957 (Washington, D.C.: NASA).

Oldham, G.R., Hackman, J.R. and Pearce, J.L., 1976, Conditions under which employees respond positively to enriched work. *Journal of Applied Psychology*, 61 (4), 395-403.

Parke, E.L. and Tausky, C., 1975, The mythology of job enrichment: self actualisation revisited. *Personnel*, September/October, 12-21.

Parker, S., 1971, *The Future of Work and Leisure*. (New York: Praeger Press).

Paul, W.J. and Robertson, K.B., 1970, *Job Enrichment and Employee Motivation*. (Gower Press).

Payne, R.L., 1973, Prospects for research on organisational climate. Unpublished manuscript: MRC Sheffield.

Philips (Committee on Participation), 1977, Participation—various ways of involving people in their work and work organisations. (Edited by Personnel and Industrial Relations/Europe). (Eindhoven: N.V. Philip's Gloeiampen Fabrieken).

Porter, L.W., Steers, R.M., Mowday, R.T. and Boulian, P.V., 1974, Organisational commitment, job satisfaction and turnover among psychiatric technicians. *Journal of Applied Psychology*, 59, 603-609.

Quinn, M., 1977, Bookbinding in Hong Kong. *The Hong Kong Library Association Journal*, 4, (1977).

Quinn, R.P., Staines, C.L. and McCullough, M.R., 1973, Job satisfaction in the 1970s. *Recent History and a Look to the Future*. Manpower Monograph. (Washington, D.C.: U.S. Government Printing Office).

Raffle, A. and Sell, R.G., 1970, The Victoria Line—Operational aspects. *Applied Ergonomics*, 113-120.

Rahe, R.H., McKean, J.D. and Arthur, R.J., 1967, A longitudinal study of life-change and illness patterns. *Journal of Psychosomatic Research*, 10, 355-366.

Report of the Committee of Inquiry on Industrial Democracy, Chairman, Lord Bullock, January 1977.

Rice, A.K., Hill, J.M.M. and Trist, E.L., 1950, The representation of labour turnover as a social process. *Human Relations*, 3, 349-372.

Rissler, A. and Elgerot, A., 1978, Stressreaktioner vid övertidsarbete. (Stress reactions related to overtime at work). Department of Psychology, University of Stockholm, Rapporter, No. 23).

Rohmert, W., 1969, Skalen fertigungstechnischer Mechanisierungs- und arbeitstechnischer Rationaloisierungsstufen. Ergonomics in Machine Design. *Occupational Safety and Health Series 14* (1969) Seite 777-787; (Geneva: International Labour Office).

Rohmert, W., 1971, Automation. In: *Encyclopaedia of Occupational Health and Safety 1* (1971) Seite 133-137. (Geneva: International Labour Office).

Rohmert, W., 1972, Mechanisation. In: *Encyclopaedia of Occupational Health and Safety 2* (1972) Seite 835-838. (Geneva: International Labour Office).

Rohmert, W., and Weg, F.J., (1975), *Organisation teilautonomer Gruppenarbeit*. (München 1976: Carl Hanser Verlag).

Rotter, J.B., 1966, *Generalised Expectancies for Internal Versus External Control of Reinforcement*. Psychological Monographs, Whole No. 80.

Rousseau, D.M., 1977, Technological differences in job characteristics, employee satisfaction and motivation: a synthesis of job design research and sociotechnical systems theory. *Organizational Behavior and Human Performance* 19:1, 18-42.

Rowan, J., 1976, Ethical issues in organisational change. In: Warr, P. (ed.). *Personal Goals and Work Design*. (London: Wiley).

Rowland, K.F. and Sokol, B., 1977, A review of research examining the coronary-prone behavior pattern. *Journal of Human Stress*, 3, 26-33.

Roy, D.F., 1959, Banana Time: Job satisfaction and informal interaction. *Human Organisation*, 18, 158-168.

Ruehl, G., 1974, Work structuring. *Work Study*, September, 19-22.

Ruffell-Smith, P., Ord, G. and Whitfield, D.J.C., 1977, An experiment to examine the concept of Interactive Conflict Resolution (Phase II). Report No. 454 (National Air Traffic Services: ATCEU).

Saari, J., 1977, Characteristics of tasks associated with the occurrence of accidents. *Journal of Occupational Accidents* 1 (3), 273-279.

Saari, J. and Lahtela, J., to be published, Characteristics of jobs in high and low accident frequency companies in the light metal industry. *Accident Analysis and Prevention*.

Saari, J. and Rinne, R., 1977, Accidents and working conditions in two industrial branches with different accident rates. *Control* 4 (1), 11-17.

Sackman, H., 1967, *Computers, System Science, and Evolving Society*. (New York: Wiley).

Schneider, B. and Alderfer, C.P., 1973, Three studies of need satisfaction in organisations. *Administrative Science Quarterly*, 18, 489-505.

Schneider, B., Hall, D.F. and Nygren, H.T., 1971, Self image and job characteristics as correlates of changing organisational identification. *Human Relations*, 24, 397-416.

Schuh, A.J., 1967, The predictability of employee tenure: A review of the literature. *Personnel Psychology*, 20, 133-152.

Seashore, S.E., 1975, Defining and Measuring the Quality of Working Life. In: *The Quality of Working Life, Vol. 1* (Edited by L.E. Davis and A.B. Cherns). (New York: The Free Press).

Sells, S.B., 1970, On the nature of stress. In: McGrath, J.E. (ed.), *Social and Psychological Factors in Stress*. (New York: Rinehart and Winston).

Selye, H., 1950, Stress. (Montreal: ACTA).

Seybolt, J.W. and Gruenfeld, L., 1976, The discriminant validity of work alienation and work satisfaction measures. *Journal of Occupational Psychology* 49 (3) 193-202.

Shepherd, A., 1976, An improved tabular format for task analysis. *Journal of Occupational Psychology*, 49, 93-104.

Shipley, P. and Cook, T.C., 1978, Individual Vulnerability to Occupational Stress: Some Psychological and Other Findings. Paper to Ergonomics Society Conference on 'Psychophysiological Response to Occupational Stress' at Nottingham University, September 21, 1978.

Silverstone, Rosalie A., 1974. The Office Secretary: a study of an occupational group of women office workers. Ph.D. thesis, The City University, London.

Silverstone, R.A., 1976, Office work for women: an historical review. *Business History*, 18, 98-110.

Sims, H.P. and Szilagyi, A.D., 1976, Job characteristic relationships: individual and structural moderators. *Organizational Behavior and Human Performance*, 17 (2), 211-230.

Singer, R. and Rutenfranz, J., 1971, Attitudes of Air Traffic Controllers at Frankfurt Airport towards work and the working environment. *Ergonomics*, 14 (5), 633-639.

Singer, R. and Rutenfranz, J., 1972, Job satisfaction and job-related health disturbances among Air Traffic Controllers. (English summary, German text). Internationales Archiv für Arbeitsmedizin, 30, 135-160.

Singleton, W.T., 1976, Skill and accidents. In: Occupational accident research. Arbetarskyddsfonden, Stockholm, 107-118.

Singleton, W.T., 1977, Some conceptual and operational doubts about job satisfaction. A.P. Report 73. (University of Aston in Birmingham, Applied Psychology Department).

Sivadon, P. and Amiel, R., 1969, Psychopathologie du Travail. (Paris: Les Editions Sociales Francaises).

Smith, P.C., 1955, The prediction of individual differences in susceptibility to industrial monotony. *Journal of Applied Psychology*, 39, 320-329.

Smith, P.C., Kendall, L.N. and Hulin, C.L., 1969, *The Measurement of Job Satisfaction in Work and Retirement.* (Chicago: Rand McNally).

Smith, R.C., 1973, Comparison of the job attitudes of personnel in three Air Traffic Control specialities. Aerospace Medicine, 44 (8), 918-927.

Smith, R.C., 1974, A realistic view of the people in Air Traffic Control. FAA-AM-74-12 (Oklahoma City: U.S. Department of Transportation, Office of Aviation Medicine).

Smith, R.C., Cobb, B.B. and Collins, W.E., 1971, Attitudes and motivational factors in terminal area air traffic control work. FAA-AM-71-30. (Oklahoma City, U.S. Department of Transportation, Office of Aviation Medicine).

Solomon, R.L., 1949, An extension of control group design. *Psychological Bulletin*, 46, 491-506.

Srivastva, S. *et al.*, 1975, Job Satisfaction and productivity, An evaluation of policy related research on productivity, industrial organization and job satisfaction: policy development and implementation. (Cleveland: Department of Organizational Behavior, Case Western Reserve University).

Stammers, R.B. and Patrick, J., 1975, *The Psychology of Training.* (London: Methuen).

Standing, T.E., 1973, Satisfaction with the work itself as a function of cognitive complexity. (Proceedings of 81st Annual Convention of APA, Montreal, Canada).

Stansfield, R.G., 1977(a), Typing Pools: a study in satisfactions in work. Deposited at The British Library Lending Division, Boston Spa, Yorkshire. Shelf mark F78/1795.

Stansfield, R.G., 1977(b), Typing Pools: a study in satisfactions in work. *Ergonomics*, 20, 684-685.

Steffler, B., 1966, Vocational development: Ten propositions in search of a theory. *Personnel and Guidance Journal*, 44, 611-616.

Surry, J., 1969, *Industrial Accident Research.* University of Toronto (Toronto), p. 203.

Swedish Employers Federation, 1975, *Job Reform in Sweden.* (Stockholm, Sweden: Swedish Employers Federation).

Taels, G., 1978, A critical assessment of Herzberg's two-factors theory. (Paper for a master's degree in psychology, stencilled, in Dutch). (Leuven: Catholic University of Leuven).

Taylor, F.W., 1911, *The Principles of Scientific Management.* (New York: Harper).

Taylor, J.C., 1977, Job Satisfaction and Quality of Working Life: A Reassessment. *Journal of Occupational Psychology*, 50, 243-252.

Teichner, W.H. and Whitehead, J., 1971, Development of a taxonomy of human performance: evaluation of a task classification system for generalizing research findings from a data base. (Washington: American Institutes for Research, Technical Report No. 8).

Theologus, G.C., Romashko, T. and Fleishman, E.A., 1970, Development of a taxonomy of human performance: a feasibility study of ability dimensions for classifying human tasks. (Washington: American Institutes for Research, Technical Report No. 5).

Theologus, G.C. and Fleishman, E.A., 1971, Development of a taxonomy of human performance: validation studies of ability scales for classifying human tasks. (Washington: American Institutes for Research, Technical Report No. 10).

Thierry, H.K., 1968, Loont de prestatiebeloning? (Assen: Van Gorcum).

Thorsrud, E., 1972, Job Design in the Wider Context. In: *Design of Jobs* (Edited by L.E. David and J.C. Taylor). (Harmondsworth: Penguin) pp. 451-459.

Toffler, A., 1970, Future shock. (Oxford: The Bodley Head).

Torbert, W.R., 1972, '*Being for the Most Part Puppets…*'. (Cambridge, Massachusetts: Schenkman).

Tripartite Steering Committee on Job Satisfaction, 1975, Making work more satisfying. Department of the Environment. (London: HMSO).

Turner, A.N. and Miclette, A.L., 1962, Sources of Satisfaction in repetitive work. *Journal of Occupational Psychology*, 36, 215-231.

Turner, A.N. and Lawrence, P.R., 1965, *Industrial Jobs and the Worker*. (Boston: Harvard University).

Verhaegen, P., 1977, Work satisfaction in present day working life. Ergonomics and work satisfaction. (Leuven: Psychology Department Paper).

Viteles, M.S., 1932, *Industrial Psychology*. (New York: Norton) p. 547.

Vroom, V.H., 1964, *Work and motivation*. (New York: Wiley).

Wahba, M.A. and Bridwell, L.G., 1974, Maslow reconsidered: a review of research on the need-hierarchy theory. *Academy of Management Proceedings*, 514-520.

Walker, C.R. and Guest, R.H., 1952, *The Man on the Assembly Line*. (Cambridge, Massachusetts: Harvard).

Walker, N., 1961, *Morale in the Civil Service*. (Edinburgh: Edinburgh University Press).

Wall, T.D. and Lisheron, J.A., 1977, *Worker Participation*. (London: McGraw-Hill).

Wallis, D. and Cope, D.E., 1977, Job satisfaction amongst professional workers. Paper given at the Annual Conference, British Psychological Society, Division of Occupational Psychology.

Wanous, J.P. and Lowler III, E.E., 1972, Measurement and meaning of job satisfaction. *Journal of Applied Psychology*, 56 (2), 95-105.

Wanous, J.P., 1974, A causal correlational analysis of the Job Satisfaction and Performance relationship. *Journal of Applied Psychology*, 59 (2), 139-144.

Wanous, J.P., 1976, Organisational entry: From naive expectations to realistic beliefs. *Journal of Applied Psychology*, 61, 22-29.

Warr, P.B., 1973, Better working lives: A university psychologist's view. *Journal of Occupational Psychology*, 47, 15-22.

Warr, P. (ed.), 1976, *Personal Goals and Work Design*. (London: Wiley).

Warr, P. and Wall, T., 1975, *Work and Well Being*. (London: Penguin).

Weick, K.E., 1965, Laboratory Experimentation with Organisations. In: *Handbook of Organizations* (edited by J.G. March). (New York: Rand McNally).

Weijel, J.A., 1975, Homo trudens—de expansieve mens. Tijdschrift voor Sociale Geneeskunde, 53, 842-851.

Weir, M., 1976, Redesigning jobs in Scotland: a survey. *Work Research Unit Report No. 5*. Department of Employment, United Kingdom.

Wester, P., 1978, Work structuring as a criterion in organisation renewal. Paper read at the Joint Conference of Industrial Psychologists of Great Britain and the Netherlands. (Eindhoven: Philips, Social Research Department).

Which?, September 1977, How you rate your jobs. pp. 489-493.

Wild, R., 1970, Job needs, job satisfaction and job heaviour of women manual workers. *Journal of Applied Psychology*, 54, 157-162.

Wild, R., 1973, Manpower planning and job satisfaction. *Management Decision*, 11, 11-18.

Wild, R., 1975, *Work Organization*. (London: John Wiley & Sons), p. 226.

Willebois, J.L.M.J. v.d.D.d., 1970, Work Structuring: A summary of experiments at Philips 1963-1968. (Eindhoven: Philips).

Worsley, P., 1970, *Introducing Sociology*. (London: Penguin).